KU-256-693

Revolutionary Change

SECOND EDITION

CHALMERS JOHNSON

STANFORD UNIVERSITY PRESS

Stanford, California

QM LIBRARY
(MILE END)

First edition published by Little, Brown and Company in 1966
Second edition published by Stanford University Press in 1982

Stanford University Press, Stanford, California
© 1982 by the Board of Trustees of the Leland Stanford Junior University
Printed in the United States of America
Cloth ISBN 0-8047-1144-5
Paper ISBN 0-8047-1145-3
Last figure below indicates year of this printing:
03 02 01 00

Foreword by Bernard Crick

Even before I read Professor Chalmers Johnson's lucid and important book I had formulated my iron law of revolutions: that revolutions take place because governments break down and not for the reasons that are given out by historians who are hired by the party that happens to emerge into power during the revolutionary situation—reasons that, if I may add *obiter dicta* to my law, are often taken surprisingly seriously by subsequent social scientists. My iron law is, of course, a tautology. But it is a curious kind of tautology, for whereas in a sense it is obvious that what one means by "revolution" is the breakdown or the breaking down of a government, yet it does tell one something positive: at least where to look. I think I was protesting against so many theories of revolution that concentrate on the ideologies and intentions of the revolutionaries in order to compare them with the sad or glad results. Surely the key is to be found in the pathology of the old order. Quite simply, I meet so many students who have read books on the origins of Communism, Marxism, and the Bolshevik Party, but seem to know little about the Czarist system or the First World War. Tocqueville did not make that mistake. The ideology of the party before the revolution can be, indeed, a formidable clue, among others, as to how it behaves when in power—Hitler's ideology was underestimated on this score; but it is a very poor clue as to how the party comes to power. Contingency and general causes both play a role.

Professor Johnson shows that the physiology and the pathology of politics are quite inseparable. If violence, in his argument,

is of the essence of a revolutionary situation, it is always "the
other side of the coin" of order, or functioning social interaction.
So he concentrates his analysis, far more sensibly than in my
frivolous and polemical aphorism, on the reasons why social
systems break down, why normal social interaction fails in the
specific manner we call revolutionary. "The key to both the study
and the conceptualization of revolutionary violence," he writes,
"lies in social systems analysis." Personally I would prefer to say
"clue" rather than "key"; I am not such a Parsonian as Professor
Johnson. I cannot always agree that social systems are as fully
systematic as the functional analysis always assumes or implies.
There are often huge rough edges or glaring "contradictions,"
which do not always result in collapse, still less revolution; sometimes such unsystematic systems are held together by sheer
political will and skill, sometimes one suspects through sheer
habit and inertia, even lack of serious challenge. But nonetheless,
the model Professor Johnson produces is an excellent model, so
long as one remembers that it is a model. It makes us look at the
right dimensions and at complicated interrelationships, rather
than a simple story either of cause or effect or of intention and
result. If the reader will not always give the same value to each of
the specified relationships as the author, or always see the real
world as quite so systematic, that does not matter: we are saved
from either romantic or deterministic error and led to look historically at events and conditions long before "the revolution" as
well as afterwards. His table of contents alone is worth brooding
over and decoding before plunging into reading the text: it suggests a clear and helpful framework for analysis—even if, like
Wittgenstein's famous ladder, we can sometimes kick it over *once*
we have climbed the wall, but then and only then.

Professor Johnson portrays the process of revolution on three
levels, "each involving variables that may move a potentially
revolutionary situation toward violence or away from violence."
These levels are: (i) the level of structural distortion in a social
system; (ii) a level of conscious political choice and intention; and

(iii) the level of strategies and tactics. These, in their historically varying forms, all interact with each other in a revolutionary situation; but this is not just a web of tautologous definition, for he makes clear that these levels can, to an astonishing extent, lead a life of their own. Ideologies cannot be treated, by either a subtle Marxist or a sophisticated Parsonian, as simply a product of social systems: they can be, for example, imports, influential because of a possibly discordant sub-system of intellectuals. And people do not always choose the political tactics most effective for their intentions. There are discussions about means as well as about ends in revolutionary ranks, which are often by no means trivial or predictable in their outcomes. Each instance is different, but we do not have to descend into a purely historical empiricism, as some argue, muttering or incanting that "every case is completely different" or "if you take a long enough view of it, was there really a revolution at all?" Chalmers Johnson gives us an extraordinarily clear and solid framework of analysis—as the great demand for the first edition of this book has shown; but he does not blanch, visibly or otherwise, at the thought that every application of it to an actual circumstance will be different.

Nor is he, on my reading, falling into the trap of some Parsonians of seeming to imply that any functioning social system is to be preferred to any form of instability. This simply does not follow from his analysis. He tells me that I cannot say that a regime is so stable and yet so unjust that I wish it could be overthrown; he is only saying that it is unlikely that revolution will occur unless there is already some demonstrable social instability. A social scientist cannot rule our intentions out of court; but he can legitimately remind us that they are seldom realized in the form that we abstractly conceive them. Orwell once remarked that "all revolutions are failures, but they are not all the same kind of failures." He meant to imply that some are hardly to be counted as failures at all, if judged by realistic standards, not by the idealistic standards of pre-revolutionary speculation.

Most of all, what Professor Chalmers Johnson has clarified for me is the great importance of being sure whether one is talking about the pre-revolutionary period (as hindsight sees it); the events of the revolution, or "the Revolution"; or the conduct of government in the post-revolutionary society. And that in each of these periods we have to think in terms of events, ideologies, and policies: separate but interacting factors. Personally I do not find a nine-dimensional box unduly complicated. "Revolution" is not a simple matter. There are no single explanations or theories of revolution. But we can think about them in a less cloudy and more systematic way. In this respect I think students should find this book extremely helpful, and, like a good drink on a hot day, both cooling and stimulating.

Birkbeck College
(University of London)

Preface to the Second Edition

Since this book was first published in 1966 it has gone through eleven separate printings, been translated into German, French, and Korean, and appeared in a simplified form for foreign readers unfamiliar with Western social science terminology. During that time the world also witnessed at least fifteen revolutions of diverse types. These include the ending during April 1975, with the fall of Saigon, of one phase of the thirty-year-old Vietnamese revolution; the defeat of the Tupamaros in Uruguay; the 1971 revolution that created Bangladesh out of what had been East Pakistan; the military coup of September 1973 against the government of President Salvador Allende in Chile; the leftist military coup of April 1974 in Portugal that led to the end of nearly a half century of authoritarian rule and to independence for Mozambique and Angola; the coup in Cyprus of July 1974 against the government of President Makarios, and the subsequent Turkish invasion of the country that led in turn to the ouster of the regime of General Dimitrios Ioannides in Greece and to the restoration of democratic government after seven years of military rule; the guerrilla war in Rhodesia from 1972 to 1979 and the creation of Zimbabwe during 1980; the military takeover of the government of Ethiopia in the middle of 1974 and the subsequent intervention in Ethiopia by the Soviet Union; the overthrow during July 1979 of President Anastasio Somoza in Nicaragua by the Sandinista revolutionaries after two years of insurrectionary struggle and the loss of more than 50,000 lives; the IRA rebellion in Ulster; the Iranian Revolution from January

1978 to February 1979; and the emergence of a workers' movement not controlled by the Communist Party in Poland during 1980 and 1981.

And these are only the major cases. During these same fifteen years the world was also assailed by a series of terrorist incidents, some of them revolutionary and some of them not. Significant instances include the shooting of 25 tourists at Lod Airport in Israel in May 1972; the killing of 11 Israeli athletes at the 1972 Olympic Games in Munich; the global epidemic of airplane hijacking; the rise and decline of such groups as the Baader-Meinhof gang in Germany, the Red Army in Japan, and the Symbionese Liberation Army in the United States; and the "revolutionary suicide" of more than 900 people on November 18, 1978, at Jonestown, Guyana. In addition to events such as these, assassinations and assassination attempts, bombings, political kidnappings, and hostage incidents of many kinds (including the seizure of the entire staff of the American Embassy in Teheran for more than a year by Iranian revolutionaries) captured the attention of politicians and political analysts on every continent.

Such evidence that revolution and political violence persist and continue to be major conceptual problems for political scientists suggested the need for a new edition of *Revolutionary Change*. The original aim of this book was to describe in analytic, social scientific terms what are called "revolutionary situations" and to discuss, again in analytic terms and for purposes of comparing cases, what is likely to happen when an attempt is made to carry out a revolution in either a revolutionary or nonrevolutionary situation. My intent was not so much to create another theory of revolution as to build on the classic studies, such as Crane Brinton's *The Anatomy of Revolution*, and on my own and others' investigations of particular cases in order to make the insights and conclusions contained in these studies amenable to comparative political analysis. Specifically, I tried to supply the concepts that an analyst would need to determine whether an instance of political violence was really a revolution—regardless of what either incumbent state authorities or insurgents might

choose to call it—and then to dissect and explain the few genuine cases. This book, then, is not about any particular revolution
or the "philosophy" of revolution in general. It is an extended
essay in the genre of conceptual clarification; and the primary
concepts to be clarified are the "revolutionary situation," "revolutionary action," and "revolutionary change."

In this revised edition I have retained the basic analysis contained in the original version with only minor changes; it appears in the present book as chapters one through seven. In
these original chapters I have introduced some new examples,
but I have also retained most of the original ones, particularly
those that relate to the struggle for civil rights during the 1960's
by black Americans. Contemporary readers may experience
some difficulty in recalling the murder of Viola Gregg Liuzzo
and its significance for social change in America, but this in no
way lessens its force as an illustration of what I call "elite intransigence." This period in American life should also serve to remind readers that the problems dealt with in this book are relevant to any social system.

I have omitted the old Chapter Six, "Measuring Disequilibrium," because it digressed too far from the basic purposes of
the study. In its place I have put a new chapter on terrorism—its
meaning, forms, and relationship to revolutionary struggles.
However, I return to one issue posed in "Measuring Disequilibrium"—namely, the need to separate analytically revolutionary
situations from revolutions themselves—in a new concluding
chapter. This final chapter also includes a summary discussion
of the analysis of revolution presented in this book together
with an attempt to relate it to some of the other schools of
revolutionary interpretation that have become important in recent years.

Chalmers Johnson

Contents

1

Revolution: The Implications
of a Political Concept

In 1908 Arthur Bauer of the University of Paris began his book on revolution with a definition that has withstood the tests of one of the most revolutionary centuries in history. "Les révolutions," he wrote, "sont les changements tentés ou réalisés par la force dans la constitution des sociétés."[1] All the elements of the elusive concept of revolution are here. Revolutions are social changes. Sometimes they succeed; often they fail. Revolutionary change is a special kind of social change, one that involves the intrusion of violence into civil social relations. And revolution, both as a form of behavior and as a concept, concerns the most basic level of man's communal existence—its constitution, in the Aristotelian sense of the principles of political authority and distributive justice prevailing in a particular society.

If a definition were all that is required to permit us to recognize and understand revolutions, Bauer has provided us with one. But before we can begin to appreciate the implications of Bauer's definition, we must recognize that the elements of his, or any other, definition of revolution are themselves in need of explanation and definition. What is social change, of which revolution is one particular configuration? Why do revolutions sometimes succeed, and what do we mean by success in this context? What is violence, of which insurrection—the certain mark of either rebellion or revolution—is also only one particular configuration? And what is it about formally constituted regimes that breeds internal demands for periodic renovation? The study of revolution is the attempt to ask these questions with rigor and penetration. This essay, in turn, is an attempt to continue a dialogue over these questions that is as old as man's social self-awareness.

It has sometimes been supposed that political theory has very little to say on the subject of either violence or revolution. Both are seen as signs of the failure of politics and hence outside the range of interests of the political theorist.[2] In terms of the history of Western political philosophy it is occasionally argued, for example, that Edmund Burke was the first theorist of revolution and that all serious theoretical writing on revolutions can be dated from the French Revolution and its political reverberations. On a purely historical level there is some evidence for this view. The modern age, characterized by revolutionary threats to the nation-state, did begin in 1789. Analytically speaking, however, the idea of revolution was implicit in the first organized society.

The English word "revolution" is particularly inadequate in conveying the meaning of purposive political violence. In its political sense, "revolution" did not begin to be used until the late Renaissance, but much older meanings (e.g., the "revolutions" of the planets) give the word overtones that suggest there are forces in human affairs comparable to the superhuman forces governing the universe.[3] We can come considerably closer to one of the political implications of revolution by looking at it in the oldest still used language on earth—Chinese. In Chinese "revolution" is the complement to another word referring to the right to rule—the authority—of the Chinese Emperor. *T'ienming* 天命 means literally "the mandate of heaven," whereas *keming* 革命, which we translate as revolution, means "to withdraw the mandate." The idea of revolution in Chinese is thus unintelligible without a prior knowledge of the mandate of heaven, the Confucian doctrine wherein the Emperor is alleged to possess superior virtue and is thereby authorized to rule.

Although the English word implies no such thing, the Western concept of revolution is similarly tied to a vision of political organization in which revolt is unnecessary and therefore unjustifiable. This is the first point to be made about the study of revolutions in general or of any one in particular: revolutions must be studied in the context of the social systems in which they occur. The analysis of revolution intermeshes with the analysis of viable, functioning societies, and any attempt to separate the two concepts impairs the usefulness of both. Some scholars who have failed to take the contingent nature of revolution seriously have explored revolutionary behavior as if it were a relatively isolable and discrete phenomenon. They have, in effect, reduced the sociology of revolution to the comparative study of the techniques for seizing power. Unfortunately for them there is a great deal more to the problem of revolution than the forms insurrection may take, and such questions as whether revolutionaries should or should not poison a city's water supply are among the least interesting aspects of the resort to revolution in a society.

The study of society and revolution is somewhat analogous to the study of physiology and pathology: a knowledge of morbid conditions in animals depends on a knowledge of healthy conditions. The analogy, however, is not exact. Whereas physiology and pathology are analytically distinct investigations, corresponding to different states of an organism, the sociology of functional societies comes logically before the sociology of revolution. This is true because social organization itself is intended to restrict or minimize violence among the people united in a society, both purposefully in terms of the conscious policies pursued by a society's members and functionally in terms of the results of the value-coordinated division of labor. Therefore in order to perceive why a revolution, signifying the return to a form of violence, occurs, we must have a knowledge of how and why the social barriers against violence have collapsed or have been breached.

Aristotle was the first political theorist to show that revolutions are contextually specific—that is, that the key to understanding why men want to change their social relations is to grasp how men think their society ought to be organized. Aristotle summarized his opinion on this subject by offering some examples: "The universal and chief cause of . . . revolutionary feeling [is] . . . the desire of equality, when men think that they are equal to others who have more than themselves; or, again, the desire of inequality and superiority, when conceiving themselves to be superior they think that they have not more but the same or less than their inferiors; pretensions which may and may not be just."[4] Although Aristotle uses the term "revolutionary feeling" in a much broader sense than we do—he is concerned with the more inclusive phenomenon of political instability and social change, of which violent revolution is only one important manifestation—he emphasizes that revolution requires an affirmative social order with which men have become dissatisfied. Aristotle argues that revolutionary feelings do not exist when men's conceptions of themselves are faithfully mirrored in the principles on which their society is organized.

Speaking in more general terms, we may say that the concept of revolution occupies a niche in a hierarchy of broader and more abstract concepts concerned with the organization of men's social interdependence. In order to reach this analytical niche we must begin by asking the broadest kind of questions: How are order and stability possible in human relations? What are the principles that men adopt in order to stabilize and legitimate the cooperation forced on them by their economic and political geography? In what manner do societies exist and persist? If we are able to achieve some intellectual agreement on these questions, we may then descend to the next analytical level and ask what causes stable societies to become unstable and to change. In making this progression from one category of political questions to another, we are not moving from one subject matter to another (as, for example, from physiology to pathology). The study of social change is in a sense identical with the study of the determinants of social order. As the quote from Aristotle implies, any basis for order is potentially discriminatory, and therein lies one important source of the seeds of instability. To study social change is simply to focus more carefully on the already familiar terrain of social integration; it is not a matter of shifting to an entirely different locale.

Even when concentrating on the strains in a viable society that may give rise to demands for change, we are a long way from isolating the phenomenon of revolution. Revolution is not the same thing as social change; it is a form of social change. Of equal or greater importance in understanding why violent revolutions sometimes occur is an appreciation of how the members of certain societies have been able to make basic changes *without* resorting to violence. The radical changes that occurred in the United States during the New Deal, the process whereby Japan changed from a feudal to a modern state, the modifications that English government underwent in response to industrialization, all were accomplished without resort to revolution.

Sometimes we speak of such changes as "revolutionary," using the already metaphorical word "revolution" in a still more metaphorical sense to mean changes of great magnitude (e.g., the "industrial revolution"). But the concept of revolution in political analysis refers specifically to the form of change that occurred, for example, in France in 1789, in Russia in 1917, and in China in 1949. One reason why revolutions took place in these societies is that nonrevolutionary change had already failed—a point that should demonstrate the need to study the more general phenomenon of social change before we can turn to revolution itself. Not only must we study social change, we must try to isolate the determinants of nonrevolutionary change so that we can better understand the determinants of the revolutionary situation. Aristotle has suggested that the seeds of instability and change are to be found in the form of the social structure itself, but we shall find that structurally generated dissatisfactions are only one possible source of either change or revolution.

To argue that revolutions must be studied within the context of social systems in which they occur is not to deny the value of comparative analyses of revolutions. The anthropologist A. R. Radcliffe-Brown once argued that comparison is the form that experimentation takes in the social sciences, and much of the research done on revolutions has utilized the technique of comparing revolutions. Gaetano Salvemini, for example, writing on the nature of history and the social sciences, advocates that "to determine whether revolutions are governed by constant laws, there is only one method: we must compare one with the other the greatest possible number of revolutions, . . . and we must see whether between these phenomena so far apart in time and space there can be discovered similarities or dissimilarities which are constant."[5] Crane Brinton, in his justly famous *Anatomy of Revolution*, attempted to do just that by comparing the English, American, French, and Russian revolutions.[6]

However, before the comparative method can be used effectively, there must be some agreement on what is being compared and on the variables to be used as a basis for discovering differences and similarities. Precisely because there is so little agreement on how to conceptualize revolution, and because revolution has often been treated in isolation from other political phenomena, comparative analyses of revolutions have commonly been a source of further confusion. Harry Eckstein, summarizing the conclusions of a symposium on the sociology of revolution, argues that "the most urgent pre-theoretical need in internal war [i.e., revolution] studies today is the development, even if only tentative, of basic descriptive categories in terms of which the basic features of internal wars can be identified, in terms of which their nuances and broader features can be depicted in general structural concepts, classes (or types) constructed, and resemblances of cases to one another or to types accurately assessed."[7]

By disregarding the social system (and its condition) within which a revolution occurs, some scholars have lost track of the very idea they sought to analyze. "To withdraw the mandate" does not make much sense without the prior existence of a mandate. Peasant jacqueries, urban insurrections, military coups d'état, conspiracies plotted by revolutionary associations, and domestically supported counterrevolutions are all examples of rebellion or revolution; and all are marked by the acceptance of violence by certain members of the society in order to cause the society to change. However, to compare these events merely in terms of their forms or participants is to ignore the deeper political significance of these forms, or of the fact that certain social groups and not others resorted to revolution.

The comparative method, when applied to revolutions, must be devoted to comparing potentially revolutionary societies. In order to focus on potentially revolutionary societies, we must examine societies that appear to be immune to revolution and also the circumstances in which some of them lose their immunity. The problem of conceptualizing revolutions is closely analogous to the problem of conceptualizing certain varieties of mental illness. The latter problem was solved only when scholars agreed that "mental illness can be understood—and *only* understood—in its biographical setting. [It] makes sense only in terms of the patient's attempt at solving a problem in his living and to think of it as a mere disorder in some mechanism is fruitless."[8]

Another way of stressing the contingent nature of the concept of revolution is to examine it as a form of violence. Despite all evidence to the contrary, some scholars of revolution persist in refusing to accept the idea that an irreducible element of any revolution is the resort to, or acceptance of, violence. Even many revolutionaries take pains to develop strategies of revolution that they can characterize as "nonviolent." As we shall see, "nonviolent revolution," so long as these words retain any precise meaning whatsoever, is a contradiction in terms. "Nonviolent revolution" is actually the name of a revolutionary strategy containing a built-in propaganda appeal to persons holding certain definable values. Nevertheless, it is quite true that many revolutions have been accomplished without any blood flowing in the gutters. What then, sociologically speaking, do we mean by violence? This question is also basic to the analysis of revolution.

One of the simplest things that can be said about revolutions is that they are forms of human behavior—that is, they are not something analogous to earthquakes or sunspots. As a form of human behavior, revolution is a proper object for social science research in the broad sense in which we understand all social sciences to be "behavioral sciences." Following Max Weber, we may classify human behavior into two broad types: "action" and "social action." According to Weber, action is "all human behavior when and in so far as the acting individual attaches a subjective meaning to it." In this sense bodily or mental processes of which we are not aware are not "action," although our responses to the symptoms of these processes may be. One particular form of action is "social action." Again according to Weber, "action is social in so far as by virtue of the subjective meaning attached to it by the acting individual (or individuals), it takes account of the behavior of others and is thereby oriented in its course."[9]

If we carry Weber's idea of orientation to others a stage further and say that orientation occurs because the acting individual possesses stable *expectations* of the behavior and responses of others in a full range of social situations, then we have a rough, introductory approximation of the idea of social action *in a social system*. Virtually every major theorist of society holds that the *sine qua non* of a society (both conceptually and concretely) is the possession of mutual expectations by members of the society, allowing them to orient their behavior to each other. The very concept of the division of labor depends on such mutual expectations, and man's ability to orient his behavior to that of others is a prerequisite for the complex human interaction that characterizes even the most rudimentary society.

Given this formal analysis of social action in a social system, we may define violence as action that deliberately or unintentionally disorients the behavior of others. Violence is either behavior that is impossible for others to orient themselves to or behavior that is deliberately intended to prevent orientation and the development of stable expectations with regard to it. Violence is not necessarily brutality, or insensitivity, or the antithesis of empathy; as we shall see in a later chapter, the capacity of human beings to adjust and orient themselves to these forms of behavior is almost limitless, as for example in the concentration camps of the Second World War. Violence is "antisocial action," and in a political context violence, like revolution, is a contingent concept dependent on the prior existence of a system of social action within which it takes place. Despite the fact that wars reveal many instances of systematic orientation among the belligerents, the radical ideal of war and of waging it successfully constitutes the quintessence of violence.

War and social interaction are antipodal concepts, as the greatest theorist of violence, Thomas Hobbes, sought to show in his *Leviathan*. However, the relationship between war and society is not simply that of conceptual opposites. Hobbes concluded his search for the *purpose* of society by arguing that society is intended to eliminate the ubiquity of violence among people who are not socially organized, and once people are organized, to control the resort to violence among those who undertake antisocial acts. Although today many sociologists doubt that we can speak of the "purpose" of a social system, they nevertheless parallel Hobbes in arguing that social action in the context of a system *functions* so as to allow the system to exist and persist beyond the life of any one of its members and that a certain sign of the termination of a social system is the return of war among its members. Perfect order in a social system would signify the arrival of utopia; perfect violence would signify the termination of the system (or, as we shall see later, that social behavior had lost all of its systematic quality).

Hobbes's demonstration that society is the conquest of violence rests in part on a portrayal of what life would be like without society—that is, in the "state of nature." "In such condition there is no place for industry, because the fruit thereof is uncertain: and consequently no culture of the earth; no navigation, nor use of the commodities that may be imported by sea; no commodious buildings; no instruments of moving and removing such things as require much force; no knowledge of the face of the earth; no account of time; no arts; no letters; no society; and which is worst of all, continual fear, and danger of violent death; and the life of man, solitary, poor, nasty, brutish, and short." In order to obtain the fruits of cooperation and the division of labor—which are absent in the state of nature—man must abandon violence. For it is violence, above all else, that characterizes the state of nature: "During the time men live without a common power to keep them all in awe, they are in that condition which is called war; and such a war as is of every man against every man."[10]

Hobbes may have been wrong in thinking that an awesome power creates the basis for shared expectations, but his insight into the interdependence of order and violence, of society and anarchy, is one of the basic theorems of the sociology of revolution. As Norton Long has observed, "It was the great merit of Hobbes to raise the problems of order—to recognize that the existence of order is problematic."[11] Of course, Hobbes was not the first theorist to perceive this problem. The very roots of Western political philosophy lie in the reaction of some men against the argument that "might makes right" and against man's primitive reliance on force. Some theorists have gone so far as to define the word "political" simply as that element of social organization which is concerned with minimizing and regulating the use of violence.[12]

Since violence is both the negation of, and a possibility in, all social systems, sociologists regard it as one of the major criteria for defining a social system and for evaluating the degree of the system's stability. Violence differs from the legitimate use of force within a system and even from "routinized" or legally constrained conflict, such as labor disputes (which may contribute to the functioning of the system), because violence tends to inhibit and ultimately extinguish the union of men into a division of labor, regardless of the principles—coercive and/or consensual—that may have been operating to maintain that division of labor. Nevertheless, all social systems are burdened by some degree of violence, either as a consequence of their imperfect integration or because of other functional problems inherent in social organization.

Violence, as we have been talking about it, is still a very broad category of behavior. It may range in form and intensity all the way from gratuitous insults to lunatic acts or criminal behavior directed against other members of the system (e.g., murder or banditry), and from sub-insurrectionary protest movements (such as civil disobedience, politically motivated fasts, and sit-down strikes) to full-fledged rebellion or revolution. Similarly, the effects of violence may vary from a degree of personal tension to the impaired efficiency of large groups of people, and from political instability to the total destruction of the system.

If order and violence are indeed different sides of the same coin, then an analysis of one is inescapably an analysis of the other. This is why the work of Talcott Parsons, who devoted much attention to the problem of social integration, is of direct relevance to the sociology of revolution (although the present study does not employ any single scholar's theory of integration). It is valuable to recognize, as Lewis Coser has, that "all of Parsons's work, beginning with *The Structure of Social Action*, is an extended commentary on the Hobbesian question: How is social order possible?"[13] On the relationship between the integration and disintegration of social systems, Parsons himself has written: "The maintenance of any existing status [of the social system], insofar as it is maintained at all, is clearly a relatively contingent matter. The obverse of the analysis of the mechanisms by which it is maintained is the analysis of the forces which tend to alter it. *It is impossible to study one without the other.* A fundamental potentiality of instability, an endemic possibility of change, is inherent in this approach to the analysis of social systems. Empirically, of course, the degree of instability, and hence the likelihood of actual change, will vary both with the character of the social system and of the situation in which it is placed. But in principle, propositions about the factors making for maintenance of the system are at the same time propositions about those making for change. The difference is only one of

concrete descriptive analysis. There is no difference on the analytical level."[14]

Parsons argues that stability and instability—or, at their extremes, utopia and anarchy—are related configurations in any
human grouping and that the analysis of why one condition
does or does not prevail is simultaneously the analysis of why
its antithesis does or does not prevail. It is for this reason that
the amount and nature of violence in a society have always been
regarded as indices either of the society's worth (when viewed
by moral philosophers) or of its viability (when viewed by sociologists). Such indices also point up once again the contingent
nature of the concept of revolution. Revolution is one form of
violence.* The general resort to arms and other insurrectionary
acts—such as general strikes, political assassinations, mutinies,
and the carrying out of coups d'état—are all forms of behavior
intended to disorient the behavior of others, thereby bringing
about the demise of a hated social system. Changes that occur in
society without the use or threat of violence are nonrevolutionary, and this form of change is normally preferred to the use
of revolutionary violence by men living in society. Normally,
socialized men do not resort to violence except as a last resort
(although the perception of what constitutes a last resort may be
colored by an ideology).

If acts of revolutionary violence are quixotic or inappropriate,
they will not be tolerated by other members of the system, and
instead of terminating the system they will be dealt with as
forms of crime or lunacy. Acts of revolt "differ from simple
crimes to the extent that collective support given the outlaws is
not itself the product of coercion."[15] Therefore, when revolution-

---

* It is instructive to note Lenin's opinion on the possibility of a "nonviolent
revolution." In "The Proletarian Revolution and the Renegade Kautsky," he
wrote: "Socialism is opposed to violence against nations. That is indisputable.
But socialism is opposed to violence against men in general, . . . however, no
one has yet drawn the conclusion from this that socialism is opposed to revolutionary violence. Hence, to talk about 'violence' in general, without examining
the conditions which distinguish reactionary from revolutionary violence,
means being a petty bourgeois who renounces revolution, or else it means
simply deceiving oneself and others by sophistry." *Selected Works* (New York,
1934–38), 7: 175.

aries promote and other members of the system accept the return of war, the society itself must have become worse than war; and the desire for a better society, even at the expense of a temporary return to war, must have become widespread. True revolution is neither lunacy nor crime. It is the acceptance of violence to cause the system to change when all else has failed, and the very idea of revolution is contingent on this perception of societal failure.

No one has expressed the umbilical connection between revolutionary violence and its social context more succinctly than Ortega y Gasset: "Man has always had recourse to violence; sometimes this recourse was a mere crime and does not interest us here. But at other times violence was the means resorted to by him who had previously exhausted all others in defense of the rights of justice which he thought he possessed. It may be regrettable that human nature tends on occasion to this form of violence but it is undeniable that it implies the greatest tribute to reason and justice. For this form of violence is none other than reason exasperated. Force was, in fact, the *ultima ratio*. Rather stupidly it has been the custom to take ironically this expression which clearly indicates the previous submission of force to methods of reason. Civilization is nothing else than the attempt to reduce force to being the *ultima ratio*. We are now beginning to realize this with startling clearness because 'direct action' consists in inverting the order and proclaiming violence as the *prima ratio* or strictly as the *unica ratio*."[16]

The key to both the study and the conceptualization of revolutionary violence lies in social systems analysis. Utilizing the concept of the social system, we can distinguish between instances of violence that are revolutionary and those that merely constitute criminal or other forms of violent behavior.* Focusing on

* All revolutionary behavior is violent, but not all violent behavior is revolutionary. Some subrevolutionary violence such as scattered, local, decentralized violence (e.g., looting) serves to notify a society's elites of the need for reform—in order to forestall revolution. As Albert O. Hirschman has observed, "Even if violence is a necessary condition for revolution, it is not a sufficient one; . . . it is also a common element of reform. To qualify as revolutionary, violence must be *centralized*; it must attack and conquer the central seats of political and admin-

instances of purposive political violence, we can also use the
social system as a reference point for distinguishing between
those forms of violence known as war and revolution: revolution is intrasystemic, war intersystemic.

We can also use systems analysis to isolate and compare those
instances of purposive political violence that are neither wars
nor revolutions. One irreducible characteristic of a social system
is that its members hold in common a structure of values. A
value structure symbolically legitimates—that is, makes morally
acceptable—the particular pattern of interaction and stratification of the members of a social system. By bearing in mind the
functions of value structures we can better understand certain
kinds of ethnic or intertribal violence that may occur in what is
legally a unitary state though, lacking a unified value structure,
not yet a social system. Instances of such violence have recently
been numerous in Africa and southeast Asia, as they were during the nineteenth century in Europe. As Harry Eckstein has
noted: "In the case of the new state . . . there was, in all probability, no previously shared system of norms from which to
deviate and, even more probably, no previously settled institutional pattern; there can therefore be no speaking of internal war
[revolution] in the proper sense."[17]

The converse of Eckstein's problem is the anomaly discovered
by Hannah Arendt that "revolutions, properly speaking, did
not exist prior to the modern age; they are among the most
recent of all major political data."[18] Social systems analysis is
equally instructive here. It is true that premodern intrasystemic
conflicts were not called "revolutions," but revolutions assur-
edly occurred prior to the emergence of the nation-state. There
were numerous premodern social systems with unified value
structures but not unified authority structures (for example, me-

istrative power. . . . Since violence has in part the function of signalling protest to the central authorities, an improvement in the signalling mechanism
serves to increase pressure as much as an intensification of the problem.
. . . To paraphrase Marx, decentralized, unrequited violence is frequently
found in the role of indispensable midwife to *reform.*" *Journeys Toward Progress*
(New York, 1963), pp. 257, 260. Emphasis in the original.

dieval Christendom), and much of the intrasystemic violence that occurred in them should be understood as rebellions or revolutions rather than as wars. In some cases, however, this intrasystemic violence may have been closer to routinized conflict than to rebellion or revolution (e.g., various medieval wars of succession).

The concept of the value-coordinated social system also helps us to overcome certain errors that result from using Western definitions of violence. It can, for example, solve the puzzle of Max Gluckman's "rituals of rebellion" in Zululand.[19] The violent but routinized behavior of certain factions whenever a new Zulu chieftain was chosen may have been either a ritual or a rebellion, but it cannot very well have been both. If it was a ritual, as seems likely, it constitutes an instance of functional conflict in Zulu society, meeting certain system-derived needs. However, the extraordinary (by Western standards) violence of the behavior has led Gluckman to suggest that the term "rebellion" might be equally appropriate—hence his "rituals of rebellion." But true rebellion is never routinized, being in fact a rejection of old routines; and the determinants of rebellion would be considerably different from the determinants of functional conflict. Again, what is needed is an analysis of the values that allowed Zulus to orient and develop stable expectations toward behavior that in Gluckman's culture is regarded as disorienting and violent.

In this preliminary discussion, it is not being suggested that all insurrections arise from value conflicts. Conflicts over values and conflicts over interests may both produce insurrections, and the distinction between these two kinds of conflict is related to the distinction between rebellions and revolutions. What should be stressed at this point is that any analytical penetration of the behavior characterized as "purposive political violence" must utilize as its prime tool a conception of the social context in which the violence occurs.

2

The Social System: Coercion and Values

What is society? As Dorothy Emmet has observed, society may be "a term meant simply to refer to the concrete fact that a number of people are somehow together, with as little analytic suggestion as possible as to *how* they are grouped together." In order to convey this image of society the techniques of literature, with its emphasis on immediacy and accuracy, are most appropriate. "On the other hand, when we talk about a congeries of people as a society, we may be thinking of them as grouped in virtue of systematic types of relationships, and be trying to exhibit these."[1] Since we are concerned here with analyzing revolution in the abstract, we need such an abstract conception of society—one that refers to "some form of empirical alignment which constitutes a relation between people in virtue of which we think of them as grouped."[2]

The contemporary idea of a social system, with its subordinate concepts of role, status, norm, value, structure, functional integration, and so forth, has a distinguished pedigree in the history of Western political theory. In an analogous form, it is at least as old as Montesquieu; and its use of the concept of teleological "function," wherein a part is seen as functional insofar as it contributes to the maintenance of a whole, has its logical foundation in Aristotle. However, this idea is also extremely complex. Before introducing the technical terms that will allow us to talk about the parts of a social system and how they operate, it may be useful to look historically at the way in which the idea of society as a system has developed.

According to one early and important thesis about the nature of society, society is a form of order imposed by some men on others, and maintained by coercion. Hobbes did not hold precisely this view, but he certainly contributed to its development. The major problem to which coercion theorists address themselves is the universal fact of life that all men want more out of their environment than all of them can possibly get. Hobbes has stated the result of this predicament: "If any two men desire the same thing, which nevertheless they cannot both enjoy, they become enemies; and in the way to their end (which is principally their own conservation, and sometimes their delectation [i.e., pleasure] only), endeavor to destroy, or subdue one another."[3] Given the additional Hobbesian assumption that people are approximately equal in terms of physical strength, the endemic scarcity of goods and people's unlimited desires account for the perpetual violence of the state of nature. Also this is the impasse that social organization is intended (or functions) to overcome.

Hobbes himself sought to rationalize society by appealing to the common interest people have in avoiding violence. In an organized society, he contends, people will never have all the wealth and prestige they want, but they will receive a stable share and be secure from violence in their enjoyment of it. Actually, they have no choice. Given the radical equality among men, should any one attempt to obtain more than his share by resorting to violence against his neighbors, they would respond in kind and all of them would once again return to the state of nature. There, as a consequence of the perpetual violence, they would enjoy even less than they do in the admittedly imperfect state of civil society. The monarch, who is not a party to their "social contract," has more power than any of them; but since he exercises it to control potentially violent men, all people profit from obeying him and from subjecting themselves to him.

Later theorists have argued that Hobbes was correct in pointing to the fact of universal scarcity but wrong in believing the conflicts it generated could be eliminated in civil society. Marx, for example, believed that some people's acquisition of property gave them a power over others that they then used to *enforce* an inherently unequal and therefore unstable order in society. He believed that slowly changing elements in the material environment would erode the original property basis of power and lead to the development of classes and class conflict. A new group of intrinsic possessors, in one epoch the capitalists and in another the proletarians, would then revolt and recast the structure of society so as to reflect and preserve their own interests.

Contemporary coercion theorists continue to believe that the roots of social order lie in the coercion of some men by others, but they have vastly expanded Marx's notion that private property produces an artificial scarcity which generates the need for coercion. For men to survive at all in a naturally limited material environment, these theorists argue, people must divide their labor in a stable fashion and provide for the recruitment and assignment of men and women to various tasks ultimately dictated by the material environment, of which some will be harder and more important than others.* To enforce role assignments, preserve stability, attract specially qualified men through differential rewards, and, in general, enforce the division of labor (without which all members of the society would perish or fall to a level of bare subsistence), the division of labor itself demands that some men carry out command and supervisory duties. To do this effectively, since there is no natural or rational division of labor, coercive powers are necessary; and some people must be authorized to exercise these coercive powers. As Ralf Dahrendorf, a leading exponent of coercion theory, has concluded, "The fundamental inequality of social structure, and the lasting determinant of social conflict, is the inequality of power and authority which inevitably accompanies social organization."[4]

* On this point, we may compare the conclusion of David Lockwood: "It is unnecessary to argue that all conflicts, interests, facilities and powers are 'economic' in the sense of being related to the ownership of productive means. . . . The division of labor may be generalized into a category that stands for the factual disposition and organization of socially effective means, and need not be

This view, if accepted, leads directly to a sociological interpretation of government and to the Weberian theory of the state. Society, conceived as the successful adaptation of a collectivity of people to their environment through a division of their labor, cannot succeed unless some people have power over other people. The need for coercive sanctions rises not simply from the presence of deviants, or fools, or strangers, but from the demands of social organization itself. For, although the competition for limited resources may be mitigated to some extent by the division of labor, social organization raises the question of who should exercise and profit from the powers required by society. This condition gives rise to political conflict and the potential return of violence. The true mark of society, therefore, will be institutions charged with the exercise of physical force both to ensure the perpetuation of the division of labor and to regulate the use of violence in conflicts of political interest. The most typical form of such institutions is the state. As Weber put it, "If no social institution existed which knew the use of violence, then the concept of 'state' would be eliminated, and a condition would emerge that could be designated as 'anarchy,' in the specific sense of this word. . . . A state is a human community that (successfully) claims the *monopoly of the legitimate use of physical force* within a given territory. . . . Hence, 'politics' for us means striving to share power or striving to influence the distribution of power, either among states or among groups within a state."[5]

Just as violence was endemic in the Hobbesian state of nature because of scarce means, the threat of violence is endemic in society because of inequalities in access to power. Marx was right in thinking that social organizations were inherently unstable, but the source of this instability is not changing forces of

---

equated simply with the division of functions, powers and interests associated with productive means." "Some Remarks on 'The Social System,'" *British Journal of Sociology*, 7, no. 2 (June 1956), 139. Coercive powers in a society may be held, for example, by a military caste or an ethnic group rather than solely by a propertied class. The only thing that counts, according to this view, is that *some* group has powers over others.

production but changing relations of power and authority. (The coercion theorists of today reverse Marx's idea that authority is a form of property. They argue that property is, at most, a form of the more general category of authority.)⁶ Whether or not the interests generated by the inequalities of coercive capacity will cause the system to erupt into violence ultimately depends on whether the state's monopoly of power is a genuine monopoly.

In summarizing this view of society, Dahrendorf has written: "From the point of view of coercion theory, . . . it is not voluntary cooperation or general consensus but enforced constraint that makes social organizations cohere. In institutional terms, this means that in every social organization some positions are entrusted with a right to exercise control over other positions in order to ensure effective coercion; it means, in other words, that there is a differential distribution of power and authority. . . . This differential distribution of authority invariably becomes the determining factor of systematic social conflicts of a type that is germane to class conflicts in the traditional (Marxian) sense of the term."⁷

Acknowledging that we have omitted the elements of modern coercion theory most damaging to its main premise (e.g., its emphasis on the legitimation of power and its need to distinguish between latent and manifest interests, points to which we shall return), we may contrast it with its antithesis—the value theory of society. In a sense, the stream of social theorizing that began with Weber and Durkheim and in recent times has been represented by the work of Talcott Parsons should be read as a rejoinder to Marx. It does not wholly repudiate the idea that social organization generates its own inequalities and stratification, but it does reject the view that the structure of society is maintained chiefly by the coercion of the many by the power-holding few. Instead, it stresses that society is a "moral community," a collectivity of people who share certain "definitions of the situation" (called "values") that legitimate the inequalities of social organization and cause people to accept them as morally justified.

This view contrasts sharply with that of Marx, who saw values as merely the ideological justifications of privilege advanced by the dominant class: "The ruling ideas of a period have always been nothing but the ideas of the ruling class. . . . In each epoch, the thoughts of the ruling class are the ruling thoughts; i.e., the class that is the ruling material power of society is at the same time its ruling intellectual power. The class that has the means of material production in its control, controls at the same time the means of intellectual production."[8] Value theorists, on the other hand, doubt that the ruling beliefs of a society can be reduced to the beliefs of a ruling class; and they explicitly assert that, whatever their origins, values are an independent variable contributing to, or detracting from, the organization and integration of a society.

Parsons, as a leading exponent of this view, was categorical in his rejection of coercion theory, arguing that society is not possible unless all adult members jointly adhere to some principles that render the division of labor intelligible and tolerable. "A relatively established 'politically organized community,'" he wrote, "is clearly a 'moral community' to some degree, its members sharing common norms, values, and culture—which is to say that I start with a view that repudiates the idea that any political system that rests *entirely* on self-interest, force, or a combination of them, can be stable over any considerable period of time."[9] In his major work, *The Social System*, Parsons gave his strongest expression to this view: "[The] integration of a set of common value patterns with the internalized need disposition structure of the constituent personalities [i.e., sane, socialized people playing roles in the system] is the core phenomenon of the dynamics of social systems. That the stability of any social system except the most evanescent interaction process is dependent upon a degree of such integration may be said to be the fundamental dynamic theorem of sociology. It is the major point of reference for all analysis which may claim to be a dynamic analysis of social process."[10]

Numerous problems are raised by these two quotations. Are

the same values internalized (either through adoption or inculcation) by all members of a system? Or do people agree on values somewhat in the way that earlier theorists thought people agreed to "social contracts"? Why do institutions for coercion, such as the state, exist in societies if everyone agrees on the basis of social organization? Some of these problems must be delayed until we discuss the social system in its full complexity, and others until even later when we examine the personal dimensions of systemic disequilibrium. For the present, let us look more closely at the nature of values and how they facilitate living together without violence and without an overriding dependence on coercion.

Values are both *explanations* of a social situation (it does not matter whether the explanation is causal or mythical) and *standards* of appropriate action designed to produce some desired ("envalued") resolution or management of the situation. They are, for example, the explanation of why a Hindu outcaste is assigned miserable tasks in the Indian division of labor (he has committed a crime in some previous incarnation), and they tell him, abstractly, how he ought to behave in his present position (accept his lot, thereby preparing the way for an improved status in a later incarnation). In short, values are social gestalts or paradigms that, to the extent they are held in common (i.e., possessed by a group of people who recognize each other because of their mutual possession of them), lay a foundation of shared expectations and make possible the orienting of human behavior.

There are many different definitions of values, varying chiefly according to whether one is interested in the way joint possession of values produces systematic interactions among people or in the way an individual person orients his behavior while at the same time satisfying the demands of his personality. Some approximately parallel terms or ideas include Erik Erikson's notion of "ideology," Anthony Wallace's sense of "culture" and "mazeway" (referring, respectively, to the system and to the individual), Sebastian de Grazia's "belief system," Durkheim's *conscience collective*, Aristotle's principles, or laws, of distributive justice, Carlyle's interpretation of "pagan religion," and Hannah Arendt's extended sense of "authority" and its foundations.

In the more limited realm of organized scientific research, Thomas Kuhn's "paradigms" are an almost perfect counterpart of values in the society at large. According to Kuhn, paradigms are "universally recognized scientific achievements that for a time provide model problems and solutions to a community of practitioners"; they define what are scientific facts and structure the work of normal science.[11] Parsons defines values as "the commitments of individual persons to pursue and support certain *directions* or types of action for the collectivity as a system and hence derivatively for their own roles in the collectivity."[12] A definition similar to that of Parsons, stressing commitment but also leaving room for the possible withdrawal of commitment in extremely ambiguous situations, is that of Jacob and his colleagues: values are "the normative standards by which human beings are influenced in their choice among the alternative courses of action which they perceive."[13]

We shall make use of several of these ideas throughout this study. For the moment, let us look at the problem of value sharing and individual human diversity in order to indicate more precisely how values operate. In an influential article on the "functional prerequisites of a society," D. F. Aberle and others posited that "shared cognitive orientations" were one such prerequisite.[14] This idea, and similar ones like it derived from Durkheim, Freud, Fromm, and Margaret Mead, created a good deal of confusion in social systems theory when it was confronted with the vast psychoanalytic and behavioral evidence that very few people in a social system actually do share "cognitive orientations" (e.g., motives) to any appreciable degree. Even in a highly homogeneous and isolated society, people persist in thinking their own thoughts and reveal marked personality differences. How is it possible, then, for them to hold common values—values that cause their behavior to synchronize?

Anthony Wallace has given the most serious attention to this problem. He rejects the notion that all people in a society are identically motivated and that the chief functional problem of a society is the reproduction, through socialization, of people who think alike. If this notion were accurate—and it is actually contrary both to common sense experience and to much clinical and statistical evidence—conflict and revolution in a society could have only one cause, namely, the inefficiency or failure of the mechanisms of socialization. In fact, great differences exist among people in terms of their personalities, motives, life experiences, habits, and physical and mental capacities. When this diversity is emphasized, Wallace argues, the fundamental problem of an orderly, integrated social system becomes not the replication of uniformity but the "organization of diversity."[15] People do not share motives or cognitive orientations, and value theory does not imply that they must. In fact, if everyone had the same motives, we might doubt that a stable division of labor could exist at all. An identity of motives comes closer to being a premise of the coercion theory, for that theory only makes sense if we assume the existence of identical cognitions, which are rendered incompatible by an environment of scarcity.

What is necessary for a division of labor and for social interaction generally is that "the behavior of other people under various circumstances is predictable, irrespective of knowledge of their motivations, and thus is capable of being predictably related to one's own actions."[16] The sharing of values, or of definitions of a situation, makes this mutual predictability possible. Values are somewhat analogous to final agreements, carefully hammered out in collective bargaining sessions, where precedent, tradition, and universally respected products of inspiration influence the bargainers on all sides. Values establish what Wallace calls "equivalent behavioral expectancies," or, more briefly, "implicit contracts." Using the word "culture" in the sense in which we use the word "value," he concludes: "It is *culture* which is shared (in the special sense of institutional contract) rather than personality, and culture may be conceived as an invention which makes possible the maximal organization of motivational diversity."[17]

As we have seen, two characteristics of values are that they provide people with definitions of situations and with standards of behavior, regardless of their motives. Another characteristic of values is that they provide abstract explanations of the human condition. Systems of human action can be distinguished from all other systems in that human beings have a need for believing their actions to be meaningful beyond mere physical self-maintenance. There are many other problems posed by individual personality needs within the context of the social system, and most of these are best delayed until a later stage of analysis; however, a short digression on this subject is unavoidable.

Sometimes we have spoken of the division of labor as if it were the end rather than the beginning of social organization. Actually we know that life in society means a great deal more to its participants than mere cooperative specialization in work or the enslavement of some men by others so all may eat. Physical nourishment is one basic human need; but there are other needs almost as basic. Past efforts to specify what these needs are have not met with any widespread agreement, but they have led to at least one generalization—namely, that whatever basic human needs there may be, they are arranged hierarchically, and certain needs do not emerge until more basic ones have been fulfilled. An example of such a hierarchy of needs is the one suggested by A. H. Maslow: physical needs (water, food, and sex); safety (order, predictability, and dependability of the environment); love, affection, and belongingness; self-esteem; and, finally, self-actualization.[18]

It is not necessary to follow this or any other list of "basic human needs" to accept the notion that there is a basic need for an explanation of the social and material environment in which a human organism finds itself. Presumably this need is of the second order—on the level of safety in Maslow's list—and emerges together with the appearance of sociopolitical organization in human life. We may explain this need in various ways— for example, in terms of the need for optimism or hope in order for people to do more than scavenge for food, or in terms of the inability of people to manage the tensions produced by a purposeless existence. The ultimate determinants of such a need probably lie in the greatly increased size of human cranial capacity. Whatever the final cause, people not only divide their labor but also provide themselves with (or accept) some intellectual construct that lends significance to their being together and working together. Values thus provide meanings for social action; they make sense of reality.

Religions, social myths, some moral philosophies, and numerous metaphysical beliefs all contribute to what we have been calling values. Thomas Carlyle, although he seems to have exaggerated wildly both the extent to which the act of myth-making requires "genius" and the extent to which it is deserving of being worshiped as "heroic," understood better than most social scientists the need for myths. In his own highly distinctive style, he wrote: "Pagan religion is indeed an Allegory, a Symbol of what men felt and knew about the Universe; and all Religions are Symbols of that, altering always as that alters: but it seems to me a radical perversion, and even *in*version, of the business, to put that forward as the origin and moving cause, when it was rather the result and termination. To get beautiful allegories, a perfect poetic symbol, was not the want of men; but to know what they were to believe about this Universe, what course they were to steer in it; what, in this mysterious Life of theirs, they had to hope and to fear, to do and to forbear doing."[19]

Carlyle recognized intuitively that the possession of a mythical or causal explanation of life is one of the attributes of socialized human beings. Unfortunately, such explanations are not, as he contends, "altering always as that [the life situation] alters." Sometimes they do change in relative synchronization with the environment of a society, and it is greatly to the advantage of social stability that they should. At other times, however, they may change (e.g., as a result of cultural borrowings or innovations in scientific paradigms) while the empirical situation remains unchanged; or they may remain unchanged while the empirical situation is being transformed (e.g., as a result of technical innovation or foreign conquest). These circumstances of noncongruence pose the greatest threat to the stability and ultimate viability of a social system. Values, in the present sense of abstract interpretations of reality, are governed by a principle rather analogous to that of the state conceived as a monopoly of force; both had better maintain their monopolies if they are not to be subverted and, possibly, overthrown. It is for this reason, as we shall see, that the explanatory or definitional function of values has such great relevance to the sociology of revolution.

With regard to the division of labor, values obviate the need to maintain discrimination primarily by coercion.[20] For example, in societies that consider competition and achievement the just way to determine winners, the resulting stratification of winners and losers is morally acceptable to both strata. It is not necessary to force the losers' stratum to perform the less desirable jobs, only to include compensatory values for the losers. "The meek shall inherit the earth," the myth of the noble poor, and popular beliefs that contrast the responsibilities of the powerful with the freedom of the unencumbered illustrate such compensatory values. In a similar fashion, societies with ascriptive values do not generate conflict when the eldest son of a ruler succeeds his father; and they normally tolerate, or systematically compensate for, the inefficiency that results if the son does not possess the temperament of a good ruler. As these examples also illustrate, the types of values a society has provide the basis for a typology of societies.

The most important function of the value system in a society is to authorize or legitimate the use of force. Although the distinction between power and authority is almost as old as political theory itself, the precise relationship between the use of force and the two facets of this behavior known as "power" and "authority" remains imprecise in social systems analysis. Too often social theorists have merely followed Weber, who defined power as the "probability that one actor within a social relationship will be in a position to carry out his own will despite resistance, regardless of the basis on which this probability rests," and authority as "the probability that a command with a given specific content will be obeyed by a given group of persons."[21] This distinction leads directly to the rather misleading conclusion that "the important difference between power and authority consists in the fact that whereas power is essentially tied to the personality of individuals, authority is always associated with social positions or roles. . . . While power is merely a factual relationship, authority is a legitimate relation of domination and subjection."[22]

Translated into value theory, such a distinction between power and authority is roughly the same as the distinction between the state of nature and the value-coordinated moral community. As Weber well knew, however, both power and authority exist—concretely and conceptually—within a moral community. What is needed, therefore, is a threefold distinction between strength, power, and authority. In the state of nature—an ideal realm of human interaction not coordinated by shared values—strength is the touchstone in determining the outcome of any social conflict. We may conceive of this strength as more or less equally distributed among men, as Hobbes did, and argue that violence is therefore a continuous phenomenon in the state of nature, unrelieved by the domination of one man over others. Or we may argue that even in the state of nature one armed man or a group of kinsmen can establish some order through the coercion of others. In either case, however, such relationships are mediated by a calculus of strength (including the effect of strength to create some order through deterrence), and strength is always a personal characteristic of the dominant party. Questions of legitimacy play no part whatsoever in this pure calculus of strength.*

Power and authority, by contrast, both refer to relationships

* This distinction between strength and power is identical to that of Hannah Arendt: "In distinction to strength, which is the gift and the possession of every man in his isolation against all other men, power comes into being only if and when men join themselves together for the purpose of action, and it will disappear when, for whatever reason, they disperse and desert one another." *On Revolution* (New York, 1963), p. 174.

of legitimacy, the first being a generalized kind of legitimate relationship and the second being a highly specific institution charged with regulating tests of legitimacy when they occur and exercising physical coercion in order to preserve the division of labor. Let us try to elucidate the differences between these two concepts within a value-coordinated system. In a stable social system, as we have seen, the members share values that permit them, through mutual expectations, to orient their behavior. That is to say, value sharing establishes a degree of trust and confidence in the normalcy of a particular pattern of social inter-action and in the likelihood of its continuing. This trust, which is a characteristic of all moral communities, permits members greatly to expand their activities because they do not have to make continuous appeals to supervisory and commanding or-gans for decisions. In a moral community most of the funda-mental questions of how to organize social action have been settled, at least temporarily, and members can therefore get on with the daily business of life.

Within such communities, the expansion and proliferation of activities are not random. They are carried out in conformity with what Parsons calls "generalized [i.e., standardized] media of the interaction process," which may also be understood as alternative but complementary regulators of behavior, or tech-niques of social control.[23] All these media rest in major degree on the trust and confidence generated by value sharing. Parsons suggests that there are four types of social control, each one utilizing specific media of interaction. They are: the offer of posi-tive advantages, or inducement, using the media of economic exchange (e.g., a monetary system); the invocation of obliga-tions, or power, using the media that threaten disadvantage (e.g., coercion); the use of persuasion, or influence; and the appeal to conscience, or the direct invocation of the moral stan-dards of right and wrong within a value system.

It is not necessary for us to argue here that this list is exhaus-tive or that it could not be formulated in some other way. We are satisfied that it conceptualizes a phenomenon easily observed empirically: that communities in which trust and confidence prevail are far more active and productive than coercive communities. The idea directly relevant to studies of violence is that power is one generalized medium of interaction. In order to illustrate its properties as a medium of interaction and to stress its reliance on the trust and confidence of value-coordinated societies, Parsons compares power to another generalized medium—money.

A basic theorem in economics and a concrete principle in the daily operations of central banks is that "the primary basis of the value of money is general confidence that expectations of the productivity of the system will be realized."[24] Power, as a generalized medium, operates in a way analogous to the functioning of money. "The money held by a social unit is, we may say, the unit's capacity, through market channels under given rules of procedure, to command goods and services in exchange, which for its own reasons it desires. Correspondingly, the power of a unit is its capacity, through invoking binding obligations [e.g., civic obligations such as military service, contractual obligations, the obligation to follow vested leadership, and so forth] to contribute to collective goals, to bring about collective goal-inputs that the 'constituents' of the collective action in question desire. . . . Once units are brought within the relevant context of collective organization, power is the medium of invoking their obligations to contribute to collective functioning. . . . [Like monetary systems, power systems] depend on the continuing willingness of their members to entrust their status in and interpretations of the collective interest to an impersonal process in which binding decisions are made without the members being in a position to control them [directly]."[25]

Power and money are greatly expandable in systems in which the mediation of values generates conditions of trust and confidence. But the viability of neither power nor money rests solely on trust. There will always be some people, for reasons to be explained later, who refuse to honor obligations or accept legal tender or bank drafts. In the first instance, those who exercise power resort to imposing progressively greater disadvantages (negative sanctions), just as the authors of rejected bank drafts either arrange to pay increasing amounts of their debts in monetized bullion or reduce their debts by contracting economic operations. However, "the question of whether [force] is or is not the 'basis' of power is ambiguous in a sense exactly parallel to that of the question of 'basing' the value of money on command of gold reserves."[26] Trust in the system itself is as important in the operation of these media as the supply of force or gold. And it is the joint possession of a value system (in the specific sense of shared "culture") that lays the ultimate foundation of trust.

Since occasionally there will be "deflations" in the power system, similar to monetary deflations, society needs institutions authorized to exercise force in order to reestablish confidence. The most typical form of this institution is the state. The state is the institutionalization of *authority*, which is a special form of power. Authorities may themselves invoke obligations (exercise power), but if they are not obeyed they may also use force to ensure compliance. Moreover, since they maintain a monopoly over the use of force they are the final appeal for individuals lacking the authority to use force, whose own exercise of power has been thwarted. Those entrusted with authority are keepers of the *ultima ratio*, but they do not exercise all power within a system. The concentration of all power and all authority in the hands of the government would be, in fact, an ideal definition of totalitarianism. In the stable, value-sharing community, the distribution of power produces a relatively much higher level of effective collective action than in the tyrannous state, or in the state so oriented toward a single goal that the totalitarian form of organization becomes tolerable.

The value system defines the roles and statuses of authority, and at the same time is the source of this authority's legitimacy.

When force is used by authorities in a manner understood or expected by those sharing the system of values—that is, in a way to which all value-sharers are committed—it is said to be legitimate. Any other use of force, including that by persons who exercise power but not authority, is condemned as violence and is itself subject to a negative obligation (exercise of power) and to suppression by legitimate force (exercise of authority).

The capacity of authorities to maintain confidence in the power system does not, of course, rest solely on the use of force; that only becomes true in the last resort. The possession of a true monopoly over the legitimate use of force allows the authorities to exercise control through coercion, of which the use of force is only the final and extreme form in a hierarchy of means. Coercion includes deterrence by threat or warning, the prevention of actions by means of physical confinement, other forms of punishment (e.g., fining), a symbolic demonstration of the capacity to act by the maintenance of superior means of force, and, finally, the use of force itself.[27] Since one of the purposes (or functions) of the value-coordinated social system is to release communal energies by generating confidence (or stable expectations), the use of force in the exercise of authority is rare and carefully circumscribed. If it is used capriciously, even though the commander of the force may be authorized to use it by the rules of the system (the distinction between rules, or norms, and values will be introduced later), this use of force will be disorienting and condemned as violence (a military coup d'état is an extreme example). Legitimacy is a function of the value structure, not a carte blanche for the occupants of certain statuses to compel obedience to their orders.

Since this threefold distinction between strength, power, and authority covers a greater range of behavior than is generally included under the Weberian definitions of power and authority, it is particularly useful for conceptualizing dysfunctional and potentially revolutionary conditions in a value-coordinated social system. The prime characteristic of revolutionary conditions, in the opinion of many political theorists, is the "loss of authority." Hannah Arendt, for example, has written, "No revolution ever succeeded, [and] few rebellions ever started, so long as the authority of the body politic was truly intact."[28] In a different context, she has concluded, "Generally speaking, we may say that no revolution is even possible where the authority of the body politic is truly intact, and this means, under modern conditions, where the armed forces can be trusted to obey the civil authorities."[29]

At a later point we shall explore in detail the ramifications of the "loss of authority." However, simply in terms of our present distinctions, we can see that it implies above all a "power deflation." Ever-increasing demands for the use of the *ultima ratio* as well as a great contraction of the media of interaction within a system are, empirically, danger signals indicating the proximity of revolution. When confidence has evaporated to the extent that the exercise of power is futile, when the authority of the status-holders entrusted with supervision and command rests *only* on their monopoly of force, and when there is no foreseeable prospect of a processual change in this situation, revolution is at hand. Since superior strength is now the sole basis for social order, there will usually be an increase in the strength of the police and the army.* Such superior force may delay the eruption of violence; nevertheless, a division of labor maintained by Cossacks is no longer a community of value-sharers, and in such a situation revolution is endemic and insurrection inevitable. This fact reveals once again the necessity of investigating a system's value structure and its problems in order to conceptualize the revolutionary situation in any theoretically meaningful way.

---

* The conclusion of Stanislaw Andrzejewski offers a comparison: "Government not based on naked force can function only if certain beliefs are accepted by the overwhelming majority of the population; if there is an agreement on the right to command and duty to obey. If such agreement does not exist, either because of ethnic heterogeneity or in consequence of an internal schism, naked force must remain the argument of last resort, and the distribution of military might the principal determinant of social structure." *Military Organization and Society* (London, 1954), p. 123.

Sociological value theory explicitly rejects the notion that social cooperation is coerced; in its conception of a system's integration, the authoritative or legitimate use of force is limited to
situations where the consensus on values has broken down and,
even then, only as a last resort. The question raised by this kind
of value theory is why institutions of authority should be
needed at all in a community based on value sharing, in which
the basic questions of justice and equity have been settled. Why
do some men withdraw their commitment to a system's values?
Why do some people refuse to honor obligations or accept bank
drafts? Why, in short, do "power deflations" sometimes occur?

Contemporary value theorists address themselves to this
problem chiefly through the concept of "deviant behavior" (i.e.,
deviant from the point of view of the standards prescribed by a
value system). According to value theorists, the major causes of
deviancy within the value-coordinated division of labor are
three: imperfect socialization, meaning that the values of the
system have been imperfectly imparted to new members; "role
strain," resulting from the attempt to integrate one system (the
human being), with its own needs, into another system (the
society), which can lead to socially caused mental illness; and
normative discord, resulting from conflicting norms or ambigui-
ties within the value system itself—for example, the dilemma of
the physician who is committed to relieving the suffering of rich
and poor alike in a system that also values the acquisition of
wealth through profit taking.[30]

These are extremely important sources of potential conflict,
violence, and even revolt; and they are sufficient in themselves
to warrant institutions of authority to enforce social behavior.
However, it is extremely misleading to conceive of the sources
of antisocial behavior (and the need for coercive institutions)
only in this way. From the point of view of the logic of value
theory, these kinds of deviancy could all, in principle, be eliminated from the social system. They are not generated by the
structure of society itself, but by imperfections in the structure—
for example, by unstandardized socialization procedures, im-

perfect role assignments, or inconsistencies in legal and normative codes. Efficient social engineering, such as that envisaged
by Aldous Huxley in his *Brave New World*, could eliminate these
flaws and thereby eliminate the need for the state.

The greatest weakness of value theory, when it is used as the
sole analytical tool in conceptualizing the social system, is its
inability to conceive of any form of antisocial behavior other
than deviancy. This becomes more evident when we push the
implications of value sharing to their extremes. Unalloyed value
theory, as it was conceived by some nineteenth-century writers,
provides the basis for the ideal of the historical Anarchist movement and for Marx's vision of true communism. As the Anarchist writer Anselme Bellegarrigue stated in 1848: "Anarchy is
order, government is civil war."[31] Few social scientists today
would equate anarchy with order, since to them anarchy means
the condition in which social actors hold incompatible and in-
congruous definitions of a situation of social action.[32] To the
Anarchists, however, the word meant precisely the opposite.

Wilhelm Weitling, for example, as quoted by Bakunin, said:
"The perfect society has no government, only an administration, no laws only obligations, no punishments only means of
correction."[33] And how is this society to be achieved? The answer is obvious. So long as men agree on the need for an equita-
ble division of labor and for cooperation (i.e., so long as they
share the same values), coercive institutions become unnecessary and even pernicious. Seen from the Anarchist perspective,
authority appears in a new light: it is the instrument of exploitation used by a truly antisocial ruling class.

Pure value theory is only slightly dissimilar. It takes a tragic
view of authority, arguing that it is an inescapable consequence
of man's imperfectibility, a necessary antidote to "deviancy."
That Anarchism and an extreme statement of value theory do
coincide is strongly suggested by Proudhon's answer to the
question, "What guarantees the observance of justice [in Anarchist society]?" "The same thing that guarantees that the mer-
chant will respect the coin—faith in reciprocity, that is to say,

justice itself. Justice is for intelligent and free beings the supreme cause of their decisions."[34]

What is wrong with these views? Why should so powerful a tool of social analysis as value theory lead to such an absurd conclusion? The answer is that value theory is unable to conceive of sources of interest and conflicts of interest other than the interest men have in conforming to a value system's definition of a situation. A fully articulated model of the social system must therefore go beyond simple value theory and supplement it with an analysis of nonnormative conflict occurring in and having an effect on the value-coordinated social system.

As we have seen, value sharing makes possible an expansion of collective action well beyond the level of coerced cooperation, but values and the people united by them never exist in a vacuum. A system of social action has for its setting a complex social, economic, and political environment (i.e., an economic geography and the presence of other, often hostile, social systems). The values of the system are, so to speak, addressed to this "environment," and they can either facilitate or retard attempts to exploit and adapt to it. Values themselves cannot be *derived* entirely from the existential determinants of societies, except within the broadest limits (e.g., the values appropriate to a peasant society would be dysfunctional among hunters and gatherers); but values do interact (and optimally synchronize) with a concrete sociopolitical environment. The influence of the environment—the "substratum" of social action, or the tangible facts of life that the value structure explains and makes intelligible—must be considered on a par with the influence of the value system in any analysis of the determinants of a particular social system.

Values and the requirements of environmental adaptation determine a social structure; they also produce conflicts within it. As we indicated earlier, social organization has as its primary purpose (or function) the maintenance of order, or the transcendence of violence. Violence (in the sense of a purposive strategy of violence, or more generally, any form of behavior to which people are unable to orient themselves) is caused by *relations of conflict*. These relations of conflict are, in Dahrendorf's definition, "all relations between sets of individuals that involve an incompatible difference of objective."[35] To reduce the amount of violence among its members, a social system must eliminate some relations of conflict and "routinize" others—that is, envelop them in rules accepted by both sides so that the relationship becomes competitive (a "game") or ceremonial and therefore not disorienting. Certainly all social conflict does not lead to violence; it is often an agreed-on method for reaching decisions without violence (e.g., collective bargaining), and much of it contributes to the maintenance of the system.* However, any relationship involving conflict can lead to violence, and the extent to which a system eliminates or routinizes relations of conflict is therefore a measure of its viability (one possible cause of its demise being the return of the war of all against all).

Relations of conflict resolved by violence are ubiquitous in the state of nature. Relations of conflict resolved by means other than violence are ubiquitous in society. A specific value system synchronized with a specific pattern of environmental adaptation (i.e., a division of labor that copes with its particular socioeconomic terrain) inescapably gives rise to conflicts at the same time that it provides the means for eliminating or routinizing them. The problem of social conflict and its resolution cannot be understood unless both the value and environmental *sources* of conflict are considered and unless the conflict-regulating *capacity* of a system is considered in the context of how its values legitimate the particular way the system adapts to its environment.

---

* Weber's distinctions on these points are helpful: "A social relationship will be referred to as 'conflict' in so far as action within it is oriented intentionally to carrying out the actor's own will against the resistance of the other party or parties. The term 'peaceful' conflict will be applied to cases in which actual physical violence is not employed. A peaceful conflict is 'competition' in so far as it consists in a formally peaceful attempt to attain control over opportunities and advantages which are also desired by others. A competitive process is 'regulated' competition to the extent that its ends and means are oriented to an order." *The Theory of Social and Economic Organization* (New York, 1964), pp. 132–33.

We have already mentioned some of the conflicts that the value system itself may generate (i.e., those caused by faulty socialization, role strain, and normative discord). The environment also generates conflicts. One form of these, conflicts of interest, stems from the competition for scarce goods. Value sharing mitigates these conflicts to some extent, but never eliminates them entirely. The value system may cause people to accept the broad differentials in rewards among social strata, but conflicts of interest will still be generated among individuals or groups occupying the same stratum and in the process of exchange among strata. To prevent these conflicts of material interest from leading to violence, the system will derive norms of bargaining and compromise from the overall value structure. If these norms prove unequal to the resolution of such conflicts, thereby generating further disagreements (this time over "the normative status of social objects"),[36] the conflicts must then be presented to the authorities for their action. They can resolve the conflicts either by deciding them on the basis of existing laws or norms, or by legislating new and more acceptable laws. Whatever they decide, they may have to enforce their decisions by force. The existence of these sorts of conflicts thus demands that the society entrust certain people with authority; and the stability of the society will depend, in one measure, on the success of its authorities in "routinizing" the acceptance of their decisions and in preventing some conflicts from developing through the routine reform of norms.[37]

Another environmental source of conflict is created by the successful management of the first. The very fact that relationships of power and authority do exist in a system creates the basis for conflicts of political interest. Power and authority, by definition, involve relationships of command and obedience—that is, of inequality. The presence of power thus automatically initiates a competition for it, and these political conflicts may become violent. The value system will eliminate certain of the conflicts by providing jointly understood definitions of the type of person who ought to occupy a particular power position. It will attempt to routinize the remaining conflicts by articulating rules for regulating or institutionalizing the competition for power. If, however, those who enjoy power betray the values of the system by employing violence, in the process of either acquiring or occupying a power status, an attempt will be made by other power holders to punish them for their behavior through the use of legitimate force. If the betrayal cannot be rectified, it may produce a rebellion.

Still a third form of social conflict is interstratum disputes, which often concern both the distribution of scarce goods and the allegedly excessive powers of the ruling stratum (e.g., "class warfare"). The value structure plays a crucial role in preventing such conflicts. It explains and legitimates the stratification of the system, and at the same time attempts to reduce the likelihood of interstratum conflict by developing norms such as equal opportunity, social mobility, co-option, and philanthropy. When conflicts do develop, the authorities must take action to relieve them. The only remedy for this kind of conflict is social change of either the value structure or the pattern of the division of labor or both, in order to bring them back into synchronization. During the time this change is being accomplished, a power deflation is likely to develop, requiring the use of force to maintain order. If the authorities fail to recognize such a situation or fail by their actions to correct it, other things being equal, a revolution will ensue.

Conflict theorists acknowledge the role of value sharing in reducing the likelihood of interstratum conflicts of interest. They do this through a distinction between "latent and manifest interests."[38] Latent interests, a purely analytical construct, are the interests any player of a subordinate role or occupant of a subordinate status (or groups of such people) *might* have if the value system did not make his position in the hierarchy acceptable. Manifest interests, or what Marx called "class consciousness," are interests in preserving or altering a *status quo* that are self-consciously perceived by parties to an interstratum conflict. According to this distinction, latent interests will never become manifest so long as the value structure remains synchronized with the demands of environmental adaptation. If they do become manifest, the society must either change in the direction of resynchronization or explode into violent revolution. The actions of the authorities are obviously central in determining which will occur.

In considering whether or not relations of conflict will lead to social violence, the main dynamic condition we must explore is the synchronization between the value system and the division of labor. Values and the division of labor are both independent variables determining this condition. It is not enough to study either the one or the other, or both separately; we must study the way each does, or does not, complement the other. David Lockwood has expressed the reasoning behind this approach as follows: "Just as the problem of order is not just a function of the existence of a normative order and the social mechanisms which procure motivation to conform with it [e.g., socialization] but also of the existence of a social substratum [division of labor] which structures interests differentially in the social system, so the problem of conflict is not reducible to the analysis of the division of labor and the group interests consequent on it. It is rather that both conflict and order are a function of the interaction of norm and substratum."[39] To conceptualize these relationships, we need a model of the social system that synthesizes the coercion theory and the value theory of social integration. Such a model provides the key to analyzing the changing society— one that may be threatened with revolution.

The Social System: Structure and Function

We began the last chapter by asking "What is society?" Now we shall rephrase this question using the more analytical language of social science and ask "What is a social system?" The word "system," when properly used, describes any group of variables arranged to form a whole (e.g., a solar system) and having a particular kind of relationship with each other—namely, they are mutually influencing ("interdependent") and they tend to maintain the relationship they have with each other over time ("equilibrium").[1] Because human societies often display these characteristics, social scientists have found it intellectually profitable to conceive of the order displayed by human societies as a "systematic" type of order. In studying the systematic order of human societies, we must specify, on the one hand, the interdependent variables that constitute the structure of social action and, on the other hand, the work these variables must perform in order to create and maintain an equilibrium. That is, we must specify what are sometimes called the functional prerequisites of a social system.

In this book we are not interested in all human situations that could be described as social systems or subsystems (e.g., churches, armies, families), but only in those social systems that constitute whole human societies. The defining characteristics of such societies are that they exist longer than the life span of any one individual contributing to them, form self-sufficient wholes, and replenish their supplies of contributing actors, at least in part, through sexual reproduction.[2] Our problem, therefore, is to describe analytically the parts, their interdependence, and the equilibrium of a self-reproducing, self-sufficient system of human behavior that persists beyond the life span of any one member.

The parts that constitute a social system of cooperative action are patterns of behavior to which members of the system are oriented by virtue of such patterns of behavior being expected. They are the tasks that are divided up and assigned in the division of labor, and they are known as roles. No person's life is taken up entirely with maintaining or reproducing the system of social action he or she belongs to, but all actions that have any significance from the perspective of the social system (the perspective taken by the systems analyst) are actions in conformity with, or in violation of, a role. Role analysis is the study of the consequences, intentional or unintentional, for the maintenance of the total system, of a particular ensemble of roles and the ways they are performed.

The idea of role does not depend on the motivation of the actor. As David Riesman has observed, "Roles within a social system may harness various types of personalities. To put it more specifically, you can get the same kind of political behavior, for instance, out of quite different human types. Although the behavior has different meanings for these people, the understanding of their differences and those different meanings may be quite irrelevant to their political and public role."[3] A player of a role may understand his role simply as a series of obligations and rights that are socially recognized and that, being so recognized, allow him to determine his own behavior and to orient himself to the behavior of others.

Behavior in roles is sometimes institutionalized. An institutionalized role may be one whose rules of performance have been codified or made legally explicit (with specific sanctions attached for nonperformance)—for example, a tax collector. Or it may be one whose standards of performance are so widely known and agreed on throughout the society that only relatively limited variations in execution are allowed—for example, the roles inherent in the institution of marriage and the family. Institutions may also refer to sets of roles whose standardized expectations of behavior have been made explicit—for example, a government bureaucracy.

No role is absolutely rigid in its standards of performance. Even a constitutionally defined role such as Supreme Court justice has changed as a result of conscious innovations and specific performances by various incumbents, even though the role requirements have remained the same.[4] However, variations in performing a role can never be entirely separated from the way the role is defined by the social system, regardless of who may be its incumbent. "Role requirements . . . constitute ranges of tolerable behavior rather than highly precise behavioral limitations. Extremes will normally be subject to negative sanctions, with considerable latitude in between."[5]

Role requirements, or standards of expected performance that govern roles, are norms. They are positive rules of behavior, appropriate to a particular role and elaborated in accordance with a system's value structure; and they may be created through codification or inherited from custom, or both. Codified norms control institutionalized roles. A common way in some societies to institutionalize a role is to codify its norms through a legitimate, authoritatively enforced legal system (e.g., military roles are codified in most nation-states today, but they depended on custom in most feudal societies). Values, as we have seen, differ from norms in that they are the general moral and definitional symbols which, when shared, establish the conscious solidarity that characterizes people joined together in a moral community. Thus the value of "private property" or "freedom of expression" is given normative expression by specific rules that say what kinds of social transactions and events should be sanctioned in order to realize such values. The concrete rules of behavior attached to various roles (e.g., the taboo against incest, or the legal and customary obligations controlling economic exchange) and the institutionalized sets of norms that guide the allocation and assignment of roles of authority (e.g., political constitutions) are inspired and legitimated by the system's value structure. Since values themselves interact with the demands of environmental adaptation, norms derived from a value structure will provide morally acceptable (i.e., legitimate) rules for performing the roles dictated by a particular division of labor.

The efficiency of norms in controlling role behavior is particularly sensitive to the degree of congruence between the value structure and the environment. In societies in which the two are perfectly synchronized, the rules of behavior will hardly appear to be rules at all, and new rules will be the result of political consensus rather than political conflict. In societies in which values and the division of labor are dissynchronized, norms, and particularly institutionalized norms, will be far more salient. And when values are insecure as a result of social change, norms themselves—partially legitimated by the crumbling value structure but also buttressed by coercive enforcement—become the basic principles for organizing the work of the society. Since they no longer rest on a solid basis of shared values, they will be subject to frequent violations, taxing the abilities of authorities to enforce them; and their content will become a major focus of attention and argument. In stable times, by contrast, norms are accepted unquestioningly as envalued definitions of the environment.

In addition to having roles and norms governing these roles, a society must differentiate among the various activities required by its values and environment in such a way that a workable ensemble of roles exists. Age and sex differences alone impose a degree of natural role differentiation on any society; no individual can perform all the roles of a society through his or her own labor, no matter how simple the tasks required.[6] However, in differentiating among roles, assigning people to them, settling conflicts of interest based on scarcity, and solving the disputes arising from multiple role playing and role confusion (e.g., the concrete problems that occur when one person simultaneously plays the roles of legislator and businessman, and the systemic problems posed by the conflicting roles of priest and scientist), the society must entrust some roles with supervisory powers and with the authority to enforce decisions. As we saw in the last chapter, conflicts of interest over the differential rewards attached to various roles create a primary need for authority. The existence of supervisory powers themselves creates further conflicts of political interest that require still more managerial and supervisory roles capable of exercising coercive authority.

The inevitable result of solving problems of role differentiation, role assignment, and conflict is the creation of a ranking or hierarchy of roles. The basis of the hierarchy is a value-derived determination of the importance of each role, and the product is a stratified system of roles in which different roles carry different amounts of prestige. The position occupied by each role within a network of stratification is called its status.

Status is the structural dimension of the dynamic concept of role. A status is a social position endowed with certain rights and obligations, whereas the exercise of these rights and obligations by the occupant of the status is the performance of his or her role. Like role, status is a social concept; a person cannot occupy a status or play a role all by himself.[7] Since each status, as well as the whole network of stratification, is legitimated by the value structure, and since a system of roles must also come to grips with the realities of a society's environment, the stability of the status hierarchy depends on the degree of synchronization between the value structure and adaptation to the environment. Similarly, the inputs into the value-environmental nexus establish the limits within which the particular configuration of a given status hierarchy may vary (e.g., merchants always occupy low statuses in peasant societies, but their precise status varies among peasant societies). Status and role are, respectively, the static and dynamic aspects of the basic concept of the division of labor. Value explanations and definitions of the division of labor make the discriminations between various statuses morally acceptable. However, to the extent that the value structure fails to render legitimate the hierarchy of stratification, status protests will develop, threatening the entire status structure and leading potentially to a recasting of the division of labor.

Using the ideas of role, norm, and status, we are able to conceptualize the structural nature of a system of social action. A social system is composed of roles (actions) played from statuses and guided by norms. As Dahrendorf has put it, "The basic unit of structural analysis . . . is that of role, i.e., a complex of behavioral expectancies which are associated with a given social position or status. In structural analysis, the human individual in the fullness of his expressions figures only as an incumbent of such positions, and 'player' of roles."[8] A structure, however, is not a system; a system has a structure. Once we have stated what a system's structure is, we are still left with the complex question of how this structure functions to meet the needs of the system (determined by value and environmental interaction) and to maintain an equilibrium.

The phrase "to meet the needs of the system" raises one of the truly controversial questions in the history of social analysis. The very word "needs" implies the question "needs for what?" What are the ends of a social system that generate a need to reach, or fulfill, them? To suggest that social systems have needs is to imply that social systems have ends. Yet many political philosophers and most social scientists deny that the ends of society are, or can be, known by human beings. Today, in fact, most social scientists reject the notion that a social system has any end—in the sense of a purpose or an intention—at all.

True, actors or groups within a social system do have ends. As Emmet points out: "Politics is . . . a signal example of an activity in which those who engage in it will talk and think in terms of purpose; and when we are meaning by 'politics' political science as the study of this activity, we shall need sometimes at any rate to put questions in purposive terms and to ask what people are trying to do when they act politically, or what they have set up some particular institution for." There is nothing illogical about such research, and we shall utilize this approach in a later chapter. It is perfectly appropriate to ask human beings what their purposes or ends are when we are attempting to make statements about the causes of their actions. However, it is not appropriate to ask a social system the same question; a system of social action does not have a "general will" and cannot have a purpose in the same way a human being can. As Emmet reminds us, "The classical tradition in political theory was written in terms of the notion of 'the purpose of the state,' and the purposes of particular institutions within it, and so under-estimated the part played by customs whose unintended but socially important consequences are better studied in functional terms."[9]

When we make a causal statement about someone's actions in terms of the ends he or she has in mind, we are engaging in a form of teleological reasoning—that is, reasoning in which "a *future* event which has not yet happened must be named among the causal factors of a present event."[10] According to modern scientific logic, the only valid form of teleological reasoning is the conscious teleology of purposeful action by a human being; however, some logicians would still prefer a nomological explanation of human action (i.e., an explanation in terms of antecedent events and general laws), and they argue that this is possible if we regard the actor's motives as antecedent events. Since social systems, as systems, demonstrably do not have purposes or motives in the way a reasoning organism does, many social scientists have totally rejected the tradition of political philosophy that speaks of the purposes of the state or society. They point out that this kind of theory has been forced to make its final argument the existence of some metaphysical being, such as God, who could have a purpose. These theorists insist that the only kind of valid explanation of a social event, or of any other event for that matter, is a historical one. Unfortunately, historians have yet to discover a single social law, and we are still a long way from a nomological social science.

Taking a cue from the biological sciences, social science has attempted to overcome this dilemma by reintroducing a modified form of teleological reasoning—namely, the logic of "functionalism." Using the concept of function, we can talk about the function of a part within a system even when we do not know, or when we doubt, that it has a conscious purpose. Functional logic has been a great boon to anthropologists, for example, in studying primitive societies. These societies had often institutionalized behavior that was incomprehensible from the point of view of the experiences of a Western-trained anthropologist. When a cultural anthropologist asked questions about the purpose of a funeral, a potlatch, a sacrifice, or a puberty rite in such a society, he usually received an answer that left him as mystified as ever. Only through careful analysis of the particular social system in which the behavior occurred could he say what function the behavior served for the "ends" of the system.* As Emmet has remarked, "The 'function' may be the unintended consequence of something which people think they are doing for some quite different reason, or may have no clear idea of the reason for which they are doing it. . . . What can be stated in terms of the functional concepts, but not in terms of purposive ones, are the consequences of people's actions which work out in a way which helps maintain a form of society without their being intended to do so."[11]

Emmet's last sentence is crucial to the logical integrity of functional analysis. Functionalism is a kind of nonpurposive teleology and, as in any reasoning from ends, an analyst who says that some action has a function must also name the end for which the action is allegedly functional. No behavior is simply

---

* Werner Stark describes this method of explanation as follows: "Confronted with many phenomena which at first sight appear strange, nay ridiculous—for instance the widespread custom called *couvade* according to which the father must take to his bed while his wife is delivered of the child—[cultural anthropologists] have invariably tried to come to a proper comprehension by seeing the puzzling pieces of behavior as part and parcel of a wider, interlocking system of culture, and asking what possible function the mysterious actions to be explained can conceivably have within the common life. The fundamental idea which guides the effort is clearly the conviction that a social system can meaningfully be described as a unity—a unity within which every element can shed light on every other because they are all organically—or, as it is usually expressed, functionally—related." *The Fundamental Forms of Social Thought* (London, 1962), p. 76.

"functional," and any true functional analysis must specify both the system within which the behavior takes place and the end it satisfies. In ascribing a function to a role in a social system, we mean in every case that it serves either the survival, or the adjustment, or the maintenance of the system. This is the most commonly assumed end in social systems analysis, and it conforms to the empirical generalization that societies generally persist beyond the life span of individual members.*

Failure to bear in mind the need to "relativize" statements of functionality has led in the past to various errors that have reflected adversely on functionalism. Some analysts are so sure that all social activity, bizarre as well as routine, is functional that they blind themselves to instances of genuinely disruptive or dysfunctional behavior. The use of functional explanations without specific reference to a system's ends may produce this kind of insidious "normative functionalism," in which the analyst winds up pleading that even patently antisocial behavior or the disruptive consequences of some form of organization must be tolerated because they are functional. However, no action is functional per se, and the analyst must show that a role or an institution is, or is not, functional for the existence and persistence of the system.[12] Although Parsons has been mistaken by some readers for a normative functionalist, he himself warned against the dangers of not making functions relative to an end: "The most essential condition of successful dynamic analysis is continual and systematic reference of every problem to the state of the system as a whole. . . . Functional significance in this

---

* We may note the conclusions on this point of two leading analysts of functionalism. Dorothy Emmet writes: "But where the purpose is not specified, or where we are reluctant to ascribe deliberate purpose at all, as in the case of biological organisms, the unexpressed presumption is likely to be that the function of an element is to be considered as the way in which it helps the system to persist and maintain itself in some form of recognizable continuity." *Function, Purpose, and Powers* (London, 1958), pp. 46–47. Carl Hempel asserts categorically, "It is essential . . . for functional analysis as a scientific procedure that its key concepts be explicitly construed as relative to some standard of survival or adjustment." "The Logic of Functional Analysis," in Llewellyn Gross, ed., *Symposium on Sociological Theory* (New York, 1959), pp. 295–96.

context is inherently teleological. A process or set of conditions either 'contributes' to the maintenance (or development) of the system or it is 'dysfunctional' in that it detracts from the integration and effectiveness of the system."[13]

Another error sometimes committed by functionalists is to use the organic analogy uncritically. The biological sciences have long employed and continue to make extensive use of systems theory. For example, physiologists speak of the function of a part, such as the heart, in maintaining the life of a living organism; and the organism is seen as a systematic arrangement of such parts. Using the method of analogy, social scientists have sometimes studied societies as if they too were living organisms. As Alvin Gouldner has observed, however, "The recurrent use of organismic models by leading contributors to functionalism, such as Durkheim and Radcliffe-Brown, has its major intellectual justification in the fact that organisms are *examples* of systems. To the extent that the organismic model has proved fruitful in sociological analysis it has become so because the organism was a paradigmatic case of a system. . . . Indeed, we might say that the organismic model has been misleading in sociological analysis precisely insofar as it led to a focus on characteristics which were peculiar to the organism but not inherent in a generalized notion of a 'system.'"[14]

Examples of such misplaced organic analogies include the belief that social systems have life cycles (birth, adolescence, maturity, old age, and death) and the belief that social systems cannot freely change their structures because individual organisms cannot freely change theirs. Even the belief of the "normative functionalists" that all behavior would be functional if only we understood the entire system is a product of the organic analogy badly conceived. None of these ideas is basic to systems theory; and functionalism, as a method for analyzing how systems operate, is not in any way dependent on the organic analogy for its intellectual rationale.

Having assumed that a social system serves the end of its own persistence, a view confirmed by empirical observation of both animal and human societies, let us try to conceptualize how this end is achieved. What work must the actors in a social system accomplish for their system to survive? Or, to put it another way, what is the minimal content of the roles that are to be differentiated, assigned, and legitimated in a functional social system? Social scientists have proposed various lists of "functional prerequisites for a social system," but the problem remains a major research topic on the theoretical frontiers of political science, sociology, and anthropology. Aberle and his colleagues attempted to solve it by identifying four conditions, any one of which if realized would terminate a social system. These four conditions are: the biological extinction or dispersion of the members; the apathy of the members (a condition that appears to be similar to Durkheim's *anomie**); the war of all against all; and the absorption of the society into another society.

To prevent or avoid any or all of these conditions, according to Aberle et al., a social system must perform nine functions. It must: (1) make provision for an adequate relation of the system to the environment and for sexual recruitment; (2) differentiate and make assignments to roles; (3) provide facilities for communication, e.g., speech and writing; (4) provide a basis for "shared cognitive orientations" among its members; (5) articulate and legitimate the society's goal or goals; (6) regulate normatively the means of interaction in the society (including the resolution of conflicts); (7) regulate affective expressions, e.g., anger, love, lust; (8) socialize newcomers; and (9) control disruptive forms of behavior, that is, control deviants.[15]

This is a suggestive list, but one with certain difficulties. As we pointed out in Chapter Two, "shared cognitive orientations" need not exist in any social system so long as individuals can predict each other's overt behavior. Another difficulty of the

---

* Sebastian de Grazia writes, with regard to *anomie*, "It stands in contrast to *solidarité*, the expression Durkheim used to designate the perfect integration of a society with clear-cut values that define the status of each member of the community." *The Political Community: A Study of Anomie* (Chicago, 1948), p. 4.

Aberle prerequisites is that several of them should be combined and reduced to a single, more fundamental requirement. It is important that functional imperatives be conceived abstractly, for if a list is merely descriptive, it will suggest concrete roles that may be required in one system but not in all systems. We therefore need a more analytical conceptualization of functional prerequisites.

Talcott Parsons has suggested four sets of functional needs that must be met by any social system if it is to exist and persist.[16] The first of these is "pattern maintenance," or socialization. In meeting this need, the system must ensure that its values and norms are transmitted to children and immigrants. In the case of children, this is accomplished chiefly by inculcating within their maturing personalities a conscience, or superego, and by training them in the habits of discipline ("deferred gratification") and socially tolerated forms of behavior (e.g., competitive activities) for reducing the personal tensions generated by socialized life. Socialization is carried out chiefly through the institutions of the family and formal education, and through the daily experiencing of societal norms that define conformity.

A second functional need is that of adaptation to the environment, including the differentiation and assignment of roles, the distribution of scarce resources, and the anticipation of environmental changes. The roles and norms of economic activity are devoted to meeting this functional need (e.g., markets, central planning institutions, and technological institutes). Closely related to adaptation is the third functional requirement—"goal attainment." Each actor, group, and subsystem within an integrated social system has one or more goals—for example, businesses seek to make money, churches to win converts, schools to educate students, mothers to protect their children, and armies to win battles—and the system as a whole has goals, for example, in relation to other systems.

Obviously, these goals often conflict with each other. Goal attainment involves processing particular wills to produce a consensus, usually temporary and often artificial, on priorities and policies for achieving goals. Goal attainment also involves mobilizing and allocating a system's resources as required by its policies. Political institutions are explicitly concerned with solving this functional problem, but political types of relationships (i.e., the use of power and influence by some people to manipulate the behavior of others) may exist at all levels of a society as individuals try to reach decisions or achieve a consensus on their particular goals.

Parsons's fourth functional prerequisite is that of integration and social control. This prerequisite is fulfilled positively by roles and institutions that perpetuate, assert, or demonstrate the basic values of the system, on which integration is based—for example, the roles and institutions of statesmen, judicial courts of last resort, religious leaders, artists, creative interpreters of the culture, and even social critics. It is also fulfilled negatively through the exercise of authority to control deviancy, regulate conflict, and adjudicate disputes. The ultimate integrative organ of a social system is the state—that is, the institutionalized set of roles entrusted with the authoritative exercise of force.

The functional prerequisite of integration is of the greatest interest to the student of revolution. As we have seen, if there were only two functional prerequisites, integration and socialization, then the need for integrative action would decline as socialization approached perfect efficiency. If values were completely consistent with each other and if they were perfectly transmitted to each member of a system (assuming biological equality), deviancy would disappear. However, a society must not only socialize newcomers into the value structure; it must also adapt to its environment. Adaptation itself generates conflicts of interest, which the integrative institutions must regulate. Equally important, the relationship between the particular values socialized into actors and the roles these actors play in adapting to the environment generates varying demands for integrative action. When the socialized values and the requirements of adaptation virtually coincide, integrative tasks will decline to residual problems of deviancy and the authoritative resolution of conflicts of interest. As socialized values and the requirements of adaptation diverge, however, the tasks of integration become proportionately more difficult.

In these situations, truly creative action by the leaders of a system is required. They must maintain some degree of integration, even if only through the exercise of physical force; at the same time, they must mobilize and inspire innovations in all roles in order to resynchronize values and environment. They may attempt these tasks by entering the policy-making arena and advancing a positive program of reform, or they may try to achieve some coherence in roles by replacing a system's irreconcilable goals with a single, apocalyptic one, such as the overcoming of a foreign threat. They may also consciously advance a surrogate for the old value structure, such as a claim to "charismatic" authority, and this may later be routinized as a form of stable authority (e.g., the Emperor myth of Meiji Japan). Whatever is attempted, in times of change the integrative institutions become the vital center, where threats of revolution will either remain benign or become malignant.

To survive, then, a system must perform four functions: socialization, adaptation, goal-attainment, and integration. But what precisely do we mean by survive? As Hempel has said, "For the sake of objective testability of functional hypotheses, it is essential . . . that definitions of needs or functional prerequisites be supplemented by reasonably clear and objectively applicable criteria of what is to be considered a healthy state or a normal working order of the systems under consideration; and that the vague and sweeping notion of survival then be construed in the relativized sense of survival in a healthy state as specified."[17]

There are various ways in which social scientists have tried to conceptualize the healthy state of the social system. One of these is through the notion of equilibrium. According to Emmet, the term "'equilibrium' should only be used where it is possible to show that customs [norms], institutions, and the social activities related to them [roles] dovetail in together in certain spec-

ified ways so that one provides a corrective to disruptive ten-
dencies in another. It should also be possible to show how, if
these functional relationships are lacking, a form of social life
will break down; and also to show how a reacting tendency may
go too far."[18] Equilibrium as used by Emmet, and as we shall use
it here, thus means "homeostatic equilibrium." Homeostasis, a
concept borrowed from physiology, refers to the fact that "processes within the body control and counteract variations which
would destroy the system if they exceeded more than a limited
range."[19] Wallace, in defining the principle of homeostasis as it
is used in social systems analysis, has said that it consists of
"coordinated actions (including 'cultural' actions [legitimate
actions]) by all or some of [a social system's] parts, to preserve
its own integrity by maintaining a minimally fluctuating, life-
supporting matrix for its individual members, and [that] will,
under stress, take emergency measures to preserve the con-
stancy of this matrix."[20]

We have already discussed several of the homeostatic or ma-
trix-maintaining processes that take place within a social system—for example, the control of deviancy, the avoidance and
routinization of relations of conflict, coercive actions to maintain
integration during a power deflation, and normative definitions
of social mobility. We have also mentioned that value sharing
endows a social system with a homeostatic capacity. An example of how this works can be found in the rules of competition
by which a system brings relationships of conflict under control.
As Dahrendorf has observed, "For effective conflict regulation
to be possible, both parties to a conflict have to recognize the
necessity and reality of the conflict situation and, in this sense,
the fundamental justice of the cause of the opponent."[21] The
antagonists must, in short, share some of the same values. Only
when they share values can they agree on norms that in turn
will allow them to pursue their conflict of interest without resorting to violence. Since values are an independent variable,
but one that interacts with the concrete requirements of adaptation to the environment, the homeostatic capacity of a system

will be determined by value sharing *and* by the potency of these values with respect to a given environment.

Obviously, a homeostatic equilibrium is not a static equilibrium, and to call it a "moving equilibrium," as some social theorists do, is to avoid most of the difficult questions. What is meant by a "moving equilibrium"? Although it is rarely defined, a moving equilibrium appears to resemble the physicists' concept of "dynamic equilibrium," in which mass and velocity remain the same, as for example in a spinning top. The concept of homeostatic equilibrium in a social system, however, does not depend on some notion of a constant social mass moving at a constant velocity. A social system in equilibrium is perfectly capable of absorbing new actors into the system of action and of altering the tempo of interactions in order to meet its functional prerequisites. Homeostatic equilibrium differs from either static or dynamic equilibrium in that it depends solely on the existence and stability of the various processes for fulfilling the functional prerequisites of a social system and for solving, short of violence, a series of problems that arise and are predictable within a particular cultural setting.

Can a homeostatic equilibrium change? Among systems theorists, most of whom recognize that societal equilibrium must be homeostatic, there are numerous disagreements over this question. Most theorists would agree in defining change as differences in structural configurations that have been observed over time. The argument is over whether homeostatic processes can accommodate real structural changes. Dahrendorf, for example, thinks not: "By change . . . we do not mean the occurrence of certain processes within a given structural pattern, for this is accounted for by the category of structure in any case. Regular processes within objects that have a structure—such as the processes of role allocation, or of socialization of new members of society—are indeed an essential element of every structure. Structural analysis is essentially the analysis of such processes [i.e., homeostatic processes]. What is meant [by change] is, rather, that the entire structural arrangement of so-called forms of society can change."[22]

In contrast to this view of Dahrendorf's, the position taken here is that homeostatic equilibrium is fully compatible with one form (although not with all forms) of observed structural change. As we have already seen, role requirements consist of ranges of tolerable behavior. Innovations occurring within these ranges may in time lead to slight modifications of the ranges themselves. Similarly, personal differences and slight variations in socialization over a period of time will give rise to sequences of small changes that taken together may result in partial or total changes of structure. Processes of growth or differentiation (increased functional specificity of roles) are changes of this sort, and they may ultimately produce an entirely different social structure.

These kinds of changes in systems may occur without disturbing a homeostatic equilibrium so long as the value structure and the environment *change in synchronization with each other*. An environmental change, such as the introduction of agriculture into a hunting and gathering economy, need not destroy the society's equilibrium so long as the value structure alters to accommodate the gradually changing division of labor. However, it is perfectly possible that the old value structure cannot accommodate such a change. In many hunting and gathering societies, for example, it is considered the women's role to collect vegetables. If agriculture is introduced so rapidly that men cannot reevaluate their own roles in terms of agricultural labor, equilibrium will be destroyed. But there is nothing in the concept of homeostatic equilibrium to suggest that such changes must automatically destroy the equilibrium. Examples of gradual structural change within the context of homeostatic equilibrium are the integration of immigrant communities into the United States' division of labor during the past century and the broadening of roles available to either sex in many countries during the 1970's.

The equilibrium of a social system depends on the degree of synchronization between its values and its division of labor. Since these two variables also determine a system's structure, as they change, social structure will change. Dahrendorf's belief that routine social processes (which taken together create a homeostatic equilibrium) are somehow different from structural changes derives in part from a misapplication of the organic analogy. It is true that an organism cannot change the structure of its organs (e.g., its liver, heart, stomach). However, though a healthy organism is a system in homeostatic equilibrium, not every system in homeostatic equilibrium is an organism. A *social* system can change its structure and still remain equilibrated.*

A different and more important criticism of the equilibrium model is that homeostatic equilibrium is incompatible with purposeful change of a social structure. This point is valid, but it does not destroy the usefulness of the equilibrium model; it merely expands the category of social change. So far we have argued that homeostatic social processes often result in small, incremental changes, which over time may amount to a change of structure. Nevertheless, the actors who make these adjustments have no intention of bringing about a structural change in the system. They are merely concerned with mild reforms, such as resolving a dispute, rewarding a novel performance of a familiar role, or removing an inconsistency in a norm.

A very different kind of change occurs when actors recognize that an internal innovation, an external threat, or some other pressure is destroying the system's equilibrium and that structural change is necessary if the society is to survive. In these

---

* Just as homeostatic equilibrium is compatible with a form of structural change, it is also compatible with structural changes initiated from within a system. Those critics of structural-functionalism who contend that equilibrium rules out all but external sources of change are looking at the structural-functional model only in its pure value theory formulation, which we have modified. For examples of the opinion that equilibrium is inconsistent with endogenous change, see Wilbert Moore, "A Reconsideration of Theories of Social Change," *American Sociological Review*, 25 (December 1960), 811; and Ralf Dahrendorf, "Out of Utopia," *American Journal of Sociology*, 64 (September 1958), 121. The exogenous/endogenous distinction is taken up in detail in the next chapter.

cases, the concern of the actor, as well as of the analyst, is not with homeostatic processes but with conscious policies and the processes of policy formation (e.g., the purposes of American leaders in issuing the Emancipation Proclamation to end slavery). Structure-changing *policies* are needed precisely because some sudden or unfamiliar situation has exceeded the capacities of customary homeostatic practices. Only in such situations does the threat of revolution exist, and the analyst of revolution must accordingly be concerned with both the determinants of such a situation and the *purposive* responses to it.

To make a revolution is to use violence to change the system; more exactly, it is the purposive use of a strategy of violence to effect a change in social structure. Revolution also develops in part because some people have purposes contrary to those of the revolutionaries regarding the desirability, amount, and direction of change. However, these cross-purposes *concerning structural change* do not arise in a system that enjoys homeostatic equilibrium. They arise only in the dysfunctional social system, the one whose values do not synchronize with its division of labor.

The distinction between changes undertaken routinely to maintain an equilibrium and changes undertaken in order to recreate an equilibrium provides the key for a typology of social changes. The basis of the typology is the factor of purposive change of social structure. One kind of change, the only kind that is compatible with homeostatic equilibrium, is "evolutionary" change. Evolutionary changes are made by actors in systems, but the intentions of the actors in making them are not to bring about structural changes, evolutionary or otherwise. If structural change occurs under these circumstances, it is an *unintended consequence* of actions undertaken for different purposes. Unintentional, evolutionary changes thus constitute one class of structural changes, and they are the only class that may occur without disturbing the equilibrium of a system.

The other main class of changes includes the results of conscious policies of structural change pursued by actors within the system. This second class of changes can be subdivided into two types: "conservative" change, which serves the ends of both structural change and the avoidance of violence; and "revolutionary" change, which serves only the end of change itself. Both these types of change occur only in the already disequilibrated social system, and they occur chiefly as a consequence of the system's being in disequilibrium. However, the occurrence and the quality of conservative change directly influence the likelihood of whether revolutionary change will ever occur at all.

4

The Disequilibrated Social System

Eric Hoffer has observed, "We are usually told that revolutions are set in motion to realize radical changes. Actually, it is drastic change which sets the stage for revolution. The revolutionary mood and temper are generated by the irritations, difficulties, hungers, and frustrations inherent in the realization of drastic change. Where things have not changed at all, there is the least likelihood of revolution."[1] After surveying military revolutions from ancient times to the twentieth century, T. H. Wintringham reached a similar conclusion: "The puzzle becomes not why did the mutiny occur, but why did men, for years or generations, endure the torments against which in the end they revolted."[2] The point of both these comments is that people in societies are not inherently mutinous. Society is a form of human interaction that sublimates violence, of which one form is revolution. Revolutions are in this sense antisocial, testifying to extraordinary dissatisfactions with a particular form of society. They do not occur randomly, and they need not occur at all. Revolution can be rationally contemplated only in a society that is undergoing radical structural change and that is in need of still further change.

Many societies have undertaken radical changes very rapidly without experiencing revolution (e.g., the United States during the Great Depression). An analysis of the causes and the configurations of a changing society, therefore, cannot provide a complete explanation of the occurrence of revolution. But such an analysis is the first step toward explaining a revolution: a changing society is a necessary but not a sufficient cause of revolution; and political violence that occurs in an equilibrated society, although it may be called "revolutionary," requires a different but related form of analysis (e.g., the analysis of subversion, nonrevolutionary coups d'état, or palace "revolutions"). In order to portray the changing society, we must explore the disequilibrated social system in both its systemic (macroscopic) and personal (microscopic) dimensions. The previous discussion of the functional social system provides us with the tools and criteria for describing the disequilibrated social system—the stage on which revolutionary action takes place.

So long as a society's values and the realities with which it must deal are in harmony with each other, the society is immune from revolution. When a society is in homeostatic equilibrium, it is continuously receiving stimuli from its members and from the outside that cause it to make adjustments in its division of labor and its structure of values. It may go on receiving these stimuli (e.g., innovations, new tastes, cultural borrowings) and making the necessary changes indefinitely, without experiencing revolution, so long as it keeps its values and its environment in synchronization. Change of this sort is evolutionary and does not directly interest us here.

On certain occasions, however, social systems previously in equilibrium move out of equilibrium. These situations pose a threat, not necessarily immediate but still a threat, to the continuation of the system. Purposeful changes must be undertaken to recreate a homeostatic equilibrium, and if a new equilibrium is reached it will usually differ from the old one. Before considering policies of change and how they may succeed or fail, let us look at some of the ways a society can lose its equilibrium.

For many years social scientists have been compiling lists of circumstances that appear to have been the causes of revolutionary situations. In 1944, Gottschalk suggested the following list of what are actually both causes and effects of revolutions: "land hunger, taxation, high fees for services rendered and for services not rendered, exclusion from certain kinds of prestige or from certain kinds of office, misgovernment, bad roads, commercial restrictions, corruption, military or diplomatic defeat, famine, high prices, low wages, and unemployment."[3] Without in the least questioning that all these phenomena have, at various times and in various societies, promoted revolutionary conditions, we must conclude that this list is useless. For one thing, it is in no way oriented toward relative standards (e.g., how a people may have envisaged good roads), which would allow us to infer that a change in either values or environment had occurred.

Anthony Wallace approaches the problem somewhat more analytically. "The severe disorganization of a socio-cultural system," he writes, "may be caused by the impact of any one or combination of a variety of forces which push the system beyond the limits of equilibrium. Some of these forces are: climatic or faunal changes which destroy the economic basis of its existence; epidemic disease which grossly alters the population structure; wars which exhaust the society's resources of manpower or result in defeat or invasion; internal conflict among interest groups which results in extreme disadvantage for at least one group; and, very commonly, a position of perceived subordination and inferiority with respect to an adjacent society."[4] This list is more valuable than Gottschalk's since it links forces that can disrupt either the values or the division of labor, or both, to a social system's equilibrium. Nevertheless, Wallace's list can only be regarded as suggestive. It makes no distinction between forces that impinge on values and those that affect environment, and it offers no clue about why the disruption of values or the environment produces disequilibrium.

A much older and entirely different conception of the changing society derives from Alexis de Tocqueville's classic study of the French Revolution. This used to be known as the "feudal reaction" theory, but in its present-day form, it is more commonly called "the 'revolution' of rising expectations." Among Tocqueville's numerous discoveries in his social history of the eighteenth century was the fact that the people of France were enjoying relative prosperity on the eve of the 1789 revolution. In a passage that has been repeatedly quoted, Tocqueville observed: "It was precisely in those parts of France where there had been most improvement that popular discontent ran highest. This may seem illogical—but history is full of such paradoxes. For it is not always when things are going from bad to worse that revolution breaks out. On the contrary, it oftener happens that when a people which has put up with an oppressive rule over a long period without protest suddenly finds the government relaxing its pressure, it takes up arms against it."[5]

Tocqueville argued that real economic conditions were slightly improved just prior to the revolution, but that the nobility, already weakened by the growth of economic power in the third estate and undercut by an increasingly ineffective central government, thrust itself into this expanding economy in an effort to recapture some of its medieval privileges. This "feudal reaction" allegedly caused the revolution. It is very important to understand that Tocqueville did not rest his case on this single line of analysis; he also gave great weight to popular dissatisfaction with the clergy, to the influence of powerful revolutionary ideologues, and to monarchical practices that the people resented as much as they did the privileges of the nobility. Moreover, his idea of a "feudal reaction" is more an analysis of the final causes of insurrection than of the remote causes of a changing society.

Nevertheless, some students of revolution have seized on Tocqueville's idea of frustrated expectations in a period of improving economic conditions to generalize about the causes of revolution. Thus James Davies writes: "Revolutions are most likely to occur when a prolonged period of objective economic and social development is followed by a short period of sharp reversal. . . . The crucial factor is the vague or specific fear that ground gained over a long period of time will be quickly lost." And: "The background for political instability is economic and social progress. A populace in a static socio-economic condition is very unlikely to listen to the trumpet or siren call to rebellion.

. . . Progress in other words is most of the time a necessary but insufficient cause for violent political change."[6]

Though there is no doubt that socioeconomic *change* lies behind any revolution, is this change of a "progressive" sort? No noticeable progress led to the Chinese revolution of 1949, the Vietnamese Communist revolution of the 1970's, or the Sandinista revolution in Nicaragua during 1979. However, a form of "progress," or at any rate a period of very rapid material change led by the Shah, seems to have influenced the Iranian revolution of 1978–79. Change in a system whose values and environment are in synchronization can be either progressive or regressive without a revolution occurring; but if its values and environment are dissynchronized, regardless of the direction in which the one or the other has moved, a threat of revolution always exists. The theory of "rising expectations" contributes something to this basic analytical proposition, but it is overgeneralized and fails to explain changes in expectations, regardless of whether they rise or decline.

Another challenge to the theory of rising expectations is the traditional view that revolutions are caused by extreme inequities in the distribution of income. One variant of this view identifies economic decline, unequally shared within the system, as the principal cause of revolutions. Representative of the general view is Alfred Meusel's contribution to the *Encyclopedia of the Social Sciences*: "The quality of the change characterized as revolution cannot be grasped without consideration of the type of society in which it occurs. This may be described in highly simplified terms as a society torn by an internal antagonism between a small upper class which by virtue of its proprietary claims to certain sources of income receives a considerable portion of the social product and a large lower class which performs all the manual, routine labor and subsists in relative poverty."[7]

One obvious drawback of Meusel's analysis is that some of the most stable societies on earth have been characterized by extreme differences of income among social strata. In China, for example, no antagonisms existed among these strata for centu-

ries-long periods. Antagonisms did develop on certain occasions, but Meusel's description offers us neither an understanding of why this happened nor a basis for distinguishing between
conditions of inequality without antagonism and conditions of
inequality with antagonism. On the basis of his hypothesis we
should expect to find that black slaves in America or Hindu
outcastes in India were historically the most rebellious social
groups. Actually we know that both these groups were among
the least rebellious so long as their values and their environment
synchronized with each other. Neither can the American Civil
War or the Satsuma Rebellion in Japan (1877) be understood
simply as a war of the poor against the rich. Barnett's conclusion
on the effects of depriving people of "essential" material products is inescapable: " 'Deprivation' . . . refers to the elimination
of something that a person believes he has the right to expect.
. . . 'Essentials' is an entirely relative term. It takes on meaning
only in the light of the system of values of a specific ethnic
group."[8]

A much more promising approach to this problem is to construct an analytical typology that recognizes as the primary determinant of a social system's equilibrium the degree of value-
environmental synchronization. Wilbert Moore suggested this
method by breaking down sources of change into two categories: "the ubiquity of the 'environmental challenge,' and . . .
the ubiquity of non-conformity and of failure to achieve ideal
values."[9] Although we must adjust Moore's second category to
stress the functions of values in providing an abstract interpretation of reality, these two categories, combined with a further
distinction between exogenous (externally derived) and endogenous (arising within the system) sources of change, can provide
us with a theoretically meaningful typology of the pressures that
may destroy a system's equilibrium. We shall refer to such pressures as "sources of change" and study them under four head-
ings: (1) exogenous value-changing sources; (2) endogenous
value-changing sources; (3) exogenous environment-changing
sources; and (4) endogenous environment-changing sources.

After examining each category separately, we shall then investigate why, together or individually, the pressures they describe sometimes swamp the homeostatic capacities of a social system.

Exogenous sources of value change are very familiar. Global communications, the rise of external "reference groups" (e.g., the effects of the French and Russian revolutions on neighboring populations, or the effects of black African republics on the values of colored populations everywhere), the internal mobilizations and refugee migrations caused by wars, and the work of groups such as Christian missionaries, communist parties, the Peace Corps, and UNESCO—all have led to culture contact and to the invidious comparisons this generates. It is of course true that the effects of culture contact in dissolving particular value structures have usually been reinforced by exogenous sources of environmental change (notably by colonialism). Without environment-changing sources to "open" a society to external influences, a functional domestic value structure would be likely to cause a population to reject foreign values, much as Frenchmen in Pascal's day believed in the existence of "vérité en deçà des Pyrénées, erreur au delà."[10] Even so, exogenous sources of value change should be distinguished analytically, and this is relatively easy in the context of narrow time spans or individual lives. For example, the effect of foreign education and travel on many students from European colonies was primarily to alter their values.

Endogenous sources of value change are equally familiar, but they are considerably harder to conceptualize. They include, for example, the displacement of religious authorities by secular monarchs in both the early modern Christian and Islamic worlds; Henry VIII's impact on England while he was trying to resolve his marital difficulties; the corrosive effects on Scholasticism of the theories of Bacon, Descartes, and others; and, generally speaking, changes in values that are brought about as a result of intellectual developments and the acceptance of creative innovations. These changes are hard to conceptualize because values, by their very nature, are resistant to changes other than homeostatic ones. Being definitional and explanatory, values claim universality and exclusive jurisdiction: they have the power to brand alternatives as heresies or mental aberrations, and defenders of a value structure frequently exercise this power (note, for example, the role of the Ayatollah Khomeini in the Iranian revolution).

Endogenous sources of value change consist primarily of internal "innovations" that affect the value structure much as technological innovations (e.g., the invention of the cotton gin) affect adaptation to the environment. In fact, care must be taken not to confuse these two sources of endogenous change. By endogenous sources of value change we mean those innovations that impinge directly on a value structure, and not those that influence values secondarily, as a result of changes in the environment. When the environment changes, for whatever reason, it becomes dissynchronized with the value structure, encouraging men to formulate expressions of value that lead to changes in the value structure and that resynchronize values with the pattern of environmental adaptation. These resynchronizing changes may be produced homeostatically, or by purposeful nonviolent processes, or by revolution. But when the actual source of change in a system impinges initially on the environment, it should be classified as either exogenous or endogenous environmental change. This point is equally valid in reverse. Initial changes of values, for whatever reason (e.g., the conversion of a people to Catholicism), will produce reverberatory changes in the division of labor (e.g., larger families, more celibate men and women, and higher church attendance on Sunday and on other religious occasions).

There have always been two main problems in studying either value or technological innovation: how to account for creative or innovative behavior itself, and how to account for the acceptance or rejection of the products of innovation. These questions continue to be the subjects of philosophical, psychological, and social science research; and at present there is only a modicum of agreement on answers to them. With regard to the origins of innovative behavior, most scholarship has concentrated on the determinants of the innovator's personality, or on answering the question: "Who are the innovators?" There are several theories, probably the most famous being Erik Erikson's, here summarized by Everett Hagen. "A reformer," Hagen writes, "is an individual who learned when a child a pattern of solution of a personal problem that caused him intense anxiety. . . . When the individual faced in adult life a social force . . . parallel to the deeply troublesome force of his childhood, his anxiety was rearoused and he reacted as he had learned to react in childhood. If the evil discerned by an individual who has thus been sensitized in his childhood is also perceived by enough fellow members of his society as an evil, they will follow his lead and he may accomplish a great social change and become an historic figure for good or evil."[11] In his well-known book *Young Man Luther*, Erikson applied this theory to analyze the value innovations made by Martin Luther.

In addition to Erikson's analysis, there are several other positive theories of innovation, including those that postulate human instincts to play, to explore, to "satisfy curiosity," and so forth.[12] In this present context, we need only assume that human beings do possess an unevenly distributed capacity to innovate—that is, to alter or recombine what Barnett calls "mental configurations."[13] The more serious problem then becomes what happens to the products of innovation. Why are they sometimes accepted, and why are they more often rejected?

Social systems normally control innovations by attracting them into certain fields through the offer of rewards to innovators. This has the effect of "routinizing" innovation. As Barnett points out, "Innovation flourishes in an atmosphere of anticipation of it."[14] Thus, in Western culture we reward the "creative" arts and distinguish between a creative composer and a re-creative performer (who may nevertheless make small changes in his role). In recent decades, a process of rewarding and anticipating innovations in the physical and biological sciences has developed because such innovations have been found to serve market and defense functions in the contemporary nation-state.

Only occasionally is an innovation produced or accepted in an unexpected sphere, such as the value structure. There are two alternative but complementary schools of opinion that attempt to explain this occurrence.[15] One is the "marginal man" or "cultural hybrid" hypothesis, according to which persons who occupy new, poorly defined, or ambiguous statuses are likely to be innovators or receptive to innovations. It is argued that such people need to reduce personal tensions and that ambiguous status affords them an emancipated view of the social structure and its stereotypes. Cultural hybrids (e.g., the Jew emerging from the ghetto) may be produced through homeostatic processes (e.g., social mobility, or co-option into an elite) or as a result of historical "accidents" (e.g., through adoption or being orphaned). When an innovator belongs to a marginal group, his innovations may be accepted throughout the group. The group may then present a challenge to the value structure, and this confrontation may cause a competition over values. More commonly, if the innovative values of the marginal group are attractive to the general society, they will be incorporated and legitimated within the overall value structure, producing a value change (e.g., the absorption of some Taoist perspectives into the predominantly Confucian values of traditional China).

The complement to the "marginal man" hypothesis is that of the high-status or "prestige-laden" innovator. Often a person with creative abilities in Erikson's sense will occupy a status that already commands respect regardless of its occupant. He may then implement his innovations simply by exercising his influence. Alternatively, the occupant of an authority status may carry out an innovation, if necessary through physical force. In both cases innovation depends on the difference in status between the innovator and other members of society. Examples include the value changes made by reform-minded monarchs, Japanese samurai of the nineteenth century, some Popes, "modernizing oligarchs" in some Afro-Asian countries today,[16] and so forth. The prestige-laden person need not, of course, possess creative talents himself in order to bring about change. Conflicts within a value structure resulting from independent lines of intellectual inquiry (e.g., scientific challenges to religious values) have often been resolved in favor of change when an innovator gained the ear of a monarch. Whether or not the changed values can then be synchronized successfully with the environment depends on other circumstances.[17]

Marginal men or innovating elites may, of course, arise as a result of exogenous sources of change (e.g., through the processes of "social mobilization" described by Karl Deutsch).[18] However, successful innovators may also develop within a system and make their influence felt through the system's normal homeostatic processes. It is a naive or overly formal model of the social system that demands they arise solely as a result of external influences.

Innovative ability is never allowed full rein in a society but can never be entirely suppressed. As Eric Hoffer has written, "To make of human affairs a coherent, precise, predictable whole one must ignore or suppress man as he really is, and treat human nature as a mere aspect of nature. The theoreticians do it by limiting the shaping forces of man's destiny to nonhuman factors: providence, the cosmic spirit, geography, climate, economic or physiochemical factors. The practical men of power try to eliminate the human variable by inculcating iron discipline or blind faith, by dissolving the unpredictable individual in a compact group, by subjecting the individual's judgment and will to a ceaseless barrage of propaganda, and by sheer coercion."[19] Unfortunately, the successful transcendence of a state of nature and the prosperity generated by a division of labor depend on the very routinization Hoffer deplores. It is all the more surprising that some people do occasionally throw off the harness and, despite the mechanisms of social control, make innovations. Even more unusual, such innovations are occasionally influential.

Exogenous influences on the pattern of adaptation to the environment are obvious. They include the introduction of modern medical knowledge into underdeveloped countries, which often rapidly alters birth and mortality rates; market stimulation as a result of foreign trade; imported technologies and skills; the migration of populations; and intersystemic diplomatic relations. One particularly important exogenous source of change is military conquest, which introduces new actors, who automatically fill the statuses of authority, into a division of labor. Much time is required for new values to develop that will synchronize with this new division of labor, and until they do develop a permanent "power deflation" exists (e.g., as in Afghanistan after the Soviet invasion of December 1979). Sources of endogenous environmental change refer to internal technological innovations, such as the invention of the wheel or the railroad; and an analysis of the origins and acceptance of such innovations is identical with that already made with respect to values. Like innovations in values, technical innovations may be ignored, accepted as toys (as was gunpowder in China), or incorporated into the division of labor, in which case they will produce environmental change and a reverberatory effect on values.

The present fourfold typology—endogenous and exogenous value-changing forces, and endogenous and exogenous environment-changing forces—is one theoretically consistent way to analyze the causes of disequilibrium in a social system. The typology organizes the diverse pressures on a system according to where they originate and what they do. According to this formulation, pressures originate either in the operations of a social system itself or through culture contact, and their influence depends on their effects on the two main determinants of a system's equilibrium: its values and its environment. This is not to say that a particular change-inducing pressure cannot belong to more than one category (e.g., colonialism affects both values and environment), or that more than one change-inducing pressure cannot impinge on the system at any given time. The typology should aid analysis, not inhibit it. For example, a single cause of change, such as imperialism, may have to be broken down into several parts (e.g., into the pressures of foreign merchants and the pressures of foreign missionaries); and to determine the precise role of an innovator's actions within a system, the analyst will need both biographical and historical information. Should Peter the Great be considered an endogenous source of change within Russia; or should we view the impact of Western ideas on his thinking as an exogenous source of change felt in Russia largely through his mediating efforts? Obviously, he cannot be fitted neatly into either category, but the typology at least provides the conceptual tools required for understanding the exogenous and endogenous proportions of his overall contribution to change.

When sources of change do impinge on a social system, one of two circumstances will result: either homeostatic changes will keep the system in equilibrium, or the pressure will exceed the homeostatic capacity of the system, thereby producing value-environmental dissynchronization and system disequilibrium. The cause of disequilibrium is the failure of homeostatic mechanisms to work—that is to say, the pressure has been so sudden, intense, or unprecedented that it has incapacitated the routine institutional procedures and arrangements of a system for self-maintenance. It is then up to the vested leadership of a system to develop policies that will result in resynchronization; for example, changed values may demand a revised arrangement for land distribution, or changed environmental conditions may require that greater political powers be granted to organized labor. As we shall see in the next chapter, whether resynchronization or revolution occurs depends in large measure on the abilities of these leaders, including their ability to perceive that the system is disequilibrated. Until they act, however, and during the period in which their policies are being implemented, the system will labor under varying degrees of disequilibrium.

A brief example will illustrate some of the uses of our fourfold typology and its relationship to social systems analysis. A popular belief of many Americans is that the causes of the black protest movement in the United States after 1954 were primarily a lack of constitutionally provided civil rights and the systematic segregation of blacks, as a race, from the rest of the community. Actually these factors became salient as a result of certain policies that the system's leaders attempted to implement in order to resynchronize the system on a new basis. If we can accept the opinions of many black observers (for example, Richard Wright and James Baldwin) on black conditions, the tragedy of the American race situation was that both blacks and whites accepted a stable, envalued definition of black inferiority—and consequent role assignments—for most of the century after the Civil War. Because blacks accepted the value structure's explanation of their status, the main body of the black population did not support innovations developed by marginal people from their own group, and the resulting relative stability of the system reinforced the stereotypes held by whites, including both those whites who exploited the blacks and those whose roles did not directly involve black labor.

The sources of change that destroyed this equilibrium were primarily ones that affected black values. These sources included the mobilizing experiences of black soldiers and domestic migrants during the Second World War, the rise of reference groups in the form of socially mobile blacks in America and of black African republics with representatives in the United Nations, basic changes in the division of labor of the southeastern states that produced reverberatory changes in values, and several others. The effect of these sources of change was to mobilize a large, chiefly urban black population that came to have values roughly identical with those existing in the general society. Given these values, blacks could no longer continue to accept assignments to roles in the division of labor that were not based on general achievement criteria. Similarly, they had to protest, as any normally socialized Americans would have, those processes that worked to exclude them from political participation, economic markets, and equal educational opportunities. Such processes no longer synchronized with their value structure, and thereby became illegitimate.

This situation could not be repaired homeostatically—court

decisions were not routinely obeyed in many states, and new segregation laws in the South, as well as laws to defend white property elsewhere, could not recreate the old equilibrium—so that the system became dysfunctional in several of its processes (e.g., a threat to the power of the Supreme Court developed). The potentiality of revolution arose in many sectors (the Black Muslims, the Black Panthers, and other groups), but was forestalled by policies of reform intended to bring the position of blacks in the division of labor into line with the values newly acquired by many blacks and by the voting majority of the white population. These policies included new legal norms ending segregation, guarantees of political rights, educational reform intended to provide blacks with the skills required by the roles that they now felt were attainable, the "war on poverty," and so forth. Without the change in black values—which led to a change of a different order in white values—these policies would not have been functional and would not have been undertaken (as they were not in the century after the Civil War).[20]

The single, most generalized characteristic of the disequilibrated system is that values no longer provide an acceptable explanation of existence. This condition has been experienced and described intuitively by many writers over the centuries, one of the most famous descriptions being John Donne's seventeenth-century lament:

> And new philosophy calls all in doubt,
> The element of fire is quite put out;
> The sun is lost, and th'earth, and no man's wit
> Can well direct him where to look for it.
> And freely men confess that this world's spent,
> When in the planets and the firmament
> They seek so many new; they see that this
> Is crumbled out again to his atomies.
> 'Tis all in pieces, all coherence gone.

The analytical problem presented by Donne's poem is to know how many of his contemporaries felt the way he did and to know what some of them did about it. As Pettee has phrased it,

"Given that cramp exists, that is, that institutions are out of adjustment to life in a given society, individual purposes feel maladjusted. The consciousness of maladjustment creates an individual tension which leads the maladjusted individual to ponder his situation. Given his imaginative and intellectual powers, this may result in anything from getting drunk to writing a book."[21]

The idea of personal "internal tension" opens up an entirely new range of problems for social systems analysis and for the analysis of revolution because the individual human being constitutes a personality system that is not identical with the social system. Our earlier discussion of the organization of motivational diversity and the concept of role in social organization was based on this inescapable conclusion. But what do we mean by personality system? We mean the structure of perceptions and images held by a single person and created by the interaction of his organic system with the processes of the social system (processes like socialization, role assignment, and social control). Personality is what Wallace has called the "mazeway," or the "perceptions of both the maze of physical objects of the environment (internal and external, human and nonhuman) and also of the ways in which this maze can be manipulated by the self and others in order to minimize stress. The mazeway is nature, society, culture, personality, and body image, as seen by one person."[22] According to Wallace, "The intersection of a cultural [social] and non-cultural [biological, e.g., libidinous] system, within an individual locus, inevitably generates a third system: the personality system of the individual,"[23] and it is the business of personality psychology to describe the process whereby this personality system, or mazeway, is created.

Wallace's "mazeway" is an attempt to conceptualize a phenomenon described many years ago by Durkheim: "Because beliefs and social practices . . . come to us from without, it does not follow that we receive them passively or without modification. In reflecting on collective institutions and assimilating them for ourselves, we individualize them and impart to them more or less personal characteristics. . . . It is for this reason that each one of us creates, in a measure, his own morality, religion, and mode of life. There is no conformity to social convention that does not comprise an entire range of individual shades."[24] The personality system is thus connected with the social system, but it is never a one-to-one reflection of it. An individual actor, having made some reconciliation between his personal needs and social interaction, may nevertheless appear deviant or insane from the perspective of the social system, even though the social system's values are perfectly synchronized with its division of labor.

As Durkheim has argued, the personalities of the actors in a social system vary over a wide range; but this range is not infinite, and the distance between its outer limits is determined by the functional requisites of the system. In a functional system, the outer limits of personality variability are set chiefly by means of the value structure's definitions of "crime" and "sickness." As Parsons has observed, "Defining an act as a crime, *so long as that definition is accepted in the community,* is an effective way of discouraging other people from following that example."[25] In a study of the motives of embezzlers, Cressey comes to a similar conclusion: "The *words* that the potential embezzler uses in his conversations with himself are actually the most important elements in the process which gets him into trouble, or keeps him out of trouble. If he sees a possibility for embezzlement, it is because he has defined the relationship between [his] unshareable problem and an illegal solution in language that lets him look on trust violation as something other than trust violation [e.g., 'borrowing,' 'business is business,' etc.]. If he cannot do this, he does not become an embezzler."[26]

Similarly, with regard to the other main category for classifying deviant behavior—physical or mental illness—Parsons has written: "[Sickness] is, in a certain sense, a functional equivalent of crime, of revolutionary movements, of escapism in the form of some kinds of religious cultism, and so on. . . . In therapy the combination of the sick role and the therapeutic role as part of the social structure constitutes a complex, intricate mechanism of defense against deviance so that deviance that occurs can be channeled into relatively harmless channels. The sick person is isolated from others. It is a very important point that sick people are a category and not a movement. From the point of view of the stability of the social system this is very important indeed."[27]

When the system is disequilibrated, however, the envalued definitions of crime and sickness—that is, the outer limits on personality variability—are relaxed, and this relaxation presents a serious analytical problem for the student of revolution. In a stable system acts of deviancy beyond the limits of toleration will be identified as criminal or lunatic, even though the actors themselves may label their acts as "revolutionary." But in the disequilibrated system, some degree of personal tension will be experienced by every actor, possibly leading him to relieve it through behavior that he would have considered deviant before the system lost its equilibrium. Moreover, at these times it becomes increasingly difficult for other actors in a system to differentiate between behavior that represents a dysfunction-inspired protest and behavior that represents the now disguised deviancy of a formerly eccentric personality. In a disequilibrated situation, some people will engage in antisocial action because of dysfunction-induced tensions and others will participate because their personalities embody a socially intolerable resolution of biological and cultural demands. The latter group would have been considered deviants in the equilibrated system, and they will again be controlled as deviants after equilibrium is restored by revolution or otherwise.

The problem is further complicated by the fact that disequilibrated conditions do not normally give rise at once to marked changes in behavior. The behavior of socialized, nondeviant actors will change only slowly and erratically in response to disequilibrium. Since personality and the social system are related, as one changes, so the other must change—but not necessarily at the same rate. This is why a disequilibrated system may persist for some time without undergoing immediate disintegration or revolution, and also why the leaders of a social system often fail to perceive the seriousness of a disequilibrated situation until the forces of revolution are well organized. On this point, Herbert Phillips has argued for "the necessity of recognizing theoretically the capacity of individuals in non-congruent situations to bear considerable psychological strain, and still function effectively, maintaining both their prevailing personality patterns and established social structure. . . . Because of the human capacity to resolve psychological strain *internally*, by the use of well-established unconscious psychological defense mechanisms such as repression, denial, etc., much of the behavioral change that we often expect to follow conditions of noncongruence may in fact not occur."[28]

Failure to take into account the systemic inputs into personality and the system's role in defining deviancy has often led to psychological reductionism, particularly in studies of revolutionary behavior.[29] A psychologically reductionist argument ignores that personality is a "third system" and tends to explain all action in terms of Freudian-derived concepts of personal motivation. One particularly heady example is quoted by Harold Lasswell in his *Psychopathology and Politics*: "'Distrust of father was the chief cause of the [1927] Vienna riot,' said Paul Federn, onetime president of the Psychoanalytical Society. From a psychoanalytical standpoint all authority is the father, and this formerly for Austria was incorporated in the imposing figure of Emperor Franz Josef. But during the war the father deceived and maltreated his children, and only the material preoccupations of life and the joyous outburst when at the close of the war the old authority broke asunder prevented Austria from having a revolution then. . . . Once the police fired, blood flowed and the mob reacted savagely, responding to the ancient fear of castration by the father which is present in all of us unconsciously in the face of the punishing authority. . . . The Vienna riots were in the deepest sense a family row."[30]

Psychological reductionism refuses to distinguish between

acts of political violence that stem from the needs of an abnormal personality and those that stem from tensions generated by a disequilibrated social system. Instead, psychologically reductionist theories tend to explain all political violence in terms of the displacement onto public objects of private and probably childhood-derived neurotic needs. Psychological reductionism is particularly dangerous in the analysis of, and in practical attempts to routinize, social conflict within or between functional systems. Many social psychologists have tried to explain all conflict, notably war, in terms of the release of tensions generated by psychosexual maturation. This is undoubtedly a vast oversimplification. Just as an individual personality cannot be derived entirely from the social system in which it is formed, the social system and its needs and processes cannot be derived entirely from a study of the personalities that exist within it. Functional social systems depend on the avoidance and routinization of conflicts among persons whose personalities are within the range of acceptable variation, while at the same time they regulate conflicts that serve the needs of abnormal personalities by establishing definitions of crime and insanity and by isolating criminals and lunatics.

Psychological data must be used in the study of revolutionary situations because heightened personal tensions are one certain indicator of systemic disequilibrium, and the personalities of revolutionaries and legitimate authorities are crucially important in determining whether an insurrection will occur and what its likely outcome will be. However, reductionism must be avoided.

There is only one correct way to utilize personality data in conjunction with social systems analysis, and that is through the macro/micro distinction. From the macroscopic perspective of the overall system, the analyst will consider disequilibrium-induced variations in role performances and policies of conflicting groups in relation to the functioning of the system, regardless of the *motivations* of the actors. In the case of the Taiping Rebellion in nineteenth-century China, for example, the analyst will consider how the ideology of the Taiping leader, Hung Hsiu-ch'üan, came to be accepted by millions of peasants as offering a way to resynchronize the system; he will ignore the fact that Hung was an epileptic and that this condition undoubtedly contributed in a major way to his behavior.[31] He will be interested to know what psychological needs may be met by subversive political activities for outcasts, déclassés, undesirables, and the "maladjusted," but his analytical focus directs him to how their social movements influence the system rather than their psychological health. The analyst of a social system never decides beforehand who is insane, a criminal, or a revolutionary; he discovers that from his study of the system.

The microanalyst, conversely, is concerned with the distinction between behavior motivated by individual personality needs and behavior motivated by disequilibrium-induced tensions. For a revolutionary situation, he will need to study both the personalities of revolutionary leaders and the tensions of their followers, and he must explain how the two complement each other. He must distinguish, as Wallace has done, between the "mazeway resynthesis" of the innovator (a stable reconstitution of the mazeway, often occurring under hallucinatory conditions and often reducible to personality factors) and the "hysterical conversion" of his followers (a reversible change in personality characteristics—e.g., the conversions of many rank-and-file Weathermen or Moonies).[32]

Although it is generally true that personality analysis must focus on individual biographies, generalizations about clusters of personalities are not ruled out. One of the main conceptual tools of the microanalyst is that of "modal personality" or "national character," a statistical construct referring to "relatively enduring personality characteristics and patterns that are modal among the adult members of the society."[33] Unfortunately, older theories of modal personality were based almost exclusively on the replication-of-uniformity image of society, and they tended to view personality wholly as a function of a social system's culture. Today it is widely acknowledged that concepts of modal personality cannot offer a guide to the behavior of any particular person; they can only be used as statistical indicators of the behavioral propensities of specific groups.

When modal personality is understood in a statistical sense, it allows one to conceptualize differences in attitudes toward authority, tolerance of ambiguity, acceptance of variations among people, and so forth. Such information is directly relevant to studies of the disequilibrated social system. For example, in systems where individualism is a pronounced modal personality trait, much of the tension induced by disequilibrium will be tolerated through "inner migration" and comparable personality defense mechanisms. Similarly, the discovery that "authoritarian personalities" are modal in all or part of a social system is of direct relevance to the rise of authoritarian revolutionary associations (of both the right and the left) under disequilibrated conditions. Disequilibrium in a society always produces personal tension, but the amount and the form of this tension varies from society to society, and modal personality offers a way to study these differences.

Social psychologists infer modal personality by collecting and analyzing data in three main areas: direct psychological reports from a sample of the population; psychological interpretations of cultural traits, such as folklore or mass-media materials, that reflect adult personality characteristics; and psychological analyses of child-rearing norms. It is absolutely essential that information collected in this way be used in conjunction with systems analysis and with microanalyses of important personalities. Particularly in the study of revolutions, attention must be paid to the congruence between modal personality and a functional social system—between the type of modal personality, the type of social system (i.e., the specific form of a value-environmental symbiosis), and the impact of a social system's disequilibrated conditions on personalities within the system. Later on in this book, we shall utilize one theorist's attempt to create modal personality categories in analyzing the psychological dimensions of revolution.

Another characteristic of the disequilibrated social system is the tendency for the society to fracture into polarized interest groups as some members of the system begin to accept ideological alternatives to the old value structure. As we have already seen, all functional societies generate a hierarchy of statuses as a concomitant of solving their problems of role allocation and assignment. This stratification is stabilized through the envalued explanation of each status's position and through such homeostatic processes as social mobility. Under disequilibrated conditions, with the stabilizing effects of the value structure impaired, status protests may develop throughout the system, even when most statuses are not affected directly by the initial source of change. That is to say, latent interests in altering the status quo (which inhere in all subordinate statuses) tend to become manifest as the value structure and the division of labor progressively dissynchronize.

This phenomenon does not take place at once. The chief systemic mechanism militating against it is multiple role playing. Normally, a person will play numerous roles—worker, father, citizen, member of a recreational association, religious communicant, labor union member, and so forth—and under conditions of equilibrium the interests of one role will counterbalance the interests of another, keeping the actor's total status interests ambiguous. As Coser has observed, "One of the traditional Protestant arguments against Catholicism in this country, as well as one of the traditional arguments against Communists, is precisely that these organizations attempt to capture the total allegiance of their members, thus insulating them against the customary cross-conflicts of American society."[34] When a system becomes disequilibrated, multiple role playing still continues to prevent an immediate revolution or disintegration of the system, but its operations become considerably more vulnerable to attack.

As the disequilibrium of a social system becomes more acute, people in all statuses experience personal tensions. Some may control these tensions by internal psychological defense mechanisms, others by deviant behavior (e.g., fantasies, crime, psychosomatic illness).[35] However, with the passage of time, these mechanisms tend to lose their efficacy, and people with highly diverse status protests will begin to combine with each other and with deviants generally to form a deviant subcultural group or movement.

Examples of this are common. One is the union of retired military officers, physicians (particularly surgeons), frustrated politicians, religious fundamentalists, taxpayers' groups, racists, and some businessmen into the so-called radical right in America. Another includes the ad hoc gathering of student idealists, black intellectuals, self-proclaimed pacifists and environmentalists, and some homosexuals to form the anarchic left in contemporary America. A theoretical formulation of this phenomenon is Kurt Riezler's "psychological class," made up of outcasts, fools, and experts.[36]

The dynamic element that overcomes the effects of multiple role playing and leads to the development of lines of cleavage is ideology. Without ideology, deviant subcultural groups, such as delinquent gangs, religious sects, and ultrapatriotic associations, will not form alliances; and the tensions that lead particular groups to form associations will be dissipated without directly influencing the social structure. Once persons whose latent interests have become manifest develop an ideology, however, the society will tend to polarize into two groups: one group with an interest in maintaining the status quo, the other with an ideology for altering it.

Let us explore the nature and effects of ideology in greater detail. Several different usages of "ideology" must be distinguished. One equates ideology with what we have been calling the value structure. Although Erik Erikson's interest in ideological constructs is directed almost exclusively to innovative ideologies (such as those of the Lutheran, Gandhian, and civil rights protest movements), his *definition* of ideology conforms more closely to the sociological conception of value structure: "Ideology [is] an unconscious tendency underlying religious and scientific as well as political thought: the tendency at a given time to make facts amenable to ideas, and ideas to facts, in order to create a world image convincing enough to support the collective and individual sense of identity. Far from being arbitrary or consciously manageable (although it is as exploitable as all of man's unconscious strivings), the total perspective created by ideological simplification reveals its strength by the dominance it exerts on the seeming logic of historical events, and by its influence on the identity formation of individuals."[37] Another theorist who uses ideology to refer to established values is Mannheim; he contrasts "ideology"—a stable structure of values—with "Utopia," which to him means an innovative belief system.

In this book we shall reserve the term ideology to refer to an *alternative* value structure, one that becomes salient only under disequilibrated conditions and is addressed to these conditions. An ideology, in this sense, may evolve into a value structure if it is instrumental in resynchronizing the system; but as an ideology, it is always a challenger, an alternative paradigm of values or a "counter-culture." An ideology has inherent in its role of challenger certain special characteristics, some of them described by Parsons: "Ideologies combine an evaluative and an empirical element in the diagnosis of social situations. Because of evaluative pressures, they tend toward selectivity and sometimes outright distortion, both in stating the case of the proponents and attacking that of the opponents. It is typical that the former are pictured as actuated by the highest of idealistic motives, while the latter are guided by the grossest forms of self interest."[38]

As Parsons's definition suggests, ideologies perform various psychological functions for the management of personal tensions created by disequilibrated conditions. Seen from a micro perspective, ideologies attempt to relieve the tensions generated by disequilibrium; seen from a macro perspective, they attempt to show the way toward value-environmental resynchronization. Ideologies arise in disequilibrated systems as the competitors to an old value structure, and they define and explain the disequilibrated system in a way comparable to the value structure's definition and explanation of a functional system. As Geertz has argued: "It is when neither a society's most general cultural orientations nor its most down-to-earth, 'pragmatic' ones suffice any longer to provide an adequate image of political process that ideologies begin to become crucial as sources of sociopolitical meanings and attitudes. In one sense, this statement is but another way of saying that ideology is a response to strain. . . . It is a loss of orientation that most directly gives rise to ideological activity, an inability, for lack of usable models, to comprehend the universe of civic rights and responsibilities in which one finds oneself located."[39]

Ideologies are incipient value structures, but they are not usually (and may never become) as developed and as inclusive as synchronized value structures. Some ideologies are simplistic intellectual constructs that provide psychological scapegoats, such as anti-Semitism and Ku Klux Klanism.* These simple tension-managing ideologies will rarely become sufficiently generalized to absorb more than a few groups of status protesters, but the appearance of a large number of them in a society is a sound indicator of systemic disequilibrium. Ideologies are typically crude rationalizations of a partially understood social situation, but over time they may become perfected and revised to the point where they constitute both a program of action and a serious alternative paradigm of values (e.g., Marxism-Leninism).

When an ideology is developed enough to be a full-blown revolutionary ideology, it will combine the ideas of "goal," "instrument," and "value." It will supply intellectually and emotionally satisfying explanations of what is wrong with the old order and who is preventing its change, how to remove the

---

* Coser directly relates ideology, in this sense, to the strain resulting from instability in the stratification network. "Some types of anti-Semitism, as do other forms of prejudice, have important functions for those who suffer from 'degrouping,' that is, from a loss of cohesion in the society of which they are a part. Anti-Semitism provides a means for pseudo-orientation in an estranged world." *The Functions of Social Conflict* (Glencoe, Ill., 1956), p. 108.

obstacles to change (that is, a strategy that promises some chance of success in the face of resistance), and what to replace the old order with (that is, a sketch of the new and more "enlightened" equilibrium). Such ideologies are what Wallace has called "goal cultures," or what we would call images of a new value-environmental symbiosis. They also define the means for reaching the goal—that is to say, they contain a "transfer culture," or "a system of operations which, if fully carried out, will transform the existing culture into the goal culture" (e.g., the seizure of power by a Leninist-type communist party and the establishment of the "dictatorship of the proletariat").[40] Revolutionary ideologies are thus composed of an analysis of the old order, a transfer culture, and a goal culture, and several alternative ideologies are usually developed in a period of disequilibrium in an effort to overcome the deficiencies of the existing culture.

Ideologies are not policies. Policies are programs of action intended to achieve resynchronization, often by conserving parts of the old value structure in order to avoid violence in the process of resynchronization. Ideologies are always replacements for the old value structure, even though they may derive from idealized versions of still earlier value structures, as in anarchistic revolutions or counterrevolutions. Since ideologies contain alternative values, they are exclusivist in their orientation toward both the old value structure and competing ideologies. The advocates of an ideology will not enter into negotiations over the contents of their ideology since they regard themselves as representatives of superindividual claims, and for this reason it is normally difficult to routinize ideological competition within a system.

A special characteristic of that part of a revolutionary ideology outlining the transfer culture—i.e., the ideologically defined methods for achieving the goal culture—is its imminentism. An ideology does not envisage postponing its realization to a later time or a superterrestrial existence; it is a program for immediate renovation in the here-and-now. This is not to say that a revolutionary ideology may not be built around a set of religious or metaphysical beliefs; all revolutionary "millenarian" ideologies, for example, are religious. But even they stress that the intervention of divine providence on the side of the revolutionaries is imminent.[41]

Because imminentism is only appropriate so long as the old value structure remains in being, problems occur when a revolutionary ideology successfully guides a revolution and then becomes the new value structure of the postrevolutionary society. As Parsons has written on this subject, "[There are] tensions involved in maintaining the ideology intact, including its utopian elements, and yet making the indispensable concessions to the exigencies of operating as a society. . . . The really radical utopian ideology may well have to give way to pressure after a struggle."[42] In the process of transforming itself into a value structure, a postrevolutionary ideology will also greatly expand its range of definitions and explanations in accordance with its basic principles. It will thus establish definitions of crime and sickness, and thereby divest the new system's authority statuses of the personal deviants who joined the movement under the guise of, or in the belief that they were, status protesters (e.g., Hitler's purge of Ernst Röhm and the Brown Shirts in June 1934).[43]

Where do ideologies come from? They are created by people who may be motivated by personal psychological needs, life experiences, disequilibrium-induced tensions, or a combination of all these. Obviously, ideologues may appear in periods in which the society is not disequilibrated; in that case, their ideological constructs will circulate only among people of marginal status and will remain unknown to larger groups within the system. A social system becomes receptive to ideological attacks on its values only when it is in disequilibrium. As Tocqueville has said, "In all periods, even in the Middle Ages, there had been leaders of revolt who, with a view to effecting certain changes in the established order, appealed to the universal laws governing all communities, and championed the natural rights of man against the State. But none of these ventures was successful; the firebrand which set all Europe ablaze in the eighteenth century had been easily extinguished in the fifteenth. For doctrines of this kind to lead to revolutions, certain changes must already have taken place in the living conditions, customs, and mores of a nation and prepared men's minds for the reception of new ideas."[44]

For ideologies to gain currency, regardless of the motives of the ideologue, the time must be, in Carlyle's phrase, "an era of prophets." "Here enters the fatal circumstance of Idolatry," he writes, "that, in the era of the Prophets, no man's mind *is* any longer honestly filled with his Idol or Symbol. Before the Prophet can arise who, seeing through it, knows it to be mere wood, many men must have begun dimly to doubt that it was little more. Condemnable Idolatry is *insincere* Idolatry. Doubt has eaten-out the heart of it: a human soul is seen clinging spasmodically to an Ark of the Covenant, which it half-feels now to have become a Phantasm. This is one of the balefulest sights. Souls are no longer *filled* with their Fetish; but only pretend to be filled, and would fain make themselves feel that they are filled. 'You do not believe,' said Coleridge; 'you only believe that you believe.' It is the final scene in all kinds of Worship and Symbolism; the sure symptom that death is now nigh. It is an equivalent to what we call Formulism, and Worship of Formulas, in these days of ours."[45]

Seen from the vantage point of social science, Carlyle's description accurately portrays the crisis of an incoherent value structure. However, we should remember that the ideologue or prophet only provides a more effective fetish. It would be unfounded to suggest that the resynchronization of a system in accordance with an ideology constitutes movement toward a more excellent form of social organization. Resynchronization does reduce personal tension and lays down a foundation of trust that produces greater efficiency in the division of labor; from the point of view of systems theory, men in disequilibrated societies listen to prophets primarily in order to achieve these ends.

A high degree of generality and insight on the part of an ideology allows it to spread beyond the single deviant group around its creator and to attract many other persons trying to cope with disequilibrium-induced tensions. Such followers will not be equally motivated or have precisely the same interests, and the group attracted by an ideology may or may not be able to organize an effective revolutionary party. Given sufficient time, however, an ideology will cause the disequilibrated society to divide into one group of allies seeking to change the structure of the system and another seeking to maintain it. It is in this environment of change, tension, and power deflation that a system's leaders must act if they wish to bring about conservative change and to forestall revolution. It is to their actions and their potential contribution to the outbreak of revolution that we shall now turn.

5

Revolution

Karl Popper once said, "Institutions are like fortresses. They must be well designed and properly manned."[1] This is certainly a sound observation, but it raises endless complications for the analyst of change and revolution. In practice, a well-designed set of institutions can go a long way toward compensating for poor elite role performances; conversely, a high order of political leadership will occasionally make the most rickety of institutions function extraordinarily well. On the other hand, perversely bad leadership often undermines an otherwise well-organized division of labor, and some social structures are so inappropriate under changing conditions that even the best leadership in the world cannot compensate for their deficiencies. Considerations of this sort demand that the analyst of revolution adopt a multilevel approach to the problems of political violence. Any attempt to reduce the phenomenon of revolution solely to social structure, political behavior, or historical accident is foredoomed to failure because it is superficial.

Machiavelli was one of the first modern political theorists to point this out. In *The Prince*, he used three basic concepts to discuss the various problems of political leadership: *virtù*, *fortuna*, and *necessita*. By *virtù*, he meant the mastery that some men acquire over forces operative in political situations; by *fortuna*, those events over which no human being has any control; and by *necessita*, the limitations placed on human choice by the society in which political decisions must be made. As he then went on to demonstrate, there can be nothing but error in the practice of a Prince—or, by extension, in the analysis of a social scientist—who relies exclusively on either virtuosity, fortune, or necessity. All three must be combined.

Dorothy Emmet extends Machiavelli's methodological insight when she argues that "no society [can] survive without elements both of the conscious teleology of purpose and of the unconscious teleology of function." According to her, and Machiavelli would agree, the social analyst must "ask not only 'what are the observable social results of this activity?' but 'what are these people trying to do?'"[2] A third element, which she omits and which we must reintroduce from Machiavelli, is the effect of capricious events—of *fortuna*—on a particular social situation in which the political actors are behaving intentionally to achieve certain definable goals.

The complicating element in all this is that, as Machiavelli also knew, virtuosity, fortune, and necessity cannot be fully isolated—that is to say, they are interdependent and mutually influencing variables. For example, the likelihood that political leaders will display high ability at any given time is directly affected by the history of the social system's functioning during the preceding years. Conversely, how the system itself functioned will have depended to some extent on the insight and acumen of political leaders during noncrisis periods. Similarly, although fortune is beyond the control of men, it may be influenced, or its influence mitigated, by the actions of men. Mastery in politics is often accompanied by good fortune in the political sphere, whereas a disequilibrated social system and narrow-minded or weak leadership seem to invite misfortune. Foreign wars coming on top of domestic conditions of social change have often led to revolutions, but the occurrence of foreign wars at such times is not wholly unforeseeable. As Machiavelli noted about that particular piece of *fortuna*: "When once the people have taken arms against you, there will never be lacking foreigners to assist them."[3]

Virtuosity, fortune, and necessity are thus interrelated, but they require separate analyses using separate conceptual tools.

In studying virtuosity, we must identify the choices open to political actors and analyze the actors' conscious purposes and underlying needs. Machiavelli described the purposes and actions of a Prince who wishes to prosper; today social scientists do the same thing, although without prescriptive intent. In studying fortune, we must analyze historical cases to see how fortune has intervened in the past. Necessity, or the limitations on choice imposed by the social system, requires still a third form of analysis: analysis of the unintended consequences of the arrangements people have chosen or inherited to organize their interdependence. Here, in short, the analysis must be sociological.

Again, it must be stressed that these inquiries are not mutually exclusive. Political actors occasionally adopt policies that run counter to sociological realities (conceived as the social requisites for the continuation of a particular system with a particular social structure), and occasionally these policies succeed in changing the structure without destroying the system's equilibrium. Hence the study of the social setting of political action is not deterministic in the philosophical sense. On the other hand, politics as a homeostatic process is "the art of the possible," and the sociological study of politics aims at determining the limits of the possible in any given social system.

These observations on the methods of social science directly inform the present analysis of revolution. We are seeking, first, to understand in a general way both the underlying and immediate causes of a revolution and, second, to understand why revolutions, when they do occur, sometimes succeed and sometimes fail. We believe that there are two clusters of underlying causes of any revolution. First, there are the pressures created by a disequilibrated social system—a society that is changing and in need of further change if it is to continue to exist. Of all the characteristics of the disequilibrated system, the one that contributes most directly to a revolution is *power deflation*—the fact that during a period of change the integration of a system depends increasingly on the deployment of force.

The second cluster of underlying causes has to do with the abilities of the society's legitimate leaders. If they are unable to develop policies that will maintain the confidence of nondeviant actors in the system, a *loss of authority* will ensue. When this happens, the use of force by the elite is no longer considered legitimate. A revolution will not occur so long as the leaders can still use the army successfully to coerce social interaction; but the power deflation will increase, producing a police state (e.g., Iran in the year preceding the fall of the Shah).

The immediate or final cause of a revolution is some ingredient, usually contributed by fortune, that deprives the elite of its chief weapon for enforcing social behavior (e.g., an army mutiny), or that leads a group of revolutionaries to *believe* that the time to strike is now. In this study, such precipitating causes are referred to as "accelerators." They are the pressures, often easily sustained in functional societies, which, when they impinge on a society experiencing power deflation and a loss of authority, immediately catalyze it into insurrection.

The conditions generated by a disequilibrated social system—"social problems"—can never in themselves be the precipitating causes of a revolution. What they do is to create demands that the system be adjusted, through political action, to the changed circumstances. While policies for adjusting the system are being created and implemented, the society will face rising rates of deviancy, increased status protests, rapid circulation of ideologies, and so forth. To control these and maintain some systemic integration under stress, the elite must use its legitimate means of force more frequently. But so long as confidence in future improvement is maintained among nondeviant actors, this increased use of force will be regarded as legitimate and tolerated as a necessary concomitant of social change. The authorities may even suppress an armed insurrection undertaken by an isolated group without bringing their authority into doubt (e.g., the suppression of an urban insurrection caused by temporary food shortages).

As Lucian Pye has commented on this point, "We [Americans] tend to suspect that any government confronted with a violent challenge to its authority is probably basically at fault and that significant numbers of rebels can only be mobilized if a people has been grossly mistreated. Often we are inclined to see insurgency and juvenile delinquency in the same light, and we suspect that, as 'there is no such thing as bad boys, only bad parents' so there are no bad peoples, only evil and corrupt governments. . . . Instead of the analogy of bad parents producing delinquent children, the classic British view has paralleled the belief that schoolboys will always misbehave if not controlled by the school master.'" Whether or not Pye has accurately portrayed the British and American attitudes toward the authoritative use of force, he is correct in suggesting that the use of force in a power deflation, so long as it remains legitimate, can be rationalized. Well-socialized actors will continue to expect authorities to control deviancy during times of change.

The crucial question is whether or not nondeviant actors—persons managing their disequilibrium-induced tensions in some private manner—continue to believe in the willingness and competence of the elite to resynchronize the system. In order to maintain widespread confidence, an elite must do two things: perceive that the system is disequilibrated, and take appropriate steps to restore equilibrium. "To govern is to choose," said former French Premier Pierre Mendès-France; and the choices that an elite makes in trying to govern during times of change directly affect whether or not that elite will become the target of revolution.

The revolution of 1848 offers an example. According to Namier, "Count Galen, the Prussian Minister, wrote from Kassel on 20 January 1847: 'The old year ended in scarcity, the new one opens with starvation. Misery, spiritual and physical, traverses Europe in ghastly shapes—the one without God, the other without bread. Woe if they join hands!' '" What happened, however, was that the elites of continental Europe prevented urban demands for republican government and rural demands for altered rules of land tenure from joining hands. Namier writes:

"The proletariat was defeated in Paris, the peasants were bought off in the Habsburg Monarchy. The social forces behind the revolution of 1848, disjointed and insufficient from the very outset, were thus practically eliminated. What remained was the middle classes led by intellectuals, and their modern ideology with which they confronted the old established powers and interests. Foremost in that ideology was their demand for a share in the government of States to be remodelled in accordance with the national principle."[6] Having perceived the situation, bought off the peasantry, and neutralized the proletariat, the elites of Germany, Poland, Italy, and parts of the Austrian Empire easily defeated the nationalist insurrections. Had they taken no steps at all, they might have succumbed to a general revolution; had they adopted still more appropriate reforms, they might have avoided even the middle-class revolts.

The courses of action open to a system's leaders during a power deflation range from conservative change to its polar opposite, complete intransigence. The successful implementation of conservative change depends primarily on two factors: the elite's familiarity with social conditions, and its ability to determine which elements of the value structure are indispensable to the continuity of the culture. On the latter point, Pettee has written: "Every myth [value structure] is embodied in a formal expression [institutionalized norms], and however much of eternal truth may be in it, the expression itself is a temporal thing, related to time and circumstance. That expression may have been nearly perfect, a quite unbetraying symbolic presentation of truth for its age. But another age may find it ambiguous, erroneous, frustrating [because values and the environment are no longer in synchronization]. The task of the elite is then to revise the applied code of good behavior of the myth, to deduce from the central truth new rules of practical conduct."[7] If it can do this, the system will move toward resynchronization, the power deflation will disappear, and no revolution will take place. Instead, we will have an example of intentional, "conservative" change, such as the New Deal in the United States, the passage of the 1832 Reform Act in England, or, more recently, the restoration of democracy in Spain by King Juan Carlos.

Elite intransigence, by contrast, always serves as an underlying cause of revolution. In its grossest form, this is the frank, willful pursuit of reactionary policies by an elite—that is, policies that exacerbate rather than rectify a dissynchronized social structure, or policies that violate the formal, envalued norms of the system the elite is charged with preserving. An example of this latter kind of intransigence was the trial in Alabama in 1965 of the alleged murderer of Mrs. Viola Gregg Liuzzo, a white civil rights worker. According to criteria laid down by the values and norms of the system itself, the evidence against the accused, Collie LeRoy Wilkins, Jr., was conclusive: he was identified as the murderer by an accomplice, who was at the same time an informer for the Federal Bureau of Investigation. Nevertheless, the local jury deadlocked and was dismissed. In this case, Wilkins was being judged only on a charge of first-degree manslaughter, the jury having already voted unanimously against a finding of first- or second-degree murder.

The Liuzzo trial was not an isolated case in which the elite betrayed the norms of the system. In 1964, two successive juries deadlocked in Mississippi in the murder trials of Byron de la Beckwith for the slaying of Medgar W. Evers. In 1959, after a masked mob of white men lynched a 23-year-old black, Charles Parker, in Poplarville, Mississippi, both federal and state grand juries refused to return indictments despite the collection of a great deal of evidence against the men. In 1955, a Mississippi grand jury did indict two men for the murder of a 14-year-old black boy, Emmett Till; but a jury acquitted them. In 1964, eighteen men, including Sheriff Lawrence A. Rainey, were indicted under a federal civil rights law for killing three civil rights workers in Philadelphia, Mississippi, but state authorities failed to return murder indictments against them. Also in 1964, a Georgia jury freed two Ku Klux Klan members accused of killing a U.S. Army reserve officer, Lemuel Penn, a black, while he was driving through the state.[8]

Such actions disorient the behavior of *all* actors. The subordinate black population lost confidence in any solution to the disequilibrium short of violence, and the white beneficiaries of these policies lost faith in the efficacy of the old values to provide the basis for an effective resynchronization. They too came to believe that violence was preferable to a restoration of the old order. Revolution in certain parts of the United States was avoided only because many actors trusted wider systemic authorities to mount legitimate actions against intransigent local elites, and because these local elites possessed overwhelming, although illegitimate, means of force. The fact that a revolution did not occur illustrates the principle that socialized actors will resort to violence only when all other means have been blocked. Other means were available in the United States, and the main effect of sporadic violence was to signal to national elites that processual change was badly needed.

Between the two poles of conservative change and utter intransigence, the policies of an elite in a disequilibrated system may vary from the barely adequate to the demonstrably incompetent. One of the most common "barely adequate" policies is the loosening of norms of social mobility in order to co-opt into the elite the actual or potential leadership of a group of organized status protesters. This often has the effect of resynchronizing the system under the old values, but it also constitutes an instance of social change because, to be effective, the criteria of the elite must be redefined to include the upwardly mobile leaders (e.g., the creation of new peers in England, and the rise of the *noblesse de la robe* in seventeenth-century France). As Pettee has observed, "The greater the degree of identity between the intrinsic and the socially recognized extrinsic elite, the less tension in society, all other things being equal."[9] The co-option of persons specially gifted with intellect has long been recognized as a sound antirevolutionary measure since it neutralizes one obvious group of people who, if they are unreconciled to their status, are capable of creating a revolutionary ideology.

The incompetent policies of an elite are more often the result of its isolation than of its antisocial intentions. Nepotism, caste, dynastic decay, blocked channels of social mobility, and evolutionary changes in the norms governing authority may isolate an elite and prevent it from becoming fully aware of conditions in the society. In these cases, the elite will be intransigent inadvertently—that is to say, it will adopt policies incommensurate with the problems it faces. If an accelerator intervenes, such an elite's efforts at reform will instantaneously be rendered irrelevant. An example was the government of China between the Boxer Rebellion of 1900 and the republican revolution of 1911–12. Led by the uneducated and incompetent Empress Dowager, it promised reforms it had no intention of carrying out, created a revolutionary group by sending thousands of students abroad, and otherwise unthinkingly pursued policies of business as usual.

In some cases an elite will recognize and acknowledge its own incompetence in the face of disequilibrated conditions. One way for it then to avoid revolution is by formal or virtual abdication, which of course constitutes a kind of nonviolent social change (e.g., the termination of the Tokugawa government in Japan, or the Weimar authorities' virtual acquiescence in Hitler's radical program of change in 1933). Abdication by an elite may usher in changes of revolutionary magnitude, but it is not an instance of revolution if all actors, including the abdicating elite, agree to the change.

When a society is beset by a power deflation and a loss of authority, the sole basis of interaction becomes the primitive logic of deterrence, maintained by the elite's monopoly of armed force. Under these conditions, the threat of revolution is at its maximum. As Andrzejewski has concluded, "The incidence of rebellions largely depends on biataxy," a condition he defines as one "in which the distribution of power and, consequently, of wealth, prestige and other desirable things . . . is settled by naked force, that is to say, by the use or threat of violence."[10] A society in such a condition still may not experience a revolution. If the elite maintains its monopoly of force intact, the society may persist until values can be created and inculcated that will legitimate the elite's status within it (many postrevolutionary societies, such as the Soviet Union prior to 1953, reveal this configuration). Of course, when a system's integration rests on armed force alone, the armed forces themselves must be greatly expanded, including the secret police, which are used to terrorize—that is, to atomize—the population.

Even in cases where new values are never developed, the society may persist without revolution. In this case, it undergoes a long-term decline brought about by its inability to generate even a modest level of systematic social interaction or to control the disequilibrium-induced personal tensions of its members. Slowly, but inexorably, such a social "system" will convert itself into a huge concentration camp, and this form of organization is unlikely to persist beyond the lifetime of the individual. As Tocqueville observed, "Even if [the French Revolution] had not taken place, the old social structure would nonetheless have been shattered everywhere sooner or later. The only difference would have been that instead of collapsing with such brutal suddenness it would have crumbled bit by bit. At one fell swoop, without warning, without transition, and without compunction, the Revolution effected what in any case was bound to happen, if by slow degrees."[11]

Given disequilibrated conditions and the elite's loss of authority, should some factor intervene to prevent the elite from maintaining its monopoly of force, a revolutionary insurrection will occur. There is surprising agreement among scholars on the immediate cause of a revolution. "It is that event," writes Gottschalk, "which demonstrates clearly that the conservative forces are no longer able to resist the revolutionary tide."[12] Peter Amann concurs: "Revolution prevails when the state's monopoly of power is effectively challenged and persists until a monopoly of power is reestablished."[13] Pettee likewise argues: "The human forces which create and maintain institutions have long been withdrawn. They have gone into new and attractive activities; for the most part they are in the new activities which contradict the old system, or into outright revolutionary activities, or into frivolity and dissipation. Under such conditions the mighty inertia of the existing institutions declines rapidly, though with almost no outward sign. The time comes when this inertia is no longer stronger in its control of behavior than the contradictory impulses of men. There the matter rests until some incident suddenly makes apparent the already real though latent situation.'"[14]

Accelerators—that is, the precipitating causes of a revolution—are thus events or ideological beliefs that make revolution possible by exposing the inability of the elite to maintain its monopoly of force. To put it another way, accelerators rupture a system's deterrence-based pseudo-integration.

Speaking generally, there are three different kinds or classes of accelerators, each requiring separate analysis. The first is military weakness or disarray. When the underlying causes of revolution have been fulfilled, a break in the effectiveness of the armed forces—in their discipline, organization, composition, or loyalty—will produce a revolution whether a revolutionary party exists or not. The second kind of accelerator is sheer confidence: the belief held by a protesting group that it can succeed in overcoming the elite's armed might. Such confidence may rest on the assumption that God will intervene on one's side, that a particular symbolic attack will rally an entire population (as in the Easter Rebellion in Dublin in 1916), that a general strike will bring the elite to its knees, or that a secessionist movement will go unchallenged. The third kind of accelerator is strategic action: operations launched against an elite's armed forces by conspirators who believe, for one reason or another, that the time is ripe. We shall postpone discussion of this final accelerator until Chapter Seven.

An analysis of the political position of a system's armed forces lies at the heart of any concrete study of a revolution. Since mounting a revolution involves the acceptance of violence to cause the system to change, revolutionaries must necessarily confront those who are entrusted, equipped, and trained to employ force within the system. "Armed insurrection in some form or other," writes Katharine Chorley, "is the classic method of making a revolution, and . . . it is bound to imply a clash with professionally trained troops equipped with all the gear of scientific warfare. History shows that, in the last resort, success or failure hinges on the attitude which those armed forces of the *status quo* government will take toward an insurrection. . . . Whatever government or party has the full allegiance of a country's armed forces is to all intents and purposes politically impregnable."[15]

In weighing the effectiveness of a system's armed forces, the analyst must consider numerous factors. Is the army a caste type of military elite, or is it organized on the basis of some other exclusivist principle (i.e., a mercenary corps, a foreign army of occupation, or a domestic army recruited among an ethnic subgroup)? Is it a mass army based on universal conscription? In what kinds of societies can a mass army be used to suppress a domestic revolt? What are the components of the armed forces available to the elite (e.g., external defense forces, militia, local police, and political police)? Does the elite possess a separate armed unit that can be used against mutinous regular troops (e.g., the Nazi Party's SS, or the Red Army's cadets)? Does an accelerator impinge on all the armed forces, or only on a part? Indeed, probably the most important generalization to be made about the position of armies in revolutionary situations is that the officer corps and the rank and file have radically different attitudes toward the social system.

Because officers commanding armed forces are charged with enforcing a system's authority, in some systems (e.g., feudal societies) the people who occupy statuses of authority also occupy positions of military command. In systems where military and authority statuses are separated, norms of role allocation and assignment must ensure that military officers do not suffer status insecurities that might cause them to exploit their status and violate the system's authority. If they do decide to exploit their status, officers can always impose their will on a system, so long as the army is united under them, because of the inability of any other group in the system to resist their armed might. One form of this usurpation of authority is an officers' revolution, but military intervention in politics is not always revolutionary. It may also take the form of an endogenous change in the division of labor, in which case it may create the disequilibrated conditions that will later contribute to a true revolution.

Military officers normally constitute at least a part of the ruling elite in a revolutionary situation. This is so because of the arrangements that are made in functional systems to avoid status protests among military officers. For example, until 1870 many British military officers, particularly in the higher ranks, purchased their commissions. Despite the injustice of a rich man buying command of a regiment over the head of a more efficient but less affluent officer—and despite the fact that many British commanders were militarily incompetent as a result—the system was justified by political theorists (notably Burke) and by military leaders (notably the Duke of Wellington) as an effective security against military insurrection. Parliament adopted the purchase system in 1683, after the Restoration, when a standing army was first formed and policy-makers were still troubled by the memory of Cromwell's major-generals. "Men were to become officers only if they could pay down a substantial sum for their commission; that is, if they were men of property with a stake in the country, not military adventurers."[16] British officers were "gentlemen," a characteristic that carried with it several disadvantages; however, Britain never suffered at the hands of a revolutionary army, and its army reliably put down any and all insurrections within the system.

Today most governments attempt to prevent military officers from exploiting their status through values and norms that stress service, separation from politics, and loyalty to the system as constituted. Great care is taken to socialize military officers in these special virtues, and most nations operate military academies for this purpose. However, since military loyalty under these circumstances rests primarily on norms rather than interests, it is not surprising that during periods of change military officers often exhibit pronounced differences of opinion from the rest of a system's elite (e.g., General MacArthur during the Korean War). Military subordination to authority may be maintained homeostatically through norms whereby an officer must leave the armed forces and enter politics as a civilian if he wants to have a voice in public affairs (e.g., Generals Eisenhower and Haig).

Part of the logic of military efficiency (as well as contributing to the reliability of the statuses entrusted with the means of coercion) is to cut off rank-and-file troops from civilian interests so that they will accept their officers' orders unquestioningly. The effectiveness of a modern army—the use of both men and weapons as instruments—depends on the creation of a least common denominator of ability in the men when they work together. All this is expressed in military science by the term "discipline." Disciplined, professional troops normally obey their officers, including the order to suppress armed insurrection.

In a situation of power deflation and loss of authority, a ruling elite can still maintain its position and the pseudo-integration of the system if it possesses a disciplined army commanded by officers who are themselves members of the elite. Insurrections that may occur in these situations will be put down by the army, and in so doing the army will exercise a deterring influence on all other potentially insurrectionary groups (e.g., in South Korea after the assassination of President Park Chung Hee in October 1979). To the extent that the military-political elite makes its intention and ability to use force truly credible, insurrections will not occur at all. However, armies are not always effective or loyal, and the analytical question therefore becomes what causes professionally trained armed forces sometimes to lose their effectiveness?

Chorley lays down as a general rule that insurrections succeed "against the opposition of the regular armed forces [only] because these are for one reason or another prevented from making use of their full resources."[17] Fraternization with the populace is one factor that may weaken army unity and allow revolutionary sentiment to enter the ranks. Regardless of whether fraternizing troops actually join a revolution, the effects of fraternization may convince an elite that it cannot rely on the army to defend the status quo. Fraternization was a factor, for example, in the Hungarian Revolution of 1956; as the United Nations Special Committee on Hungary reported, "At times the Hungarians met with sympathy from Soviet troops. Soviet troops normally stationed in Hungary or in Romania had been affected by their surroundings. . . . Some Russian officers and soldiers appear to have fought and died on the Hungarian side." Significantly, the Committee also observed that "The forces used to repress the uprising in October were not exclusively forces which had been stationed in Hungary under the Warsaw Treaty."[18]

Another group of army-connected accelerators includes army mutinies related to conditions of service and intramilitary struggles due to factional differences. Such events serve revolutionaries as windfalls. In 1929 and 1930 in China, for example, Mao Tse-tung took advantage of the revolts of generals within Chiang Kai-shek's government to launch his earliest guerrilla uprisings; and he later put part of the blame for the defeat of his early south China guerrilla bases on the communist failure to exploit the 1933 mutiny of Nationalist troops in Fukien province. Possibly the most famous example of this type of accelerator was the 1905 mutiny of the sailors on the battleship *Potemkin*, which converted the strikes of the Odessa workers into full-fledged revolt.

The army may be weakened by disputes within the elite over the policies to be pursued in a disequilibrated situation, as well as by open mutinies. Indecisiveness on the part of the elite prevents it from giving coherent orders to the armed forces, including the order to suppress revolt, and this failure of com-

mand may be as valuable to revolutionaries as an internal mutiny. As Plato observed in the eighth book of the *Republic*, "Is it
not a simple fact that in any form of government revolution
always starts from the outbreak of internal dissension in the
ruling class?"[19] The final scene of the Iranian revolution offers a
classic example. The Shah himself left Iran and went into exile
on January 16, 1979. He entrusted his government in Teheran to
Shahpour Bakhtiar, an opponent of his for some twenty-five
years but nonetheless a secular political alternative to the Ayatollah Khomeini. As the analysts of the International Institute for Strategic Studies conclude, "The leaderless military
proved indecisive, first wanting to block Khomeini's return from
exile, then acquiescing in it; first repressing demonstrations
against Bakhtiar and in favor of Khomeini's prime ministerial
nominee Mehdi Bazargan, then (as important units, particularly
in the air force, began to side with Khomeini) on February 9
announcing its neutrality in the domestic power struggle. The
armed forces were no longer a cohesive instrument of power in
the state and their abdication from loyalty to the monarchy
sealed the fate of the government."[20]

Of all the accelerators directly affecting the armed forces, by
far the most important is defeat in war. This is the one occurrence that dissolves even well-trained military formations, and
from a restricted perspective, revolution in modern times can
almost be considered an invariable complication of international
conflict. Chorley emphasizes the consequences of defeat above
all others: "Experience proves that on the whole the [army] rank
and file will never disintegrate on their own initiative through
the impact of direct political emotion. Some other and stronger
solvent is required. The supreme solvent for the disintegration
of the rank and file is an unsuccessful war. . . . There can be
little doubt that under modern conditions the last stages of an
unsuccessful war provide the surest combination of circumstances for a successful revolutionary outbreak."[21] Sometimes an
elite has been able to mobilize enough loyal forces to put down a

domestic insurrection even after a defeat in war, but the most important successful revolutions of the past century were all accelerated by military defeat in foreign wars. Examples include France in 1871; Russia in 1905 and 1917; Hungary, Germany, and Turkey in 1918; Italy (the overthrow of Mussolini) in 1943; China and Yugoslavia during the Second World War; and various French and Dutch colonies after the Second World War.[22]

Whereas the first kind of accelerator directly concerns the armed forces of an elite, the second consists of beliefs that the armed forces *can be crippled* if a particular course of action is pursued. These beliefs or theories may or may not have any empirical validity. If they are not valid and an insurrection is attempted, it will be defeated, other things being equal (e.g., the Boxer Rebellion in China, where the rebels believed they could not be pierced by bullets). Even revolutionaries certain of their success may approach the actual staging of the revolution as a calculated risk and launch it under the guise of legal or semilegal activities in order to test the resolve of the elite and its armies (e.g., strikes, parades, mass meetings). Similarly, revolutionaries will sometimes incite crowds to riot in order to test the structures of deterrence. Nevertheless, we have "no instance of a revolutionary strike which issues in armed insurrection succeeding in an overthrow of the existing system of government,"[23] and the more rational approach to toppling an elite defended by a reliable army is through a carefully planned coup d'état or through some *strategy* of revolution (see Chapter Seven).

Accelerators, of whatever type, can normally be sustained in functional societies without resulting in either a power deflation or a loss of authority; but in disequilibrated societies, they lead people to believe that coercion can no longer be maintained over them. The classic example occurred in Petrograd in March 1917. Some 200,000 demonstrators, consisting of women and workers locked out of the Putilov Metal Factory, marched through the streets. On being given the order to fire into the crowd, the soldiers of the Volinsk Regiment fired into the air, thereby end-

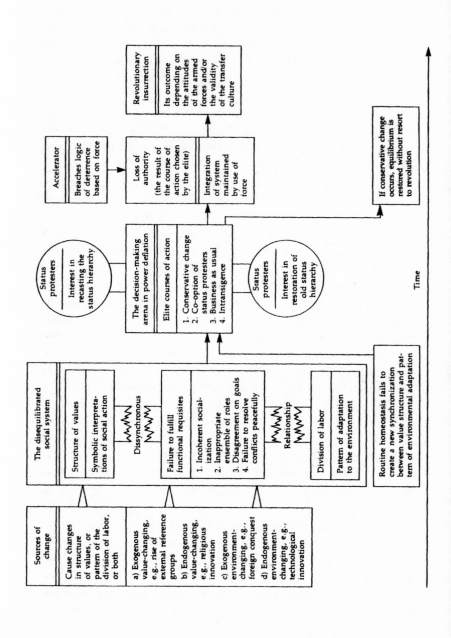

ing the monopoly of force of the Russian autocracy. Other units mutinied, the people sacked the headquarters of the Okhrana, and revolutionaries stormed into the prison fortress of St. Peter and St. Paul. Defeat in war was the factor that caused the soldiers to refuse their orders, and this refusal in turn produced the first successful Russian revolution of the modern age.

Up to this point, we have analyzed revolution from a macroscopic, or systemic, perspective—that is to say, we have avoided considering individual motives and personality changes. From this perspective we have concluded that power deflation, plus loss of authority, plus an accelerator, produces revolution (the chart on p. 108 portrays graphically the relationship among these elements).

Now let us alter the perspective and explore one theorist's attempt to provide a microscopic model of the processes of revolution. Anthony Wallace does not use the term "revolution," but instead speaks of "revitalization"—a psychological equivalent of revolution, which he defines as a "deliberate, organized attempt by some members of a society to construct a more satisfying culture by rapid acceptance of a pattern of multiple innovations."[24] In an earlier article on revitalization movements, he states that the term revitalization includes such phenomena as "revolutions," "mass movements," "nativistic movements," and "charismatic movements."[25]

The most significant characteristic of Wallace's idea of revitalization is that it is personality-oriented. "Under conditions of disorganization," he writes, "the system, *from the standpoint of at least some of its members*, is unable to make possible the reliable satisfaction of certain values which are held to be essential to continued well-being and self-respect. The mazeway of a culturally disillusioned person, accordingly, is an image of a world that is unpredictable, or barren in its simplicity, or both. His mood (depending on the precise nature of the disorganization) will be one of panic-stricken anxiety, shame, guilt, depression, or apathy."[26] The pressures that bring about these psychological states are, in Wallace's formulation, roughly equivalent to our sources of change—that is, they are endogenous or exogenous pressures on either values or the division of labor that disequili- brate a functionally integrated social system.

When people are suffering from panic-stricken anxiety, shame, guilt, depression, and so forth, as a result of systemic disequilibrium, either they will carry out a revitalization move- ment, or the whole society will slowly disintegrate. One of the problems of Wallace's conceptualization, however, is that he does not specify the immediate or final causes of a revitalization movement. The particular psychological states he describes are not in themselves sufficient to bring about a revitalization move- ment, since homeostatic or purposive processes of change might equally well relieve them. Since Wallace argues that revitaliza- tion is an extreme form of rapid change, we may infer that he assumes all other remedies for overcoming mazeway disorgani- zation have been exhausted, thereby bringing the psychological needs of the actors to the threshold of revitalization. Without such a qualification, Wallace would be arguing that *all* social change occurs via revitalization, and he certainly does not be- lieve that.

Given the condition of a disequilibrated social system, with its psychodynamic dimension of severely disorganized mazeways, Wallace proceeds to conceptualize the stages through which ac- tors pass in revitalizing their culture. He establishes various categories within which modal personality data can be fitted; and his formulation is probably the best abstract model in con- temporary social science of the nature and cause of personality change during a revolutionary movement.

His formula consists of five stages. The first is a benchmark model of the integrated social system, which Wallace calls the "steady state" and which he defines as a social system in equi- librium. Change may occur while the system retains this con- figuration, but it is change of the evolutionary variety. The pri- mary psychological characteristic of this period is that mazeway disorganization and the resulting internal tensions remain within tolerable limits for most individuals. Deviant behavior occurs among persons who are socially (through faulty socialization) or physically (through congenital malformation of the mazeway) incapable of managing the stress that exists routinely in their particular systems. "Occasional incidents of intolerable stress," says Wallace, "may stimulate a limited 'correction' of the system, but some incidence of individual ill-health and criminality [is] accepted as a price society must pay."[27]

When a source or sources of change disequilibrate this steady state, the system enters the second period, "increased individual stress." In this stage, "Anomie and disillusionment become widespread. . . . Crime and illness increase sharply in frequency as individualistic asocial responses."[28] Actually, Wallace may go too far toward suggesting that the social system and individual personalities change in synchrony. During this initial period of disequilibrium, many of the resulting psychological tensions will probably be managed through internal defense mechanisms and hence will be disguised. We should expect to see only slight rises in the rates of crime and mental illness, and even these changes may go unnoticed owing to increasing disagreement over the precise definitions of crime and deviancy. A more likely indicator of stress during this period is the increased production and circulation of ideological constructs for rationalizing the new stresses.

So long as equilibrium is not restored, the system will proceed to the third stage, "cultural distortion." Here the tensions induced by disequilibrium become fully manifest, and the behavior resulting from them is measurable. "Some members of the society attempt, piecemeal and ineffectively, to restore personal equilibrium by adopting socially dysfunctional expedients."[29] Among such expedients are alcoholism, attacking scapegoats, venality among public officials, breaches of sexual and kinship norms, and hoarding. Moreover, during this period the society will begin to divide into ideologically oriented interest groups. Various groups will accept tension-managing constructs that may offer some sense of reorientation but that cannot, because of their crudity, form the basis for reintegrating the whole system without extensive modification.

This stage finally gives way to "the period of revitalization"—

what we would call the period of revolution. There is nothing inevitable about the occurrence of a revitalization movement. As Wallace acknowledges, "Once severe cultural distortion has occurred, the society can with difficulty return to a steady state without the institution of a revitalization process." The possibility of conservative change thus remains open, although it obviously involves difficulties. If conservative change does not occur and no revitalization takes place either, "The society is apt to disintegrate as a system: the population will either die off, splinter into autonomous groups, or be absorbed into another, more stable, society."[30]

Wallace breaks down the stage of revitalization into six requisite functions. First is the "formulation of a code," or what we have called the creation of a revolutionary ideology. The code is a prescription for disoriented people, telling them two things about the culturally distorted system: what to do to change it, and what to replace it with. These two functions are performed, respectively, by what Wallace calls (as we have noted) the "transfer culture" and the "goal culture." Whether or not the goal culture can ever be achieved, its psychological importance is immense, for it opens up the possibility of liberation from the disturbing reality within which people have been trying to orient themselves.

The second requirement of a revitalization movement is communication, or the preaching of the code by its formulators with the aim of making converts. The formulators themselves will have experienced what Wallace calls "mazeway resynthesis"—a stable, usually irreversible conversion, characteristic of prophets. The converts, those who join the prophet's movement, will undergo "hysterical conversion." Hysterical conversion may last for years, but it does require periodic reinforcement and is more easily reversible.

Wallace's third and fourth requirements, organization and adaptation, refer to needs generated by small-group dynamics. "The tricornered relationship between the formulators, the disciples, and the mass followers is given an authoritarian structure

. . . by the charismatic quality of the formulator's image."[31] This means simply that the people united by an ideology go on to organize themselves as a hierarchically structured revolutionary association, regardless of the ultimate values to which they subscribe. "Adaptation" occurs as the transfer culture is hardened into a program of action. The revolutionary association now displays hostility not only toward its ideologically defined enemy but also toward nonparticipating but ideologically included members of the action party. Such persons will be branded as traitors (e.g., "Uncle Toms," "social fascists," "running dogs").

These four requirements culminate in "cultural transformation"—the overt attempt to implement the transfer culture. Whatever form this may take—revolutionary war, coup d'état, general strike, or urban insurrection—if it is successful, it "will be attended by the drastic decline of the quasi-pathological individual symptoms of anomie and by the disappearance of the cultural distortion."[32] Assuming that the initial attempt at cultural transformation succeeds, the final task of a revitalization movement becomes "routinization." The focus of the movement shifts from innovation to maintenance, with the attendant development of norms to meet all the system's functional requisites. The surest sign that routinization is occurring is the elimination of those disciples and hysterical converts who are not able to reverse their revolutionary commitments. Hannah Arendt has pointed to the irony of this situation: "If foundation was the aim and end of revolution, then the revolutionary spirit was not merely the spirit of beginning something new but of starting something permanent and enduring: [however,] a lasting institution, embodying this spirit [i.e., the spirit of innovation and beginning] and encouraging it to new achievements, would be self-defeating. From which it unfortunately seems to follow that nothing threatens the very achievements of revolution more dangerously and more acutely than the spirit which has brought them about."[33] The classic example of this phenomenon is Mao Tse-tung's "Cultural Revolution" of 1966–76, an attempt to "revitalize" a revolutionary movement that was tend-ing inexorably toward routinization. With routinization the system moves from the period of revitalization into Wallace's final conceptual stage, that of the new steady state.

There are several difficulties with Wallace's theory, but none that cannot be overcome by using it in conjunction with a macrosystemic conception of revolution. Its great virtue is that by portraying what happens to individual thought and behavior as a social system becomes progressively disequilibrated, it provides a scheme for correlating stages of systemic change with stages of personality change.

Wallace summarizes his findings in the form of a "principle of conservation of cognitive structure." This principle has three components, the first of which is that "the individual will not abandon *any* particular conception of reality (including, therefore, his culturally standard conceptions), even in the face of direct evidence of its current inutility, without having had an opportunity to construct a new mazeway."[34] This is a psychodynamic corollary of our fundamental premises that societies enjoying value-environmental synchronization are stable, that a disequilibrating source of change produces attempts to adapt prior to a resort to violence, and that revolution is purposeful, goal-oriented behavior, intended to overcome dissynchronization.

It is interesting to compare Wallace's formulation of this point with Kuhn's analysis of organized scientific research. Kuhn argues that a scientific "community" depends on the existence of a nature-defining paradigm (e.g., the Newtonian or Einsteinian paradigms) which scientists participating in a discipline jointly share. Given the existence of such an explanatory and definitive paradigm (in social systems, a value structure), "Novelty ordinarily emerges only for the man who, knowing *with precision* what he should expect, is able to recognize that something has gone wrong. Anomaly appears only against the background provided by the paradigm. . . . The decision to reject one paradigm is always simultaneously to accept another, and the judgment leading to that decision involves the comparison of both paradigms with nature *and* with each other. . . . Paradigm-testing occurs only after persistent failure to solve a noteworthy puzzle has given rise to a crisis. And even then it occurs only after the sense of crisis has evoked an alternative candidate for paradigm."[35] This alternative paradigm Wallace would call a goal culture and we would call a revolutionary ideology.

Wallace's second and third components of the principle of conservation of cognitive structure follow directly from his first: "(2) initial confrontation of the individual with evidence of inutility [anomaly, disequilibrium] will arouse an anxiety-denial syndrome, and this anxiety-denial response may continue for a considerable period of time; [and] (3) it is easier for the individual to abandon a conception if substitutes are offered and models of new mazeways are presented, than if the abandonment must be made 'blind.'"[36] We are inclined to state the third component more positively: without an alternative value structure, the old system will simply destroy itself as the members futilely persist in their familiar but now inappropriate roles, norms, and statuses.

Having discussed revolution from two perspectives of contemporary social science—that of social systems theory and that of the psychology of culture change—let us now turn to a third and contrasting perspective on revolution, namely, the viewpoint of political philosophy. Our purpose is to point out some of the similarities between our social science analyses and certain generalizations about revolution that have been preserved in the traditions of political philosophy. Since all three perspectives attempt to explain the same behavior, to the extent that the three resulting explanations tend to coincide we have a somewhat greater assurance that we have been conceptualizing revolutionary conditions accurately. The two theorists we shall consider are John Locke and Hannah Arendt.

Locke's theory of rebellion is similar to that of contemporary social systems analysis, except that he conceives of only one major source of revolutionary conditions: tyrannous behavior by a ruler or a legislature. Having thus narrowed his focus, he tends to think of the changes brought about by rebellion as restorative or preservative rather than innovative. Locke's theory of rebellion grows directly out of his theory of the "good" (we would say "functional") society. He understands the purpose of society to be the avoidance of a state of war, and he acknowledges that men must refrain from their prepolitical right to employ force in their own interest while they are living within civil society. In *The Second Treatise of Civil Government* (1690), he wrote: "The reason why men enter into society is the preservation of their property; and the end why they choose and authorize a legislative [body] is that there may be laws made and rules set as guards and fences to the properties of all the members of the society, to limit the powers and moderate the dominion of every part and member of the society; for since it can never be supposed to be the will of the society that the legislative should have a power to destroy that which every one designs to secure by entering into society, and for which the people submitted themselves to legislators of their own making. Whenever the legislators endeavour to take away and destroy the property of the people, or to reduce them to slavery under arbitrary power, they put themselves into a state of war with the people who are thereupon absolved from any further obedience, and are left to the common refuge which God hath provided for all men against force and violence."[37]

Some critics of Locke have supposed that his formulation allows for frequent and capricious resorts to rebellion, since he appears to have an extremely instrumentalist understanding of political organization (i.e., as a form of organization to which people give their support only so long as it protects their property). While under the regimen of political institutions, Locke argued, the people retain a separate, apolitical right—based on "a law antecedent and paramount to all laws of men"[38]—to judge the acts of their governors (the "legislative"). We must not suppose, however, that Locke believed people had a right to revolution. "This I am sure: whoever, either ruler or subject, by force goes about to invade the rights of either prince or people and lays the foundation for overturning the constitution and frame of any just government is highly guilty of the greatest crime I think a man is capable of."[39] Moreover, according to Locke people do not want to revolt against their government. "Such revolutions happen not upon every little mismanagement in public affairs. Great mistakes in the ruling part, many wrong and inconvenient laws, and all the slips of human frailty will be borne by the people without mutiny or murmur."[40] What, then, are the conditions under which rebellion is justified? Only, as Locke said, in the event of the return of war.

To make sense out of Locke's idea of the return of war, we must look in his work for concepts similar to our "power deflation" and "loss of authority." "Force," wrote Locke, "is to be opposed to nothing but unjust and unlawful force."[41] Unlawful force is the opposite of the authoritative use of force, and Locke's understanding of the concept of authority leads to one of the more unusual aspects of his theory—namely, his notion that the original betrayer of authority, the tyrant, is the one who actually "rebels," and not the people who overthrow him by force following this betrayal. Authority is a complementary relationship, bestowing rights and obligations on those who obey and also on those who command. As Locke put it, "Rebellion being an opposition, not to persons, but to authority which is founded only in the constitutions and laws of the government, those, whoever they be, who by force break through, and by force justify their violation of them, are truly and properly rebels; for when men, by entering into society and civil government, have excluded force and introduced laws for the preservation of property, peace, and unity amongst themselves, those who set up force again in opposition to the laws do *rebellare*— that is, bring back again the state of war—and are properly rebels."[42]

The occupant of a status of authority who exploits his authority thereby loses his authority. His exercise of force becomes illegitimate. "When a king has dethroned himself," Locke explained, "and put himself in a state of war with his people, what shall hinder them from prosecuting him who is no king, as they would any other man, who has put himself in a state of war with them?"[43] Social interaction loses its social quality in the state of war, and relations among men are once again settled solely through a calculus of force.

Given Locke's conception of the act of rebelling, we can see how similar his theory is to the conclusions of social systems analysis. Clearly, he conceived of society as a moral community, and he regarded the use of force within it as the last resort, as the recourse of men whose reason is exasperated. The problem then becomes what causes the occupants of the statuses of authority to "rebel" in the first place. Locke was peculiarly silent on this subject. He cited a series of conditions that typify the illegitimate exercise of authority—breach of trust, misuse of funds, rigged elections—but he identified the causes of these conditions only as "ambition, fear, folly, or corruption."[44] Locke thus imagined that the only possible sources of change are endogenous mutations in the division of labor, and he had no theory at all to explain change toward an unprecedented equilibrium. Rebellion for him stood at the extreme end of homeostatic processes and was undertaken only to control venality and to return the system to its original, envalued configuration. Locke's theory of rebellion contributes to a general understanding of political violence, but it is incapable of explaining all violent attacks by a people against their governors.

Hannah Arendt's language is similar to Locke's, but she differs from him in being interested in *revolution*—the use of violence to found new political communities. Her theory is a complement to Locke's analysis of the rebellious or restorative form of political violence. Arendt agrees with Locke that the most fundamental cause of revolution is a loss of authority, but she means something more general by authority than he did. Whereas Locke conceived of authority chiefly as flowing from the contractual understandings achieved by men in society for the purpose of avoiding the return of war and protecting their property, Arendt roots authority in a structure of values—in ideas and beliefs that unite men by providing shared explanations of reality. Although her analysis is culture-bound, being wholly restricted to "Western" communities, her examples of the loss of authority all refer to losses of the power of value structures to unite people and to legitimate authority among them.

"It may ultimately turn out," she writes, "that what we call revolution is precisely that transitory phase which brings about the birth of a new, secular realm. But if this is true, then it is secularization itself, and not the content of Christian teachings, which constitutes the origin of revolution."[45] Although Arendt does not discuss the forces of change that led to secularization, she is acutely concerned with the consequences of the breaking up of the medieval symbiosis between universal Christian values and a division of labor based in part on them. This rupture destroyed the old bases of legitimate political authority and thereby generated a long series of changes and revolutions aimed at establishing some new basis of authority. The earliest postmedieval attempts, she believes, failed in this respect: "European absolutism in theory and in practice, the existence of an absolute sovereign whose will is the source of both power and law, was a relatively new phenomenon; it had been the first and most conspicuous consequence of what we call secularization, namely, the emancipation of secular power from the authority of the church. . . . Absolutism . . . seemed to have found, within the political realm itself, a fully satisfactory substitute for the lost religious sanctions of secular authority in the person of the king or rather in the institution of kingship. But this solution, which the revolutions soon enough were to unmask as a pseudo-solution, served only to hide, for some centuries, the most elementary predicament of all modern political bodies, their profound instability, the result of some elementary lack of authority."[46]

Whether or not one agrees with Hannah Arendt that the absolutist regimes were inherently unstable, it is clear that by loss of authority ("the authority of the church") she is referring to a phenomenon closely comparable to our conception of a social system laboring under the effects of an unsynchronized value structure. She does not discuss in detail why the authority of the church once did provide a basis for a stable political community, but her understanding of the need for value sharing as the basis of community is identical to that discussed in this book in the language of the social system.

Turning to revolution itself—to the response generated by this "elementary lack of authority"—Arendt describes it as an act of "liberation," and she envisages a successful revolution in terms of the "foundation of freedom." "Violence," she writes, "is no more adequate to describe the phenomenon of revolution than change; only where change occurs in the sense of a new beginning, where violence is used to constitute an altogether different form of government, to bring about the formation of a new body politic, where the liberation from oppression aims at least at the constitution of freedom can we speak of revolution."[47] By liberation, she means the "passionate hatred of masters, the longing of the oppressed for liberation."[48] Although she says at one point that this longing is as old as human history, such a statement would appear to contradict her idea of authority. It is precisely because the religious bases of authority no longer explain and make tolerable the status hierarchy that the oppressed come to think of themselves as oppressed and to long for liberation. Thus, by the phrase "longing for liberation," she appears to mean something equivalent to the desire for a reduction in the tensions experienced by people living in a disequilibrated social system.

Arendt argues that a people longing for liberation may be provoked to "blind violence," or mere rebellion, and that this kind of behavior must be carefully distinguished from true revolution. Though the longing for liberation may be a prerequisite for revolution, revolution also involves purpose. The revolutionaries must possess an ideology of the future, an alternative conception of the bases of authority. Arendt thinks that this ideology can take only one form; to her a popular desire for liberation is revolutionary only if it is informed by the "central idea of revolution, which is the foundation of freedom."[49] And, she adds, "Political freedom, generally speaking, means the right 'to be a participator in government,' or it means nothing."[50]

Although one may be willing to grant Arendt her definition of political freedom, there have been genuine revolutions that have had different goal cultures. Freedom, in her sense, was not the central idea of the Chinese revolution of 1949, and this was certainly a true revolution according to all her other criteria. Moreover, by freedom does Arendt mean only political participation, or does it also involve certain so-called checks and balances over the various occupants of the statuses of authority? If so, does the theory, held by some sociologists, that all government is oligarchic—the so-called "iron law of oligarchy"—make all revolutions in the name of freedom hopeless? We raise these questions not to answer them, but to indicate the extreme vagueness of Arendt's idea of freedom used to *define* revolution.

From the perspective of a general theory of revolution, we must assume that Arendt is using the "foundation of freedom" as an elaborate example, or archetype, of what we have been calling "revolutionary ideology" or "goal culture." In order for the desire for liberation to take a genuinely revolutionary form, she appears to be saying, the revolutionaries must have some intellectual construct, some vision, of how they want to recast society and install authority within it. Freedom, in this context, becomes the name of a particular pattern of relations of authority—one that Arendt believes the American revolutionaries successfully founded and the French Revolution failed to found.

Arendt's analysis, when it is read as a case study of an ideal type of revolution, coincides with the social science interpretations of revolution we have explored earlier. The Arendt perspective is too restricted, however, even when generalized in the present manner. But she is correct in her belief that revolution is not mere change, only one form of change, and that to understand revolution's occasional attractiveness as an alternative, it must be studied as part of the general phenomenon of social change.

6

Varieties of Revolution

On the evening of July 14, 1789, the Duc de La Rochefoucauld-Liancourt told King Louis XVI of the fall of the Bastille, to which the King responded, "Mais, c'est une révolte!" "Non, sire," the Duke corrected him, "ce n'est pas une révolte, c'est une révolution." In so doing he gave classic expression to the now universal distinction between "rebellion" and "revolution." Writing in 1854, Thomas Meadows perpetuated this old contrast in his often repeated observation that the Chinese were (then) the most rebellious and the least revolutionary people on earth. The problem with both La Rochefoucauld and Meadows is that there has always been a great deal of confusion about what they were distinguishing: today we call Fidel Castro's seizure of power the Cuban "revolution," but we refer to the massive peasant war of nineteenth-century China as the Taiping "rebellion," and we call the Budapest insurrection of 1956 either the Hungarian Rebellion or the Hungarian Revolution. Further confounding the picture, we refer to the Indian "Mutiny," the Paris "Commune," the American "Civil War," and the Kapp "Putsch." Why resorts to political violence take different forms is an extremely complex problem. One way to begin to penetrate it, however, is by sharpening the traditional distinction between rebellion and revolution.

"Medieval and post-medieval theory," writes Hannah Arendt, "knew of legitimate rebellion, of rise against established authority, of open defiance and disobedience. But the aim of such rebellions was not a challenge of authority or the established order of things as such; it was always a matter of exchanging the person who happened to be in authority, be it the exchange of a usurper for the legitimate king or the exchange of a tyrant who had abused his power for a lawful ruler."[1] Here is the simplest and clearest meaning of rebellion. Political principles inform the actions of the rebels, but the rebellion is not caused by a dispute over fundamental principles. The rebels know how the society ought to be governed—namely, in the way they remember or imagine its having been governed before the usurper or tyrant betrayed the trust that the society had placed in him. Rebellion in this sense is an act of social surgery; it is intended to cut out one or more members who are offending against the joint commitments to maintain a particular social structure. Locke used the term rebellion in precisely this sense; in fact, he thought that it was the tyrant who rebelled and that the act of deposing him was no rebellion. Simple rebellion, we may say, is without ideology; its ideology is actually a functioning structure of values that informs people about the presence of a usurper or a tyrant.

The classic example of a simple rebellion is a jacquerie. Both the historic Jacquerie in France in 1358 and subsequent rebellions similar to it were motivated by a belief that the system had been betrayed by its elite; violence was invoked to purge the system of its violators and, so to speak, to set it back on the tracks. Masses rebelling to restore an *ancien régime*, or one patterned after it, are not alienated from the description of reality embedded in the old value structure. Jacqueries have usually been carried out in the name of a king or church, against the allegedly unworthy local agents of that king or church, or against agents of a foreign king or church. E. I. Pugachev, for example, the leader of the large-scale Russian peasant rebellion of 1773–75, exploited the popular belief that Peter III had not been murdered and declared that he was rebelling in the name of the rightful Tsar. He united behind this banner peasants, cossacks, runaway serfs, and Tartar bands—all of whom were rebelling against the progressive curtailment of the rights of the lower strata during the eighteenth century.

Concerning jacquerie ideology, Hobsbawm has written: "The peasants did not rise for the real king, whom they hardly knew, but for the ideal of the just king who, if he only knew, would punish the transgressions of his underlings and lords; though often they did rise for the real church. For the village priest was one of them, the saints were certainly theirs and nobody else's, and even the tumbledown ecclesiastical estates were sometimes more tolerable than the grasping laymen."[2] Potential jacquerie conditions may persist for a long time until some occurrence—such as humiliation by a foreign power, open banditry, or rebellion elsewhere in the realm—reveals that the existing elites are incapable of performing their roles. The typical remedy for these conditions will be a purge of the elites by the masses.

Sometimes, however, ideologies of rebellion may seek to "restore" patterns of social organization that in fact never really existed. Examples include the ideology of the Confederate rebels in the American Civil War, the ideology of the Franco forces in the Spanish Civil War, and the attempt to establish an Islamic Republic in Iran. In describing these cases we shall continue to use the term "rebellion," although it is clear that they involve changes of greater magnitude than the removal of offending personnel.

The historical European Anarchist movement offers us an example of the ideology encountered in this type of rebellion. As Woodcock has observed, "It [Anarchism] was a protest, a dedicated resistance to the worldwide trend since the middle of the eighteenth century toward political and economic centralization, with all it implies in terms of the replacement of personal values by collective values, of the subordination of the individual to the state. . . . They [the Anarchists] drew their support mainly from those social classes which were out of tune with the dominant historical trend and which were steadily declining in numbers."[3] The Anarchists articulated goals for the future that derived from an idealized but increasingly redundant past. They hoped to escape from the tensions generated by rapid social change by restoring a simpler, prenational, preindustrial life that placed greater reliance on cooperation than on authority. Anarchist rebellions were, in this sense, restorative rather than revolutionary.

When the goal culture of an insurrectionary ideology envisions recasting the social division of labor according to a pattern that is clearly unprecedented in a particular social system, then we should use the term "revolution." Revolutions of course also involve attacks on certain persons; all insurrections have that as a goal. But revolution intends to accomplish more. It is distinguished from its nearest rival, the ideological rebellion, by its conscious espousal of a new social order, be it a society based on "The Rights of Man and Citizen," the ideal of "self-determination," or the principle "From each according to his ability, to each according to his needs."

As the distinction between simple and ideological rebellions was necessary, so also is there a need to distinguish between simple and total revolutions. Some revolutionary ideologies are restricted to fundamental changes in only a few values (e.g., values governing authority, economic exchange, or the resolution of conflicting goals) but do not contemplate alterations in others (e.g., religious beliefs, basic political identity, or sex- and age-based status differences). The goals of simple revolutions can sometimes be achieved simply by promulgating or rewriting a political constitution for the system, as was done in General de Gaulle's seizure of power in 1958 and, to a large extent, in the American Revolution. Of course, the implementation of demands for revolutionary changes in certain values may give rise over time to either homeostatic or deliberate reinterpretations of most of the other values in a system in order to maintain a coherent and integrated social structure. But changes subsequent to, and arising as a consequence of, revolutionary change need not themselves be revolutionary. On the other hand, a simple revolution intended to resolve certain dissynchronized conditions may produce new conditions of disequilibrium that the elite is unable or unwilling to relieve through policies of change, thereby setting the stage for a later total revolution.

Total revolutions, such as the one in France that began in 1789 or the one that has transformed China during this century, aim at supplanting the entire structure of values and at recasting the entire division of labor. In France between 1789 and 1797, the people employed violence to change the systems of landholding, taxation, choice of occupation, education, prestige symbols, military organization, and virtually every other characteristic of the social system. The effect was to transform Provençals, Bretons, Alsatians, and so forth, into Frenchmen. This is the kind of revolution that, when successful, alters the social system from one major type to another—for example, from feudalism to capitalism, or from peasant community to national community. This type is, of course, extremely rare. Changes in basic political and social consciousness seldom occur at once (viz., the slowness of change in both white and black attitudes vis-à-vis the "integration" of blacks into the American social system), and the extent to which changes of such magnitude have ever been achieved through revolution remains a controversial matter. Nevertheless, some revolutionary ideologies, such as that of Chinese communism, do envisage a total reformulation of a society's value structure and pattern of environmental adaptation. Our immediate criterion for differentiating between rebellion and revolution will therefore be, following Hannah Arendt, the aims or goal cultures of the various movements.

The differences between simple and ideological rebellions and simple and total revolutions should not, of course, be treated as dichotomies. Every revolution reveals shades of difference from all other cases; and many rebellions turned into revolutions only as they encountered difficulties in actually securing the changes demanded (e.g., the American Revolution). Simple rebellion and total revolution should thus be understood as polar extremes along a continuum.

The differences between rebellion and revolution may be made clearer if they are viewed in terms of the levels of sociopolitical organization on which they impinge. The idea of "levels" of society has been formulated in many different ways in the past, but for our purposes a simple threefold distinction among the levels of *government*, *regime*, and *community* is sufficient.[4] By "government," we mean the formal political and administrative institutions that make and execute decisions for the society—that is to say, the institutionalized expressions of the statuses of authority. Resorts to violence to cause changes at this level will be simple rebellions; they seek to replace persons who are believed to be occupying various authority positions illegitimately.

"Regime" refers to the fundamental rules of the political game in a society. Democracy, dictatorship, monarchy, oligarchy, federalism, constitutionalism, thus designate different kinds of regimes. Ideological rebellions and simple revolutions normally aim at this level—that is, at the normative codes governing political and economic behavior, which are thought to be in need of change. Revolts that seek to establish or broaden popular suffrage, alter the norms of land tenure, or oust foreign conquerors are attempts to change the system at the regime level.

By "community," we mean the broadest level of social organization and consciousness, the level where fundamental values cohere with the cardinal demands of environmental adaptation. If, for example, the mode of production in a society shifts from subsistence agriculture to one-crop cultivation for a market, and a revolution is required to bring its values into line with this radically different pattern of environmental adaptation, the revolution will be total. Similarly, when people cease to regard themselves primarily as members of kinship or religious communities and become members of national communities, a change in basic political consciousness has taken place. If this change occurs under revolutionary auspices, the revolution will be of the magnitude of the French or Chinese.

A typology of revolutions parallel to the one being set forth, also using the concept of levels, is that of James Rosenau. He distinguishes among revolutions in terms of the "targets" of the revolutionaries, and on this basis he identifies three types (he uses the term internal war instead of revolution): personnel wars, authority wars, and structural wars.[5] His personnel wars and structural wars correspond, respectively, to our revolutions aimed at the levels of government and the community. His "authority" wars, while corresponding roughly to our revolutions aimed at the regime, are perhaps unfortunately named, since, as we have seen earlier, *all* rebellions and revolutions involve challenges to the authority of ruling elites.

Still another attempt to distinguish types of revolutions according to ideology is by Anthony Wallace. The three types he suggests are: "Movements which profess to *revive* a traditional culture now fallen into desuetude; movements which profess to *import* a foreign cultural system; and movements which profess neither revival nor importation, but conceive that the desired cultural end-state, which has never been enjoyed by ancestors or foreigners, will be realized for the first time in a future *Utopia*."[6]

Wallace's first category corresponds exactly to the traditional idea of rebellion, according to which all rebellions seek to put back into perfect working order a social system that has, from the perspective of an earlier time, diverged from its inner logic. Similarly, Wallace's Utopian movements correspond to total revolutions, in which the revolutionaries see themselves as the instruments or creators of "progress" toward a newer and better form of communal life. However, these categories are a little too broad, and Wallace himself points out that "it is easy to demonstrate that avowedly revival movements are never entirely what they claim to be, for the image of the ancient culture to be revived is distorted by historical ignorance and by the presence of imported and innovative elements."[7] This fact suggests the need to distinguish between purely revival movements—or simple rebellions—and rebellions that consciously develop an *ideology* of earlier social perfection. Although many simple rebellions, such as some of the widespread peasant uprisings associated with changes of dynasty in traditional China, both espoused and succeeded in reestablishing a virtual mirror image of the social *status quo ante*, there have also been rebellions based on more developed ideologies, such as those of the Boxers or the Mau Mau, which should be distinguished from the Lockean type of revolt. By the same token, some revolutions are genuinely Utopian, but many others, typically those occurring at the level of the regime, demand innovations that fall well short of reconstituting the system.

The greatest problem with Wallace's typology is his belief that the importation of ideology makes a difference. It seems highly unlikely that any successful movement ever professed to be the agent of a foreign cultural system; the history of international communism since the Russian Revolution alone suggests that such an avowal is tantamount to ideological suicide. Imported ideological constructs always undergo a process of domestication: what Mao Tse-tung did for Marxism in a modern Chinese context, Hung Hsiu-ch'üan did a century earlier for Christianity in a Taiping context (he declared himself to be the younger brother of Jesus Christ). As we observed earlier, the endogenous or exogenous nature of *sources of change* is highly relevant to discovering the causes of a system's disequilibrium, but this factor cannot be shown to determine what kind of revolution will occur.

The distinction between rebellion and revolution provides a beginning for a typology of revolts, and its usefulness may be improved through the addition of various relevant criteria, such as the levels at which revolutionary activity is aimed. However, even when perfected, any typology of this sort runs the danger of excessive abstraction and superficiality. This is because of the contingent nature of revolution (using the word "revolution" in its generic sense rather than as one *kind* of political violence), a characteristic that has been stressed throughout this book. Revolution is a response to a particular crisis in a particular social system, and any attempt to compare revolutions that does not at the same time compare social systems is theoretically inconsistent. The fundamental factors that give rise to variation among revolutions are the types of system in which they occur and the conditions of systemic disequilibrium that they seek to over-

come. These two elements must form the foundation for serious
study of any revolution.[8]

Unfortunately, generalizing about types of social systems is
still extremely difficult. In this volume we cannot hope to do
more than suggest several approaches to the problem, but it
should be evident from our earlier analysis that the study of
types of revolutions and the study of types of social systems are
inseparable. We may be able to define abstractly the different
meanings of the words "rebellion" and "revolution," but we
can never compare the Algerian and Vietnamese revolutions
without thoroughly investigating the Algerian and Vietnamese
social systems.

The best-known social scientific attempt to categorize societies
is that of Marx. Basing his analysis on the alleged primacy of the
pattern of environmental adaptation—the "modes of production"—he discovered six types of societies, which he called
primitive communism, slavery, feudalism, capitalism, socialism, and communism. These were linked, he argued, in an evolutionary chain of development, and the dynamic elements that
caused one type to change into the next were the dialectical
creation of social classes, followed by class warfare and revolutionary change. He also noted some types of societies that stood
outside his evolutionary framework—for example, "Oriental
Despotism," or the "Asiatic mode of production"—but he did
nothing more than identify them as anomalies. Contemporary
social scientists studying the same problems have reacted
strongly against the Marxist conception—against the idea of an
evolutionary chain of development, for which the evidence is
lacking, and against the use of economic criteria as the primary
categorizing principles.

Parsons, for example, attempted to distinguish social systems
on the basis of their value structures by the use of criteria he
called "pattern variables" or "dilemmas of orientation." He posited a series of five value dichotomies in terms of which each
society can be placed: (1) affectivity vs. affective neutrality; (2)
collectivity-orientation vs. self-orientation; (3) particularism vs.

universalism; (4) ascription vs. achievement; and (5) functional diffuseness vs. functional specificity.* As is readily apparent, the values of affectivity, collectivity-orientation, particularism, ascription, and functional diffuseness typify societies often called "traditional"; whereas affective neutrality, self-orientation, universalism, achievement, and functional specificity are traits of societies popularly called "modern." These variables are, to this extent, an attempt to refine the older sociological distinction between gemeinschaft (a community characterized by face-to-face personal relationships and ascribed, or intrinsic, statuses) and gesellschaft (an atomized, secularized society that assigns persons to statuses on the basis of their achievements).

Parsons did not intend, however, that his five dichotomies should constitute one overarching dichotomy—the broadest possible distinction between two societies on the basis of all five pattern variables should be conceived only as constituting the opposite poles of a continuum—and he rejected the notion of a unitary evolutionary path from one pole to the other. For example, some basically traditional societies may nevertheless use achievement to assign individuals to certain statuses, as was partly true of the classical Chinese examination system for selecting imperial officials; and many so-called modern societies retain particularistic features, such as buying done on the basis of friendship, trust, or habit, or the persistence of school and regional ties. The pattern variables thus make an advance over the old traditional/modern distinction by providing the basis for differentiating within the larger groupings.

Of all the pattern variables, the most relevant to the varieties of revolution is functional diffuseness vs. functional specificity. In traditional societies it is very difficult to employ such concepts as "economic man" or "political man," or to make clear distinc-

* These relationships may be described somewhat less succinctly as follows: (1) the saliency of public emotional ties vs. private emotional ties; (2) the primacy of group interests vs. individual interests; (3) the basing of decisions on nonscientific, ungeneralized knowledge vs. allegedly scientific laws; (4) the assignment of people to statuses on the basis of who they are vs. what they do; and (5) a lack of role specialization vs. role multiplicity and compartmentalization.

tions among the roles of father, citizen, farmer, and civic leader. Persons living in these societies do not themselves distinguish among, for example, religion, philosophy, and science, and the roles required for fulfilling the system's functional prerequisites are not characterized by internal specialization within the system's broad strata. We use the word "peasant" to refer to a whole congeries of roles and norms, whereas the word "farmer" refers specifically to the role of agricultural production. The role of farmer does not necessarily indicate anything about the other roles that a farmer may perform, whereas the role of peasant implies a whole way of life.

There is some evidence to suggest that functionally diffuse societies are more likely to experience rebellions, whereas functionally specific societies are more likely to experience revolutions. Diffuse societies are characterized by an almost homogeneous spreading of the system's values among all its members and, owing to the lack of role specialization, by a relatively low interdependence among its parts and a relatively high degree of equilibrium.[10] Because of the homogeneity and stability of values, dissynchronized conditions are more likely to produce efforts at restoration than innovation; and because of the low degree of interdependence, exogenous sources of change are likely to have only a localized impact, which the elite may isolate or eradicate. Many so-called primitive (preliterate) and traditional (literate but having at best a pre-Newtonian science and technology) societies thus have histories of rebellion but not of revolution.

The functionally specific or differentiated society is one in which values and the pattern of environmental adaptation demand a highly complex ensemble of roles. The sources of change that may generate these roles include the rise of a centralized state governing a large territory, the acceptance of a religion with a professional priesthood, the control of water for irrigation and flood prevention, the development of towns as the loci of markets or intellectual centers, and the production of goods in a factory system.[11] As a result of such changes, certain types of work become separated from kinship, religious, regional, and other relationships; and this initial separation in turn causes further major role differentiation.

Differentiation, or "the formation of social positions specialized in different segments of [an] activity, and the subdivision of existing social positions into more specialized ones," is directly relevant to the production of *revolutionary* ideologies.[12] Differentiation generates subsystems, which, in performing their particular functions, often emphasize or modify the system's values in such a way that they begin to diverge markedly from other subsystems. As Arnold Feldman has written: "Differentiation (1) increases the number of social systems that constitute a society; (2) increases the salience of the particular system to which a norm belongs, which increases the salience of subsystem goals and values; [and] (3) increases the discontinuity between subsystems as the normative content of each is purified and decontaminated."[13] By decontamination, Feldman means the extent to which subsystem values come to be understood by members of the subsystem in terms of structural characteristics of the system and not simply as the personal preferences or anomalies of a group of people.

Functionally differentiated societies also differ from diffuse societies in that their segments are highly interdependent and their equilibrium is more fragile. Here the roles of the system are not duplicated throughout each stratum; they diverge widely both individually and in accordance with specific functional requirements. The relationship among roles is one of coordination rather than simple complementarity, and new roles charged with coordinating the numerous functions must be articulated. Because of this high degree of interdependence and the ease with which differences over the meanings and priorities of values may arise, if the system's values become dissynchronized with its division of labor, an ideology proposing revolutionary changes in either the values or the division of labor is likely to develop. Rebellion presupposes a fair degree of agreement among participants on how the society should be organized.

Revolution is a manifestation of basic disagreements among many sectors of the society on precisely this point; the revolution is often an attempt to settle these disagreements by force in favor of one or another position.

The effects of differentiation are, of course, offset by patterns of multiple role playing, which will normally cause differences in value saliency to cancel each other out in the minds of individual actors. Moreover, the differentiated society will itself develop values and norms for the toleration of differences, for the peaceful resolution of conflicts, and for the routine settlement of differences arising from value saliency as an element of maintaining a homeostatic equilibrium in a complex division of labor. However, if the preconditions for violent social change arise in such a system, the system's very complexity is more likely to suggest the need for revolutionary than for rebellious action. Probably for this reason Hannah Arendt noted the modernity of the concept of revolution; although the idea is not restricted to highly complex societies, it is considerably more relevant to them.

Parsons's pattern variables constitute only one of many attempts to create a typology of societies. Though it is perhaps the most useful for our purposes, even it is not completely satisfactory. As we have argued earlier, the ultimate determinant of social structure is the interrelationship between a particular structure of values and the demands of adaptation in a particular sociopolitical environment. A typology of social structures must be informed by the many variables that go to make up this subtle relationship. Such a typology does not exist, and it would constitute more than a digression to attempt to create one here.

Lacking firm agreement on the types of social systems and, more narrowly, on the varieties of disequilibrated conditions that may arise in them, we must retreat from any claim to exhaustive study of the types of revolutions. Revolutions are determined by an extremely numerous set of variables; and, given the present state of social science theory, it is virtually impossible to isolate and recombine all these variables into various abstract models. A more satisfactory "middle range" approach is the attempt to categorize differences among a few salient variables. We did this earlier in terms of the goal culture components of revolutionary ideologies. The distinction between renovation and innovation—or, more simply, the distinction between rebellion and revolution—remains the most widely used classification in studies of political violence. It must be reiterated, however, that none of the forms of the rebellion/revolution distinction is the equivalent of a true typology based on social systems principles.

7

Strategies of Revolution

Whereas the distinction between rebellion and revolution rests on differences in the ideologies of various movements, another time-honored way of classifying revolutions is by the different tactics of violence adopted by the revolutionaries. Thus we describe the Bolshevik Revolution as a coup d'état, the Russian revolution of 1905 as a spontaneous popular insurrection, and the Chinese and Algerian revolutions as guerrilla wars. Moreover, we attempt to create subclasses among major categories of insurrectionary tactics, speaking of "regular" revolutionary wars, rural guerrilla wars, military coups d'état, urban insurrections, and so forth.

As should now be apparent, to classify revolutions by their tactical characteristics is even more reductionist than to explain their variability by the single factor of ideology. A revolutionary ideology often offers insights into the conditions of disequilibrium that have breached a system's defenses against violence; demands for land reform, for example, indicate the need to examine a society's system of land tenure. Technologies of violence, however, are much further removed from the major variables that produce differences in form. In fact, the practice of differentiating among revolutions on a tactical basis is partly responsible for the widespread confusion over the very meaning of revolution. Not all coups d'état are revolutionary, even when they "succeed" (for example, palace revolutions and military *pronunciamientos*, or *juntas*). Moreover, some guerrilla wars are actually international policies of subversion—disguised as revolution—undertaken by one social system against another. The labeling of such activities as "revolutions" by their sponsors is merely a conscious element of political warfare in modern international conflict (e.g., several Chinese Communist-sponsored "wars of national liberation," or the U.S. Central Intelligence Agency's sponsored revolution at the Bay of Pigs in Cuba). The fact that some conspirators call themselves revolutionaries does not, from the point of view of systems theory, make them so.

By contrast, some coups d'état are genuinely revolutionary; they constitute the first stage in the relief of systemic disequilibrium and the initiation of revolutionary social change (e.g., the Bolshevik seizure of power, the Italian Fascists' march on Rome in 1922, and the coup d'état of Gamal Abdal Nasser in Egypt in 1952). Similarly, guerrilla wars that are *supported* by foreign governments should be carefully distinguished from guerrilla wars that are *sponsored* by foreign governments, and it should be recognized that degrees of support and sponsorship can and do change over time, thereby altering the nature of a movement.

Nonrevolutionary coups d'état and acts of international subversion disguised as revolutions (the classic example is the Nazi Party's use of persons of German descent residing in Czechoslovakia and throughout Europe) ought to be understood, from a systems theory perspective, as either endogenous or exogenous sources of change. Very often these so-called revolutions create the conditions for a subsequent true revolution. The seizure of power by the Hungarian Communist Party after the Second World War, for example, was the primary source of the disequilibrated conditions that caused the Hungarian Rebellion of 1956. Similarly, a military coup d'état against President Juan Bosch of the Dominican Republic set the stage for the Santo Domingo revolution of 1965. When nonrevolutionary resorts to violence fail, as they often do, they are treated as the acts of traitors or as instances of international subversion. It is therefore inconsistent to regard them as revolutions simply because their perpetrators sometimes bring to bear overwhelming force and, as a result, are said to have "won."

The element that distinguishes the acts of criminals or lunatics (e.g., Conrad's *Secret Agent*) from a revolutionary coup d'état or a mass uprising is the functional condition of the social system in which they occur. This condition should be determined independently of the success or failure of violence against a system's elite. If the condition of the system is one of power deflation and a loss of authority, violent attacks against it are to be expected. Whether these attacks take the form of a coup d'état or a civil war is of secondary importance.

The tactics of a revolutionary outbreak, however, can sometimes tell us a good deal about the conditions that prevail in a disequilibrated system. If there is widespread agreement on the need for change and if the ruling elite is relatively isolated and undefended, a coup d'état is the most economical and welcome violent way of altering the system's structure. If the elite, through its possession of overwhelming armed force, is able to frustrate all demands for change, then revolution may take the form of a prolonged revolutionary war. The choice of revolutionary method will depend on what actions the revolutionaries perceive to be necessary to implement their goal culture—or, in other words, differences in tactics illustrate differences in the "transfer cultures" of revolutionary ideologies.

The transfer culture of a revolutionary ideology—that element which tells the revolutionaries what to do and how to do it in order to usher in the new order—in some cases dictates what will be the sufficient cause, or accelerator, of a revolution. The remote causes of a revolution, namely power deflation and a loss of authority, may exist without a revolution occurring, in which case the integration of a system will rest on the elite's monopoly of armed force—on its ability to prevent revolutionaries from organizing and on its maintenance of role performances through deterrence. In these circumstances the final cause of a revolutionary resort to arms is some event that holds forth the promise to the revolutionaries that they can break the elite's monopoly of force. This accelerator may be some factor beyond the control of the revolutionaries, such as the crippling of the armed forces; it may be a belief that the forces of a ruling elite can be incapacitated through direct action against them; or it may be the launching of a careful strategy of revolution.

The distinction among these accelerators, however, is analytical rather than empirical. The internal dissolution of the armed forces may accompany either one of the other two accelerators; for example, the strategy of a revolutionary coup d'état often involves exploiting or exacerbating an elite's temporary loss of its armed strength. Similarly, both ideological and strategic accelerators are parts of "transfer cultures." The differences between them lie in the fact that the latter are amenable to strategic analysis. According to the widely accepted view of Thomas Schelling, "Among diverse theories of conflict—corresponding to the diverse meanings of the word 'conflict'—a main dividing line is between those that treat conflict as a pathological state and seek its causes and treatment, and those that take conflict for granted and study the behavior associated with it. Among the latter there is a further division between those that examine the participants in a conflict in all their complexity—with regard to both 'rational' and 'irrational' behavior, conscious and unconscious, and to motivations as well as calculations—and those that focus on the more rational, conscious, artful kind of behavior. Crudely speaking, the latter treat conflict as a kind of contest, in which the participants are trying to 'win.' A study of conscious, intelligent, sophisticated conflict behavior—of successful behavior—is like a search for rules of 'correct' behavior in a contest-winning sense. We can call this field of study the *strategy* of conflict."[1]

Strategic accelerators differ from ideological accelerators in their degree of rationality. By the rational quality of strategy, we mean merely that *both* sides to a conflict recognize particular courses of behavior as promoting or impeding victory, and that one side's behavior is modified in response to the behavior of its opponent—as in the strategy of an end game in chess. On the other hand, ideological accelerators—such as the belief that certain initiation rites endow one with supernatural powers—are not rational in this sense; they are the products of wishful thinking, recklessness, emotional frenzy, and so forth.

A strategy of revolution derives from a rational calculation of the forces that the ruling elite has mobilized against the possibility of revolution, and it elaborates courses of action intended to disarm this military preparedness. Clearly, strategies of revolution demand leadership, organization, and communications among the revolutionaries. When implemented, a strategy may or may not succeed, but both sides of the struggle take each other's actions seriously. Success or failure depends on numerous variables that both parties will have tried to calculate, including the military variables of morale, competence of command, training, equipment, and intelligence.

Not all revolutions are accelerated by strategies, nor are all revolutions organized, led, or informed by a directorate. Probably the simplest kind of accelerator is the "incident," which reveals to the mob that the armed forces arrayed against it have been incapacitated or causes the mob to believe that its combined strength can overcome the armed police. Schelling comments on the differences between strategic and mob action as follows: "It is usually the essence of mob formation that the potential members have to know not only where and when to meet but just when to act so that they act in concert. Overt leadership solves the problem; but leadership can often be identified and eliminated by the authority trying to prevent mob action. In this case the mob's problem is to act in unison without overt leadership, to find some common symbol that makes everyone confident that if he acts on it, he will not be acting alone. The role of 'incidents' can thus be seen as a coordinating role; it is a substitute for overt leadership and communication. Without something like an incident, it may be difficult to get action at all, since immunity requires that all know when to act together."[2] By contrast, the actual moment of acceleration in a strategically directed revolution occurs when a leader's orders to commence operations are put into effect.

Strategies of revolution vary a great deal from one another

according to the size and quality of the armed forces that revolutionary leaders must overcome and according to the ingenuity displayed by the revolutionaries. We shall discuss here only two strategies—the coup d'état based on infiltration, and the militarized mass insurrection, or what is commonly known as "guerrilla warfare." Both have received a great deal of attention from twentieth-century strategists of revolution, particularly within the international communist movement, and both have resulted in important recent revolutions.

A coup d'état envisions the replacement of the occupants of the existing statuses of authority with revolutionaries—men who will then use their newly acquired authority to initiate changes in the structure of society, sometimes including their own positions of authority, in conformity with the goal culture of the revolutionary movement. A coup thus involves a sudden seizing and usually killing of a system's political elite; and its strategic success depends on one overriding condition—that the system's armed forces and the population at large welcome, or at least tolerate and therefore obey, the new occupants of the statuses of authority. As Janos has shown, this condition is never favorable to the revolutionaries unless they can already claim some position of respect or some element of legitimacy in the eyes of the population.[3] Not everyone can usurp the positions of authority and expect the army and the population to accept his explanations about why he has deposed the former rulers, glad though people may be to see them gone.

The inability of the leaders of a coup to assume automatically that their orders after the coup will be obeyed is the primary difficulty of the strategy. The main exceptions to this principle are military coups, in which the military forces can compel obedience after ousting the old elite. Even then, a *junta* can often expect that the people will call a general strike or otherwise retaliate against it. When that happens, the military must either back down or adopt totalitarian methods. In the case of the Bolsheviks' October Revolution, where Lenin and Trotsky had already gained a large measure of legitimacy in the eyes of the population, the Bolsheviks still had to form an army and consolidate their revolution in a prolonged civil war.

Modern coup d'état strategy involves either infiltrating revolutionaries into the elite and army, converting key members of the elite or army, completely isolating the elite from its army and people, or all of these. In the communist revolutionary tradition, these techniques are known as the "united front," of which there are two subvarieties: the united front from above, which involves the creation of a coalition government consisting of the established elite and a communist party, and the united front from below, which involves both the legitimation of the communist party through tactical alliances with labor unions, ethnic groups, patriotic associations, and so forth, and the transformation of such groups into a front against the government. United front strategy is designed to put the revolutionaries in a position to carry out a successful coup at the highest levels of authority, maintain the continuity of authority without provoking counterrevolutions, and place members of the revolutionary movement in positions where they can incapacitate any challenges to the coup.

The first requirement of this strategy is to organize the revolutionary party itself—the unit to whom the revolutionaries will owe their primary allegiance and from whom they will take orders while serving within a united front government, labor union, army unit, or peasant cooperative. Although Lenin's ideas were foreshadowed in the eighteenth and nineteenth centuries by ideas of Babeuf, Buonarroti, and Blanqui, his formulation and implementation of the qualities of the coup party are classic: hierarchy, military command relationships, secrecy, cellular primary units, and all the rest.[4]

A second requirement of this strategy is to identify and exploit issues that will lead governments or social groups to accept coalitions with communist parties—issues such as anti-fascism, anti-imperialism, and anti-militarism. To be sure, communist parties may have genuine positions on these issues, much as other groups in a society do. However, for a communist party to attain a position from which it can bring about its ultimate goals, it cannot enter a united front solely to achieve the immediate reforms advanced by the front. A united front is a tactical alliance that revolutionaries join in order to begin legitimating their movement and to position their forces for a coup d'état. A revolutionary party always has interests that go beyond the concrete issues that may allow it to form temporary alliances.

Lenin's most complete exposition and advocacy of the united front as a strategy for positioning communist parties to make coups d'état dates from 1920. In May of that year, two months before the second congress of the Communist International accepted his views as basic revolutionary strategy for the world movement, he published his *'Left-Wing' Communism, An Infantile Disorder*, subtitled *A Popular Exposition of Marxist Strategy and Tactics*. Zinoviev later compared Lenin's pamphlet to Marx's *Capital*, and Franz Borkenau commented: " *'Left-Wing' Communism* is perhaps the most powerful thing Lenin has ever written, . . . [comparable] for force of argument, realism, directness, and convincing power with Machiavelli's *Il Principe*."[5]

In this handbook of revolutionary strategy, Lenin outlines the purposes of a united front: to gain for a communist party some aura of legitimacy, and to position it for making a coup d'état against its allies when their usefulness has expired. In answer to the question, "What is the intent of the British Communist Party in entering an alliance with the Labour Party, led by Arthur Henderson, against Lloyd George?" Lenin wrote: "At present the British Communists very often find it hard to approach the masses and even to get a hearing from them. [However,] if I come out as a Communist and call upon the workers to vote for Henderson against Lloyd George, they will certainly give me a hearing. And I will be able to explain in a popular manner not only why Soviets are better than parliament and why the dictatorship of the proletariat is better than the dictatorship of Churchill (disguised by the signboard of bourgeois 'democracy'), but also that I want my vote to support Henderson *in the same way as the rope supports a hanged man*—that the impending establishment of a government of Hendersons will prove that I am right, will bring the masses over to my side, and will hasten the political death of the Hendersons and the Snowdens just as was the case with their kindred spirits in Russia and Germany."[6] Henderson, like Kerensky, was to serve as a "bridge to the new regime."

A united front is the most important but not the only element in this overall strategy. To ensure that the army will acquiesce to a coup once it has been made, various other tasks must be performed by the Leninist party. For example, one of the twenty-one conditions for the admission of a national party to the Communist International, also ratified at the second Comintern congress, stresses: "The obligation to spread Communist ideas includes the special obligation to carry on systematic and energetic propaganda in the Army. Where such agitation is prevented by emergency laws, it must be carried on illegally."[7] If the army can be neutralized by such means, the coup d'état can anticipate probable success; if not, the conspirators will probably fail.

In the history of the communist movement, the Leninist coup d'état has had only a mixed record of success. In 1927, the Chinese Communist Party had successfully infiltrated a few army units and most of the labor unions, and was fully poised to make a coup against the Kuomintang, its partner in an "antifeudal, anti-imperialist" united front, when Chiang Kai-shek carried out a coup against the communists. This development reveals the greatest weakness of the Leninist-type coup in the communist tradition: more often than not the noncommunist partner in the united front is fully aware of communist intentions and can destroy the party after using it for its own purposes. On the other hand, in Spain in 1936, the united front tactic worked only too well. Great Britain came to regard the Republican-Communist coalition government as a Soviet puppet, and its refusal to aid Madrid against the Axis-assisted fascist forces contributed to the eventual defeat of the Republicans. The Leninist-type coup d'état influenced the communist seizures of power in postwar eastern Europe, particularly in Czechoslovakia, but in all these changes of regime the crucial element was the presence of the Soviet Red Army. The Czech coup d'état should be considered a case of change due to exogenous forces more than to a revolution.

Even in the most favorable circumstances, Leninist tactics may fail as a result of accident or miscalculation. In September 1965, the Indonesian Communist Party, having thoroughly infiltrated the government of President Sukarno and the Indonesian Air Force, staged a coup d'état against the regime with the ultimate intention of establishing a so-called people's republic. The rebels accurately calculated that the army was their chief enemy, and they killed six generals in the course of implementing the coup itself. However, they did not kill Sukarno, no doubt intending to use him temporarily to legitimate their actions, and they allowed General Haris Nasution, the Defense Minister, to escape from their net. The result was predictable: the army under Nasution reacted with ruthless measures against the party, and the people were rallied against the so-called traitors. Thus, although the Indonesian system was markedly disequilibrated and the revolutionaries had carefully prepared their strategy, the coup failed as a result of numerous miscalculations and chance events.

The coup d'état is always an extremely risky venture, even when calculated in the most careful and realistic manner. Numerous chance factors can intervene—mistaken identities, changes of schedule, unforeseen treacheries, and so forth. Its most serious defect, as Trotsky pointed out, is that a coup can succeed without the army, but it cannot succeed against it.[8] These considerations caused many revolutionaries to shift their attention to an entirely different strategy of revolution—to a direct assault on the ruling elite's armed forces via guerrilla warfare. Not all guerrilla revolutions of recent decades have succeeded (those in Greece, the Philippines, and Malaya failed), but a number have been spectacularly successful, notably those in China, Yugoslavia, Cuba, Algeria, and Vietnam. Guerrilla warfare was as a consequence the most widely used and studied strategy of revolution until the 1970's, when it was replaced by terrorism.

Revolutionary guerrilla warfare is an attempt to disprove Trotsky's principle that a revolution cannot be made *against* an entrenched elite's armed forces. It is a strategy designed to answer the question, "How does a rebel party make a revolution against a regime protected by a professional army?" The answer is complex, and acting on it is difficult. The revolutionary party must begin by turning the strengths of the elite's army into weaknesses; it must then create an army of its own; and finally it must commit its members to a long struggle. This strategy requires a greater singleness of purpose on the part of the revolutionaries than any other historical program of internal political violence.[9]

Guerrilla warfare is a form of warfare in the technical sense in which all war involves the use of armed men to annihilate the men and arms of an enemy. The initiation of a revolutionary guerrilla war thus requires that an armed band of men take to the field and launch attacks against a regime's forces. Because the military situation is by definition one in which the defending forces are far superior in strength and numbers, the rebel army's tactics are dictated by this fact. Mao Tse-tung laid down the essence of these tactics in 1929: "The enemy advances, we retreat; the enemy camps, we harass; the enemy tires, we attack; the enemy retreats, we pursue."[10] Guerrilla tactics are always employed by an objectively weaker military force against an objectively stronger military force. The guerrilla compensates for his deficiencies in training, equipment, and leadership by fighting only when, as a result of concealment or the concentration of superior numbers, victory is assured. Conversely, he flees in the face of enemy counterguerrilla campaigns, and he never offers battle on terms favorable to his foe. These are the tactical truisms of guerrilla warfare; however, the strategy of guerrilla warfare concerns not *what* the guerrilla does but *how* he is able to do it and, at the same time, begin to legitimate the revolutionary party and prepare the population for accepting its goal culture.

The essence of guerrilla strategy is to entrap the status quo forces in the swamp of an overwhelmingly hostile population, and to organize this population to serve a coherent, long-range program of military conquest in which the defending force's strengths are turned into weaknesses. As Peter Paret has written: "The conquest of the population is . . . the indispensable opening of insurrectional war. Once this has been achieved, once the population has been schooled and organized for the revolutionary purpose, it becomes possible to go on to a second stage—open warfare—under conditions that are unfavorable to the enemy, even though his military forces may be larger and, according to traditional standards, better trained and equipped than those of the insurgents."[11] On this same point, Mao Tsetung has concluded, "Because guerrilla warfare basically derives from the masses and is supported by them, it can neither exist nor flourish if it separates itself from their sympathies and cooperation."[12]

How does a revolutionary party gain the "sympathies and cooperation" of the broad mass of the people? What it needs is a general ideological appeal that will bring the revolutionary party the support of the people at the same time that it disguises any elements of the party's ultimate aspirations that might conflict with the demands of the mass movement. Promises of land redistribution to poor peasants have been used with partial success in Asian revolutionary wars, but by far the most common and successful appeal is to the defense of the fatherland against alleged domestic traitors or foreign invaders. To make this appeal, the rebels may have to wait for foreign intervention, or else provoke intervention so that they can arouse antiforeign, nationalistic emotions.

Guerrillas have been known to undertake small-scale terrorism, combined with an international propaganda barrage, in order to frighten and possibly trick a foreign state into taking military action in the target system. They have also used guerrilla terror raids to intimidate a population into believing that the elite is unable to protect people from banditry, thereby causing the people in certain restricted areas temporarily to transfer their support to the guerrillas for their own safety. However, the rebels' use of terrorism to coerce support indicates that the population is basically opposed to revolutionary change, and movements based predominantly on terrorism should be analyzed as cases of subversion or crime rather than as revolutions (terrorism is discussed in Chapter Eight). If a system is basically functional—and that includes being free from foreign domination or interference—efforts at artificial mobilization will fall on barren soil and be rejected. True revolutionary conditions cannot be "imported" into a social system.

Assuming that the rebel party is able to mobilize support from the people, it must then organize them for the long haul. Organization is the complement to mobilization in the strategy of guerrilla revolution. The party's "political workers" will organize the aroused populace into groups such as workers' unions, soviets, peasants' cooperatives, militia, and ascriptive associations of women, youths, and ethnic minorities. These groups will provide military support for the full-time guerrillas and give the masses a sense of participation in the revolutionary effort, thereby initiating the habits of loyalty and obedience to the legitimate authority of the rebel leaders. The final stage of organization is the establishment of revolutionary territorial bases. The government of these bases will not yet be of the form prescribed in the revolutionaries' goal culture; instead, it will be one designed to promote maximum unity and participation in the movement by all groups. As these bases are expanded and consolidated, they become a regular guerrilla "infrastructure," or an "alternative government," supplying the rebel forces with food, sanctuary, training centers, and manpower. Such enclaves also weaken the existing regime by removing land and population from its control.

Simultaneously with mobilization and organization, the revolutionary party must begin to recruit an army. This army is at first poorly trained and inadequately equipped, but it exhibits extraordinary discipline and enjoys friendly relations with the local population. Its discipline is inculcated through rigorous political indoctrination, reinforced by the irreversibility of a soldier's commitment in joining the revolutionary movement. Every guerrilla strategist, from T. E. Lawrence to Che Guevara, has insisted on the need for intensive education of rebel soldiers. In addition to indoctrination, discipline is usually maintained by "political commissars," who are attached to and oversee each unit of a rebel army.

A well-organized guerrilla army characteristically behaves well to the civilian population, since in order to be effective against a professional army, the rebel forces must have civilians' active aid, not just their passive acquiescence. Only when the people provide intelligence, guides, recruits, and labor can the rebels set ambushes, avoid mopping-up campaigns, and maximize their mobility. Although rebels may be able to obtain supplies at gunpoint, they cannot get positive support from people if they behave like bandits.

Intimate, friendly relations with the civilian population allow guerrillas to obtain near-perfect intelligence concerning the enemy's strength and movements, which enables them to set ambushes and concentrate superior numbers at the moment of attack. The Chinese Communists regard the principle of concentration, with its attendant requisites of superior mobility and intelligence, as the key to insurrectionary warfare. A Chinese Communist theoretical publication asserts: "Starting from the basic premise of a people's war and a people's army, Mao laid down the policies and principles for building a people's army, solved a series of strategic and tactical problems concerning the way in which a people's army can defeat an enemy stronger than itself, and guided the Chinese people's armed revolutionary struggle from victory to victory. The kernel of Comrade Mao Tse-tung's thinking on the strategy and tactics of a people's war is to concentrate a superior force to destroy the enemy's forces one by one."[13] Mao himself put it more succinctly in 1937: "Our *strategy* is to pit one against ten, and our *tactics* are to pit ten against one. This is one of our fundamental principles for gaining mastery over the enemy."[14]

Guerrilla warfare is the beginning of the end of revolution, but it is not the end. Guerrilla fighting has one specific purpose: to weaken the enemy through a protracted war of attrition. The guerrilla phase of the revolution serves to offset the original weakness of the rebel armies. The certain sign that the revolution is nearing its end is the abandonment of guerrilla tactics by the rebels in favor of massed infantry and artillery. In China, the battle for Kaifeng (which fell on June 19, 1948) was the opening of the People's Liberation Army's final campaign to destroy the Kuomintang. Similarly, the battle for Dien Bien Phu (which fell to the Viet Minh on May 7, 1954) marked the end of the guerrilla phase and the beginning of traditional military operations against the French in Indochina. In the latter case, there were no defenders left who wanted to fight, and the battle of Dien Bien Phu also ended the war.

Guerrilla warfare, as a strategy of revolution, is extremely difficult to defeat once it has gone so far that the defending regime must take it seriously. By the time guerrilla activities appear threatening, counterrevolutionary measures are likely to produce warfare of such savagery that the contested social system will disintegrate instead of being "won" by either the rebel or the conservative side. By far the most effective defenses against guerrilla revolution are preventive and processual social change and efficient police protection against terrorists. True guerrilla revolutions occur only in response to the most hopelessly intransigent opposition to change; they ought never to occur. Any form of revolution testifies to the failure of politics, but guerrilla revolutions signify the perversion of politics, the need to resort to warfare in order to oust a social group blocking change.

The two strategies of revolution discussed in this chapter illustrate a variety of tactical problems that revolutionaries encounter as well as their common, overriding strategic problem:

the need to legitimate their resort to violence. Too often rebels have believed that the seizure of power was merely a technical problem—that they had only to seize the "levers" of government to achieve their objectives. Nothing could be further from the truth. The resort to violence must be in response to real needs of politically organized peoples if it is to be accepted by them as humane, logical, and tolerable behavior. If they do not accept revolutionary violence as such, although they may be cowed by the force used against them, the resulting regime will be organized more like a concentration camp than a social system. The tactics of future revolutions may vary significantly from case to case, but the primary need to legitimate revolutionary behavior will always confront those who come to power by violence.

Terrorism

"Terrorism" is often a paradoxical term, much like "opportunism." A leader is labeled an opportunist if he acts on the belief that the time is ripe for some political or revolutionary initiative and is subsequently found to have been wrong. Had he been right, he would be called a statesman, a leader, or a great revolutionary. Similarly, a terrorist is a person who seeks to create conditions of extreme fear and anxiety and manipulate them to his own advantage, but who fails. When such a person succeeds, he is no longer called a terrorist. Sir John Harington (1561–1612) made the same point about another famous political act: "Treason doth never prosper: what's the reason? / For if it prosper, none dare call it treason."

Like the coup d'état and guerrilla warfare, revolutionary terrorism is a technique or strategy. The terrorist or his sponsors believe that a particular social situation is revolutionary and that it can be altered by terrorism in ways favorable to the terrorist's cause. But unlike a coup d'état or guerrilla warfare, terrorism is not invariably revolutionary. Even when adopted for ostensibly revolutionary purposes, terrorism has many side effects—including effects on the morale and integrity of the revolutionaries—that are even harder to calculate or control than the side effects of a coup d'état or guerrilla warfare.

According to one definition, "Terrorism involves the intentional use of violence or the threat of violence by the precipitator(s) against an *instrumental* target in order to communicate to a *primary* target a threat of future violence. The object is to use intense fear or anxiety to coerce the primary target into behavior or to mold its attitudes in connection with a demanded power (political) outcome."[1] In line with this distinction between instrumental and primary targets, Raymond Aron stresses the lack of correspondence between the actual deeds of terrorists—kidnappings, bombings, hijackings, assassinations, and so forth—and the significance given to these acts by observers remote from the scene: "An action of violence is labeled 'terrorist' when its psychological effects are out of proportion to its purely physical result."[2] To Norton and Greenberg, "Terrorism is the theatre of the macabre, and the audience is only incidentally the spectator at the scene."[3]

Terrorism, then, involves violence or threats of violence against victims who may be but often are not parties to a given political conflict. It is not aimed, as war is, at the annihilation of the enemy's coercive forces, but rather seeks to wound him politically and psychologically. Since terrorism commonly involves the use of random violence against the innocent—against persons who can in no way be regarded as combatants in a contest of arms and whose deaths can in no way advance the cause of the terrorists—it is of course denounced by the defenders of an embattled regime as barbaric and demented. In response to such charges, terrorists sometimes rationalize the killing of the innocent after the fact: for example, Palestinian spokesmen argued that the Puerto Rican pilgrims killed at Lod Airport in 1972 had involved themselves in the Palestinians' struggle by accepting Israeli visas. As Brian Jenkins has put it, "They did not become victims because they were enemies, but rather they became enemies because they happened to be victims."[4] Similarly, Horst Mahler of the Baader-Meinhof gang explained the killing of two innocent bystanders as the equivalent of an automobile mishap: "When I drive off in my car, I can't know beforehand if a tire will go flat."[5]

Such statements miss the point. Revolutionary terrorism is intended to produce side effects that are out of proportion to the damage done or the risks incurred by its perpetrators. The fear created by terrorism is thus radically different from the fear of punishment, no matter how harsh, for committing proscribed acts or failing to commit prescribed acts. Terrorism is *not* the same thing as enforcing a legal or a moral order, or even taking the law into one's own hands. As Eugene Walter notes, "The conditions of legality imply that there must be a way of being innocent. If no path is left open to avoid transgression, or if people are bound to be charged falsely with offenses they did not commit, then it is not possible to be innocent. In the terror process, no one can be secure, for the category of transgression is, in reality, abolished. Anyone may be a victim, no matter what action he chooses."[6] In short, revolutionary terrorism is the use of violence against insignificant people in order to affect the behavior of significant people or their supporters.

There are at least four basic types of terrorism: political terrorism (of which revolutionary terrorism is a variant), official or state terrorism, nonpolitical terrorism, and pseudo-terrorism. Political terrorism is simply "criminal behavior designed primarily to generate fear in the community, or a substantial segment of it, for political purposes."[7] This kind of terrorism is of primary interest to us here.

State terrorism refers to a "regime of terror" or a "reign of terror." Its ultimate end is to control a population through fear. Terror regimes are created "by those who already control the ordinary institutions of power. Instead of relying entirely on authority, conventional rules, and legitimate techniques, the men in power, for various reasons, choose to initiate the process of terror."[8] Examples include the Jacobin "Reign of Terror" during the French Revolution (from which the term "terrorism" dates), the Nazi regime, the Soviet regime under Stalin, the "Cultural Revolution" period in China, Uganda under Idi Amin, and the Cambodian regime of the Khmer Rouge (1975–78). Although such reigns of terror create conditions of serious social disequilibrium, they rarely elicit revolutionary attempts to overthrow them because they atomize people, inhibit the circulation of revolutionary ideologies, and prevent the organization of protesters. A reign of state terror not terminated by the deaths of the terrorists or by foreign conquest is more likely to lead to the decay and disintegration of the social system than to revolution.

As the term suggests, nonpolitical terrorism refers to the *planned* implementation of a siege of terror for criminal or personal ends. Examples may be found among the actions of organized criminal syndicates, teenage gangs, mentally deranged persons, and nihilist associations (e.g., Charles Manson and his followers). These types of terrorist activities may become political if revolutionary terrorists form tactical alliances with the perpetrators (as, for example, the Italian Red Brigades did with the Mafia to carry out kidnappings and the like for mutual profit) or if revolutionary terrorists employ the mentally aberrant to implement terrorist raids (as, for example, the Popular Front for the Liberation of Palestine did with Kozo Okamoto, the sole surviving Japanese terrorist from the Lod Airport attack).[9] A curious case of terrorist exploitation of the mentally ill was the German Socialist Patients' Collective, organized during the 1970's by two married psychiatrists in Heidelberg to supply drug addicts, delinquents, and psychopaths to the Baader-Meinhof gang.[10]

Normally, nonpolitical terrorism consists of random felonies committed by psychopaths (e.g., "Jack the Ripper" and his innumerable successors) and the terrorism incidental to organized criminal activities. A borderline case was the seizure during March 1977 in Washington, D.C., of some hundred hostages by a group calling itself the Hanafi Muslims. The group had no known links with other terrorist organizations, and its goals were clearly nonpolitical, although clothed in political rhetoric.

Whereas nonpolitical terrorism involves the planning and execution of a siege of terror for particular nonpolitical reasons, pseudo-terrorism merely mimics the tactics of political terrorists; there is no intention of establishing a siege of terror. A typical example is the ad hoc taking of hostages during a robbery or prison riot. Although there is nothing new about pseudo-terrorism, its incidence in the United States rose dramatically during the 1970's as criminals imitated highly publicized cases of international and transnational political terrorism, commonly by hijacking airplanes to escape to a foreign country, usually Cuba. The definitive pseudo-terrorist case was the seizure in November 1971 in Portland, Oregon, of an aircraft by a man using the alias of D. B. Cooper. He successfully extorted $200,000 from the airline, parachuted from the aircraft, and was never heard from again.

Political terrorism is defined by its specific strategic objectives. The first is the attempt to turn a socially disequilibrated situation (or one so perceived by the terrorist) into a revolutionary situation by demonstrating to a wavering population that the incumbent authorities' monopoly of force has been broken and is unlikely to be restored. The idea is to disorient the mass of the population "by demonstrating through apparently indiscriminate violence that the existing regime cannot protect the people nominally under its authority. The effect on the individual is supposedly not only anxiety, but withdrawal from the relationships making up the established order of society."[11]

Following the death of Che Guevara in October 1967 and the setback to Cuban-sponsored rural guerrilla warfare in Latin America, this kind of thinking inspired so-called urban guerrillas in many countries. Such a strategy rarely works: indeed, it usually has the opposite effect of calling people's attention to the seriousness of the situation and encouraging them to support any strong reassertion of authority. The best example is probably Uruguay, which between 1968 and the middle of 1972 was ravaged by the Tupamaros. In April 1972, however, President Juan-Maria Bordaberry proclaimed a "state of internal war" and gave the army and police complete freedom in their choice of methods to wage it. The Tupamaros were easily defeated, but so was Uruguayan democracy, which has not yet been reestablished.

A second strategic objective of revolutionary terrorism is to provoke the ruling elites into a disastrous overreaction, thereby creating widespread sentiment against them. This is a classic strategy, and when it works its impact on a revolutionary situation can be devastating. Carlos Marighella, the Brazilian guerrilla leader whose writings influenced most political terrorists of the 1960's and 1970's, explains its rationale as follows: "It is necessary to turn political crisis into armed conflict by performing violent actions that will force those in power to transform the political situation of the country into a military situation. That will alienate the masses, who, from then on, will revolt against the army and the police and blame them for this state of things."[12]

Provocative terrorism, in short, is aimed at short-circuiting efforts to bring about conservative change, eliminating reformers within the embattled administration, and forcing the defenders to adopt policies of intransigence. When the social system is genuinely disequilibrated, such a strategy may turn a situation that could still be resolved through conservative change into one of revolution. It may also convert a small organization of revolutionary conspirators into a mass movement.

There are problems, however. Even if the elites overreact, they are normally strong enough to suppress both the terrorists and any other newly mobilized revolutionaries who are reacting against the excessive use of force. This outcome may well lead to a dissynchronized social system, regardless of whether the one in which the terrorist action occurred was dissynchronized or not; and this new dissynchronization may lead in turn to a future revolution. It is also possible that, given time, the overreacting elites may be able to establish their own prestige and popularity. This is clearly the strategy of President Ferdinand Marcos of the Philippines, who established martial law in 1972, and of General Chun Doo Hwan in Korea, who entered politics in December 1979 through a military coup to overcome the confusion caused by the assassination of President Park Chung Hee the previous October.

Terrorism is usually self-defeating or can be defeated by established elites; but it is historically inaccurate to proclaim, as some analysts do, "the invariable failure of terrorism to obtain its objectives."[13] Perhaps the prime example of terrorism succeeding is the Philippeville massacre of August 20, 1955, in which Algerian revolutionaries killed 123 French colonials. As a conscious act of terrorism carried out by revolutionaries who until then had enjoyed only slight popular backing, the Philippeville massacre led to French overreaction, converted one of the leading French reformers (Jacques Soustelle) into an advocate of suppression, eliminated most moderates on the Muslim side, and ultimately caused the French to adopt similar terrorist tactics (as in the Battle for Algiers), which alienated influential sections of the French public.

In his masterly history of the Algerian revolution, Alistair Horne describes Philippeville: "Immediately on hearing the news, Soustelle flew to the scene of the massacre. Nothing was concealed from his gaze; the mutilated men, the disembowelled mothers, and in Constantine hospital he visited women and children survivors 'groaning in fever and in nightmare, their fingers severed, their throats half-slit.' At the burial of the victims in Philippeville, grief and rage took over, with distraught relatives trampling on the flowers sent by the administration. . . . Certainly, from this date on determination to crush the rebellion began to assume priority over any hopes of liberal compromise. . . . And for the Algerians of both races it was a terrible Rubicon over which there was to be no return. . . . Horrible as it was, there is no doubt that—on the principle set out by Carlos Marighella—for the F.L.N. [the Algerian revolutionary party] this new Sétif was to prove a net gain. . . . What had hitherto been, in many respects, a 'phoney war'—or *drôle de révolution* as some French called it—now became a full-blooded war to the end."[14] The course of the Algerian revolution is unintelligible without an understanding of the changes wrought in all the variables by the Philippeville massacre. Something comparable, although on a lesser scale, seems to have occurred in Israel in reaction to the Palestine Liberation Organization's seizure of 85 children at Maalot in May 1974.

Another strategic objective of political terrorism is to gain publicity for the revolutionaries' grievances and for their movement. Since revolutionary terrorism is by definition aimed at sending a message to a primary but inaccessible target, many terrorist actions are planned specifically with the mass media in mind. For example, during the Christmas 1975 seizure of eleven Arab oil ministers in Vienna by a German-Palestinian team, the terrorists waited for the cameras to arrive on the scene before they left the country with their hostages. Similarly, in the 1975 kidnapping of Peter Lorenz, a candidate for mayor of West Berlin, Melvin Lasky reported: "Not the least historic aspect of this unprecedented Berlin incident was the impressment of the nation's television screens to serve the masterplan of the terrorist kidnappers. 'For 72 hours,' one T.V. editor told me, 'we just lost control of the medium. It was theirs, not ours. . . . We shifted shows in order to meet their time-table. Our cameras had to be in position to record each of the released prisoners as they boarded the plane to freedom, and our news coverage had to include prepared statements at their dictate.'"[15] Exactly the same thing had happened in California in 1974 with the kidnapping of Patricia Hearst by the "Symbionese Liberation Army."[16]

It is unquestionably true that the Palestinians, as a result of their terrorist actions, are far better known than, for example, the Kurds, who have been waging a guerrilla war of national independence against Iraq, Turkey, and Iran for decades. It is not clear, however, that this publicity has advanced their cause. The OPEC oil embargo during the 1973 Arab-Israeli war undoubtedly did more for the Palestinians than all their incessant terrorism. The real significance of terrorist "media kidnappings" seems to lie in their contagion effect, disseminating terrorist techniques to other groups and triggering actions among the unstable. Television in particular seems to contribute to the epidemics of pseudo-terrorism that follow all widely reported terrorist incidents, particularly assassinations and assassination attempts.

Still other strategic purposes of political terrorists include obtaining specific concessions from authorities—for example, ransom payments or the release of previously captured terrorists—and the enforcement of obedience, secrecy, and loyalty among followers. This enforcement function is, of course, similar to state terrorism, but it is implemented by a revolutionary movement in order to maintain control over *its* population. Perhaps the most unusual example of the use of terrorism for internal control was the killing of fourteen members of the Japanese Red Army in 1972: they were tied up and left in the snow outside a villa in Karuizawa, Japan, where they froze to death.

Though as a tactic terrorism can have significant effects on a revolutionary struggle, it is important not to overstate those effects. Terrorism most commonly backfires against those who first use it. At a minimum, a turn toward terrorism almost invariably damages the internal unity of a revolutionary movement and usually leads to a split. Examples include the division of the Irish Republican Army into "officials" and "provisionals" (the terrorists), the splitting off of the Stern Gang from the Zionist Underground Army (Irgun Zvai Leumi), and the splintering of the Palestine Liberation Movement into innumerable terrorist wings and groups. Rarely has a strategy of terrorism led directly to revolutionary change, and only occasionally has the tactical use of terrorism had a profound influence on the course of a revolutionary struggle. Even tactical successes can be avoided if the defenders of a regime are aware of the dangers of overreacting and can successfully portray the revolutionaries as mere "terrorists."

Terrorist tactics are an old form of political struggle. During the nineteenth century terrorism was the normal form of revolutionary violence practiced by Russian political radicals and European Anarchists. It also occurred in the United States. In Chicago the Haymarket Square riot of May 1886, caused by a terrorist bomb that killed some seven policemen and wounded 60 more, led to severe police reprisals against Chicago's labor organizers and to the public hanging of four suspects. (*The Bomb*, Frank Harris's 1908 novel romanticizing American Anarchists, was based on this incident.) Similarly, the Wall Street Bombing of 1920, following the "Red Scare" of 1919 and the consequent Palmer Raids (the arrest and deportation to Russia of thousands of radicals by Attorney General A. Mitchell Palmer), killed 34 people and affected the treatment of Sacco and Vanzetti in 1927. Four presidents of the United States have also been assassinated (Lincoln, Garfield, McKinley, and Kennedy); and in recent times considerable political fear and anxiety have been caused by the killings of Dr. Martin Luther King and Senator Robert F. Kennedy, and by the attempted assassinations of Governor George Wallace by Arthur Bremer, President Gerald Ford by Lynette "Squeaky" Fromme and Sara Jane Moore, and President Ronald Reagan by John Hinckley.

And yet, during most of the recent period political terrorism has not been regarded as a major problem in the United States or in most other advanced industrial democracies. Where it occurred in the ex-colonial world, it was generally associated with revolutionary movements, as in Palestine, Vietnam, Algeria, and Kenya. In the quarter century following the Second World War, the world's revolutionaries, politicians, and political analysts focused almost exclusively on guerrilla warfare as the paradigmatic form of revolutionary struggle[17] (although the military coup d'état remained, as it had been throughout the postwar era, the most common form of attempted political change through violence).[18]

Beginning about 1968, however, there appears to have been a significant increase in the number of terrorist incidents occurring in advanced democracies. One must say "appears" because of the unsatisfactory nature of the available statistical data. Reports of bombings in the United States, for example, have been systematically collected only since 1969, and the data are not reliable before 1972. Similarly, information on hostage-taking is still not collected in the United States on a nationwide basis, and it is impossible to distinguish within the available data between political terrorist incidents and pseudo-terrorist incidents.[19] Nonetheless, according to the CIA (which pioneered the effort to bring terrorist incidents under statistical control), "1968 emerges as a watershed year. At that juncture, a combination of Palestinian initiatives and the cumulative impact of the broader environmental trends . . . seems to have finally sensitized dissident groups throughout the world to their latent and growing potential for effective transnational terrorist activity."[20]

To distinguish these new types of terrorist attacks from the terrorism associated with ongoing revolutionary struggles (e.g., the Vietnam war), analysts invented the terms "international terrorism" to refer to terrorist actions carried out by individuals or groups controlled by a sovereign state (e.g., Libya or Cuba), and "transnational terrorism" to refer to terrorist actions carried out by basically autonomous actors (e.g., the Baader-Meinhof gang). They also categorized terrorist incidents into four types: those carried out inside the target regime against domestic victims (e.g., Northern Ireland); those launched from outside the target regime against domestic victims (e.g., Al Fatah's attacks on Israel); those carried out inside the target regime against international victims (e.g., Latin American kidnappings of foreign businessmen and diplomats); and those carried out outside the target regime against international victims (e.g., the European activities of the Popular Front for the Liberation of Palestine).[21]

On the basis of CIA statistics and counting only international and transnational incidents, we find that between 1965 and 1967 the number of cases remained around 10 per year. The rate then jumped to about 40 during 1968 and to well over 100 during 1969–70. It fell back to around 75 during 1971 and then ascended steeply to over 200 during 1973. It declined slightly to around 175 during 1975, and rose again to 353 during 1978 and 293 during 1979. The trend in terms of killed casualties from international and transnational terrorist incidents was also upward:

1968	34	1973	127	1978	442
1969	29	1974	344	1979	738
1970	110	1975	276	1980	642
1971	36	1976	415		
1972	157	1977	261		

Between January 1, 1968, and December 31, 1975, there were 913 unambiguous transnational terrorist incidents, including 123 kidnappings, 31 barricade and hostage episodes, 375 cases of the use of explosive devices, 95 armed assaults or ambushes, 137 hijackings of aircraft and other means of transportation, 59 incendiary attacks or cases of arson, 48 assassinations, and 45 cases of other forms of violence.[22]

What caused this shift from guerrilla warfare to terrorism? In attempting to answer this question, most analysts distinguish between two general classes of causes—direct causes and permissive causes. Direct causes refer to grievances or frustrations resulting from such things as neocolonialism, ethnic dependency, or other forms of alleged victimization (i.e., the sense of injustice experienced by people in a dissynchronized social system) that may lead activists to resort to political violence. Permissive (or enabling) causes are those factors that make terrorism possible, even easy, and that therefore recommend it as a tactic.

This distinction should not be made too rigidly. For example, the availability of publicity through the news media may be a permissive cause in one case and a direct cause in another. Some terrorists, that is, will act because the means of publicity are available, whereas others will act in direct imitation of publicized violence. The permissive and direct causes of terrorism within a given society may thus differ for a single terrorist act and a cycle or epidemic of terrorism.

The direct causes of terrorist violence are a function of the degree and nature of a social system's dissynchronization and of the quality and timeliness of the efforts of its ruling elites to rectify the dissynchronization. There is no evidence of a significant change in the direct causes of violence during the late 1960's. What seems to have led to the increase in terrorism was a series of frustrations to revolutionary efforts in the main arenas of continuing political violence (e.g., the Israeli victory in the six-day war of 1967, the death of Che Guevara, and the escalation of American intervention in the Vietnam War), along with significant changes in the permissive causes of terrorism: such elements as feasibility, efficacy, risk, popularity, and availability of targets. There are several ways to disaggregate this complex cluster of causes, but the simplest is in terms of the "three T's": targets, technology, and toleration. All three underwent certain changes beginning in the late 1960's that greatly facilitated terrorism.

As we have seen, political terrorism has two targets: a primary target, typically the ruling elite, from whom concessions are sought, and a secondary or immediate target, which consists of hostages or property to be destroyed if the primary target resists terrorist demands. However, a primary target may make itself less vulnerable to terrorist attacks by suppressing or ostracizing its internal revolutionaries, by mobilizing its population to reject terrorist demands, by building a semi-independent economy, or by other comparable policies. When this happens a third target becomes salient for terrorists: an international audience that the terrorists seek to persuade of the justness of their cause, of the incompetence and brutality of the primary target, or of the need for outside intervention to force the primary target to negotiate with its revolutionaries. Terrorist objectives remain the same as in a domestic struggle—disorientation, provocation, publicity, specific demands, and control—but they are now directed against targets outside the terrorists' own countries. This strategy is adopted because such targets—particularly the mass democracies—have not been hardened; they are more vulnerable and accessible than the primary target.

One of the changes that occurred in targets after 1968 was that terrorists began to identify more accurately the vulnerabilities and bottlenecks of open, advanced societies: such things as large aircraft, supertankers, international power grids and pipelines, transportation hubs, commercial and communications centers, democratically elected politicians, offshore oil rigs, liquefied natural gas facilities, nuclear power facilities, and computerized data banks and management systems. During the

1970's all these became the targets of terrorist attacks, particularly international airliners. As political terrorism in turn spawned pseudo-terrorism, it seemed to some that the very existence of a complex and interdependent modern world was contributing to the advance of terrorism by offering the terrorist—including the political terrorist, criminal terrorist, and psychopathic terrorist—a plethora of vulnerable targets.

As a response to the development of international and transnational terrorism, however, the victimized countries began to harden their vital centers and take antiterrorist considerations into account in the design of their facilities and systems.[23] All modern nations, for example, undertook programs to protect materials of mass destruction from falling into the hands of terrorists.[24] Most countries also developed specially trained and equipped counterterrorist forces to defend against domestic terrorist threats or to deal with terrorist attacks against their citizens outside the country.*

There were two critical changes in the area of technology. First, an array of new weapons and other devices became available to the terrorist. In addition to the traditional terrorist arsenal of time bombs, machine guns, and plastic explosives, modern technology contributed the letter bomb; the remote-controlled cache of high explosives; the bazooka and man-portable guided missile; chemical, biological, and radiological agents; and the potential use of either homemade or stolen nuclear weapons. A further contributing factor to the growth of terrorism during the 1970's was the extensive international traffic in arms, which meant the ready availability to terrorists of such sophisticated weapons as the U.S.-made M-11 hand ma-

* Some prominent examples are the Israeli counterterrorist commandos who rescued 105 hostages at Entebbe, Uganda, in July 1976; the West German counterterrorist commandos who rescued 86 hostages at Mogadishu, Somalia, in October 1977; the British Special Air Services regiment that recaptured the Iranian Embassy in London from Arab terrorists in May 1980; the United States counterterrorist unit that assisted in the rescue of 55 hostages at Bangkok, Thailand, in March 1981; and the Italian antiterrorist police who rescued U.S. General James L. Dozier from the Red Brigades in January 1982.

chine gun, the Soviet-made Kalashnikov machine gun, and the Czech-made Skorpion pistol (the weapon used in 1978 to kill Italian Premier Aldo Moro after his abduction by the Red Brigades).[25]

Second—and at least as important—a global expansion of mass media became available for terrorist exploitation. As David L. Milbank notes, "Among all the technological advances in recent years, the development of satellite communications, and in particular, their upgrading in 1968 to include a television capability have unquestionably been among the most important in making transnational activity seem attractive to terrorist groups."[26] The mass media clearly help to publicize terrorist causes, which in turn may trigger other terrorists' decisions to act. The media also facilitate the training of new terrorists (e.g., by showing them the procedures of an actual operation) and promote international links among terrorist organizations.

Under the category of changes in toleration of terrorism, we include the direct and indirect support of terrorist organizations by various nation-states, the toleration of terrorist organizations by some law-abiding nations out of fear of retaliation, the inability of international organizations to agree on countermeasures against international and transnational terrorists, and a political climate favorable to revolutionary activities among some sectors of the populations of democratic countries.

During the 1970's the Soviet Union, Czechoslovakia, East Germany, Cuba, Libya, and the Popular Democratic Republic of Yemen operated centers for the training and support of terrorists.[27] Other nations tolerated this activity because of various overriding national policies, including superpower détente, the West German government's policy of *Ostpolitik,* and the presence of large, legal communist parties in most Western European democracies. However, following the killing of the German industrial leader Hanns-Martin Schleyer by the Baader-Meinhof gang in September 1977, the killing of Italian Premier Aldo Moro in May 1978, the IRA bombing of Lord

Mountbatten in August 1979, and the holding of American hostages in Teheran from 1979 to 1981, the climate of toleration began to change. It became clear that much of the terrorism of the 1970's was not transnational but international, a form of surrogate warfare in an international system in which open warfare had become too dangerous. As Brian Jenkins has noted, not least of the attractions of international terrorism is that "a secret backer of the terrorists can also deny sponsoring them."[28]

But clandestine support of terrorists was only one aspect of toleration. The other was a persistent belief in Western countries that the resort to political violence *had* to signify the existence of intolerable social grievances and that left-wing political movements, regardless of the temporary excesses they might commit, were basically on the side of human "progress." This was particularly true in nations that had recent memories of disastrous right-wing or totalitarian regimes (e.g., Italy, Germany, Spain, Greece, and Japan). As Claire Sterling has written about Italy, "The secret of the terrorists' success lay in the decent, well-meaning citizens who formed a protective second society around them."[29] In a similar vein, James Q. Wilson observes, "We are more inclined to confound terrorists with heroes than we are to confuse psychotic killers with decent people because the former claim a political justification, and we tend to accept political justifications for acts that are otherwise unjustifiable."[30] While this political climate of toleration lasted, terrorists were able to obtain the training, safe havens, funds, equipment, and new recruits that made their attacks possible.

Though toleration is not easily quantified, the following figures are suggestive. Between 1968 and 1974, based on a study of 63 major kidnapping and barricade operations, the terrorists had an 87 percent chance of actually seizing hostages; a 79 percent chance that no members of the terrorist team would die or be punished; a 40 percent chance that all or some of their demands would be met in operations where something more than just safe passage or exit permission was demanded; and a virtually 100 percent chance that they would gain major publicity for themselves.[31] Small wonder terrorist acts proliferated.

During the 1960's and 1970's terrorists gained many apparent tactical victories. But it is well to remember that terrorism runs a high risk of turning potential revolutionary victory into defeat. The true political significance of terrorism lies in its influence on the perceived legitimacy of a revolutionary movement; and nothing has done more to embarrass or discredit revolutionary movements than their use of terrorism in gaining power (e.g., the Nazis, the Japanese Nationalists of the 1930's, or the Khmer Rouge in Cambodia). Extensive reliance on terrorism by such movements in their efforts to seize power often condemns them to a continued reliance on terror in order to rule at all.

During the 1970's several revolutionary movements with a high potential for legitimacy appealed to an international audience for understanding and support, and often received it. But one wonders whether the PLO or IRA, for example, would ever be able to overcome the heritage of their own past and exercise genuine political authority. As we have sought to demonstrate earlier in this book, a social system in equilibrium is a moral community, one based on mutual trust and on values that define roles and legitimate a division of labor. Political terrorism is a form of tyranny, not something to which people can become accustomed and thereby orient their own behavior. Can revolutionary terrorists abandon their own earlier activities? More to the point, can citizens of a regime dominated by ex-terrorists fail to repeat Cassius's question: "Upon what meat doth this our Caesar feed that he is grown so great?" Political terrorism, in short, is as likely to cause a revolution against those who use it as it is to serve them.

Theories of Revolution

The 1960's and 1970's witnessed not only an epidemic of terrorist incidents but also an explosion of writing about revolution and political violence. By one count some 2,400 books and articles on the subject were published, and even the U.S. Senate's Committee on Foreign Relations held hearings on "The Nature of Revolution," with Professor Crane Brinton of Harvard as the lead-off speaker. Interest in the subject was by no means confined to senators, government officials, and academics. Robert Dahl noticed the greatly increased use in America of the word "revolution" in its political sense; Stanislav Andreski wrote a popular paperback entitled *Prospects of a Revolution in the U.S.A.*; and Hannah Arendt published her essay "Civil Disobedience" in the *New Yorker*.[1]

This outpouring of analyses, essays, and theories of revolution, few of which agreed with each other or built on previous work, also led some scholars to attempt to categorize theories of revolution. According to Harry Eckstein, "The first and most fateful choice [in the study of revolution] lies between regarding it as 'contingent' or 'inherent' in political life."[2] Theories that regard revolution as inherent posit, following Hobbes, that social cohesiveness is always the result of coercion (what Albert Cohen has called the "killjoy theory of conformity") and that people will revolt the moment this coercion is relaxed. By contrast, contingency theories argue, as this book does, that revolution is always an unusual and disruptive event contingent on serious social disorganization and anomie. Eckstein decided that contingency theories have greater analytic force and fewer unexplained contrary cases; but because of problems in his own analysis, he came to no firm conclusion from his comparison.[3]

However, the idea of grouping theories of revolution according to larger principles is a good one. Here we will propose four basic groups: (1) actor-oriented theories; (2) structural theories; (3) conjunction theories; and (4) process theories.[4] In the following pages we will examine the major current theories of revolution in terms of these four groups.

Actor-oriented theories pose the question, What sort of individuals or groups commit revolutionary acts and why? To the extent that impersonal social situations play a part in causing people to become revolutionaries, the situations are treated as triggering or channeling circumstances for behavior that would probably find expression sooner or later in some antisocial activity. Such theories inquire into the kinds of personalities that are attracted to revolutionary movements, and they particularly stress the personal dimensions of revolutionary leadership and followership.

Some very well known actor-oriented theories rely on the Freudian conception of the "psychopath" (a person totally devoid of a moral sense) or on the less extreme idea of the "sociopath" (a person with a grasp of social situations but who is inclined to manipulate them to his or her own advantage in an antisocial way). Others invoke Harold Lasswell's research on the displacement of private motives onto public objects and his discussion of four modal types who compensate for their feelings of inadequacy and low self-esteem by various kinds of public activity (the politician, the agitator, the administrator, and the ideologue).[5] Another interesting formulation is Erik Erikson's so-called epigenetic principle—the theory that the human life cycle consists of eight distinct stages, each with its own "crisis" or "turning point"—and his elaboration of the "identity crisis," especially important in the development of revolution-

aries, that occurs between childhood and young adulthood.*
Finally, the terrorism epidemic of the 1970's inspired innumerable new personality profiles of skyjackers, assassins, hostage-takers, and pseudo-terrorists.[6]

Although actor-oriented theories can never supply complete explanations of revolutionary situations, revolutionary violence, or the outcomes of revolutions, they explain things that other theories often ignore—for example, the tensions between a revolutionary vanguard and the masses, the contributions of particular personalities to the course of a revolution, or the fact that revolutionary leaders are almost never recruited from the classes whose victimization or unrecognized intrinsic merit is the alleged cause of the revolution. As Michael Walzer has observed, "While classes differ fundamentally from one revolution to another, vanguards are sociologically similar. They are recruited from middling and professional groups."[7]

To take one example from the history of terrorism, only an actor-oriented theory can account for the leaders of the Baader-Meinhof gang in Germany during the 1970's. They included such diverse figures as Andreas Baader, the son of a civil servant and virtually apolitical until he fell in love with Gudrun Ensslin; Ulrike Meinhof, an orphan raised by a prominent teacher, a former brain surgery patient, and the divorced mother of two children; Horst Mahler, a practicing attorney with a promising career ahead of him; and Gudrun Ensslin, a Protestant minister's daughter, the author of an uncompleted doctoral dissertation on *Finnegans Wake*, and a one-time campaign worker in the Brandt-for-Chancellor Committee of the Social Democratic Party.[8] These people did not come together and terrorize several Western European countries because of the structural character-

* Erik H. Erikson, *Childhood and Society* (Harmondsworth, England, 1965), pp. 59–60, 239–66. Important applications of this theory or others in the same vein include Erikson's own *Young Man Luther* (New York, 1962), James V. Downton's *Rebel Leadership: Commitment and Charisma in the Revolutionary Process* (New York, 1973), Eric Hoffer's *The True Believer* (New York, 1951), Lucian W. Pye's *Mao Tse-tung: The Man in the Leader* (New York, 1976), and E. Victor Wolfenstein's *The Revolutionary Personality* (Princeton, N.J., 1967).

istics of the Israeli-Palestinian conflict. Similarly, the biographies of such people as Malcolm X, Jim Jones (the leader of the People's Temple, who led almost a thousand of his followers to mass suicide in Guyana), and the international terrorist Illich Ramirez-Sanchez (or "Carlos" as he came to be known) are as indispensable to our understanding of their movements as a knowledge of their followers' needs and aspirations.

Many actor-oriented theories are derived from theories of personality found in psychoanalytic literature. Personality, in this sense, refers to the lessons, behaviors, and attitudes a person has learned from "early-established, deeply-engrained, relatively enduring problems of adjustment and techniques of coping with these problems."[9] Another major subtype of actor-oriented theory, however, is based on the frustration-aggression hypothesis. Two major exponents of this form of actor-oriented theory are James C. Davies, whose ideas on the role of frustrated rising expectations were discussed in Chapter Four, and Ted R. Gurr, whose influential book *Why Men Rebel* and many subsequent articles are based on the workings of the frustration-aggression syndrome in political life.[10]

In essence, the frustration-aggression hypothesis holds that aggression is caused by the thwarting of a person's needs or aspirations—the frustration arising when "an individual does not attain what he thinks is justifiably due to him."[11] However, Edward Muller, who has made the most thorough analysis of attempts to apply this scheme, concludes: "Most kinds of frustration, not to mention sheer deprivation, are at best weakly associated with individual differences in potential or actual participation in aggressive action. The exception is frustration arising from the belief that one's just deserts are unfulfilled. This feeling of just-deserts frustration, called relative deprivation by Gurr, probably bears an indirect relationship to individual propensities for political protest and violence, but the evidence is by no means decisive even on this point."[12]

Even if such a relationship exists, we still have no way of predicting how, or against whom, the resulting aggression will be expressed. It may be directed against the self, the source of the frustration, or a substitute target; or it may be sublimated and the aggressive energy devoted to some socially acceptable or constructive cause. Moreover, the theory's focus on individual actors (even when generalized to include all members of a particular group or class), and the fact that standards of just deserts vary from culture to culture, inhibit cross-cultural comparisons. This inherent lack of comparability is the greatest weakness of actor-oriented theories, even though they are indispensable to the analysis of particular cases of revolutionary violence within a given culture.

Structural theories of revolution are the direct opposite of actor-oriented theories; they hold revolutions to be the attempts of normal or average people to respond to abnormal situations. Aberrant individuals, leaders, or parties have no place in these theories, nor do revolutionary ideologies or clandestine operations. The theories dispose of the human factor (usually implicitly) by supposing that any group of people faced with the same unusual circumstances or social obstacles would behave in more or less the same manner, and they focus directly on the structural components of the social situation that has brought about the unusual circumstances or obstacles. Because of this focus, structural theories are normally uninfluenced by cultural variables and are thus of great importance in the comparative study of revolution.

The great strength of such theories is their contribution to our understanding of why some revolutions appear to be more important than others. For this reason they are often an integral part of a theory of history, that is, of a conception that sees order or "progress" in human history. The major weakness of such theories is their inability to deal with political change that falls outside their definitions. Structural theorists usually devise a subclass of "true," "classic," or "great" revolutions, and as a result cannot characterize a development as revolutionary until several decades or generations have passed—that is, until it can be clearly seen whether the event contributed to democracy, modernization, a realignment of classes, a new mode of production, or whatever criterion is held to be the mark of true revolution.

An uncompromisingly structural theory is offered by Theda Skocpol in her *States and Social Revolutions*. Skocpol writes: "Organized revolutionary vanguards have with time become increasingly self-conscious and vociferous about their indispensable role in 'making' revolutions. It nevertheless seems to me that recent revolutionary crises, just as surely as those that launched the classic social revolutions, have come about only through inter- and intranational structural contradictions and conjunctural occurrences beyond the deliberate control of avowed revolutionaries." In contrast to the pretensions of vanguards and to authors of actor-oriented theories, Skocpol emphasizes "objective relationships and conflicts among variously situated groups and nations, rather than the interests, outlooks, or ideologies of particular actors in revolutions."[13]

Skocpol posits two structural conditions that she thinks caused the French, Russian, and Chinese revolutions (the only three cases she studies). The first is international: "Modern social revolutions have happened only in countries situated in disadvantaged positions within international arenas," their disadvantages arising from the "internationally uneven spread of capitalist economic development and nation-state formation on a world scale."[14] (This is a variant of dependency theory.) The second condition is internal: peasant revolt occurring while elites are distracted and divided by their international problems (i.e., dependency). "Administrative and military breakdowns of the autocracies inaugurated social-revolutionary transformations. . . . This result was due to the fact that widespread peasant revolts coincided with, indeed took advantage of, the hiatus of governmental supervision and sanctions. . . . Peasant revolts have been the crucial insurrectionary ingredient in virtually all actual (i.e., successful) social revolutions to date, and certainly in the French, Russian, and Chinese Revolutions."[15]

We note in passing that Skocpol seems to hold to Eckstein's "inherency" theory of revolution: peasants revolt because the controls over them have been relaxed.

Like most structuralists Skocpol is interested in outcomes. For her the central result of revolution must be the appearance of powerful, centralized, bureaucratic states enjoying greater mass support than the ones they replaced: "In each New Regime, there was much greater popular incorporation into the state-run affairs of the nation. And the new state organizations forged during the Revolutions were more centralized and rationalized than those of the Old Regime. Hence they were more potent within society and more powerful and autonomous over and against competitors within the international states system."[16]

It would be easy to quibble with some of Skocpol's historical details (particularly on the Chinese case), or to point out that a slightly different repertory of revolutions (say, the English revolution of the seventeenth century, the Nazi seizure of power, the Cuban revolution, and the Iranian revolution) would alter her structural conditions. And one might further argue that the coincidence of her two independent variables, international dependency and peasant revolt, does not occur at all uniformly in her three chosen cases.

But more important than any of these points is what Skocpol's structuralism omits from the three cases she studies. The actual *processes* of revolution made a difference in France, Russia, and China. In France the revolutionary vanguard (the Jacobins) was eventually defeated and replaced by the revolutionary class (the bourgeoisie). In Russia the revolutionary vanguard (the Bolsheviks) suppressed and terrorized the revolutionary class (the proletariat and peasantry) and continued to rule in its own interests.[17] And in China the revolutionary vanguard (the Communist Party) tried to remain in control of the revolutionary class (nationalistically aroused peasants and city-dwellers); but with the failure or repudiation of the vanguard's extremist policies, the possibility arose that China's revolutionary class might reas-

sert its supremacy. These differences cannot be explained or
predicted by a structural theory, yet they obviously have had
extremely important consequences.

Other prominent structural theories of revolution are those of
Samuel P. Huntington and Barrington Moore, Jr. Both are concerned with social "modernization" and its relationship to revolution. For Huntington, however, modernization is a structural
cause of revolution, whereas for Moore revolution is a structural
cause of modernization. Paradoxically, both are probably right.

According to Huntington, revolution "is most likely to occur
in societies which have experienced some social and economic
development and where the processes of political modernization and political development have lagged behind the processes of social and economic change."[18] Unlike Skocpol, Huntington argues that different structural conditions affected the
European revolutions of the eighteenth century and the Asian
revolutions of the twentieth century. "The Western revolution is
usually directed against a highly traditional regime headed by
an absolute monarch or dominated by a land-owning aristocracy. The revolution typically occurs when this regime comes
into severe financial straits, when it fails to assimilate the intelli-
gentsia and other urban elite elements, and when the ruling
class from which its leaders are drawn has lost its moral self-
confidence and will to rule. . . . Eastern revolutions, in contrast, are directed against at least partially modernized regimes.
These may be indigenous governments that have absorbed
some modern and vigorous middle-class elements . . . or they
may be colonial regimes in which the wealth and power of a
metropolitan country gives the local government a seemingly
overwhelming superiority in all the conventional manifestations
of political authority and military force. . . . Western revolutions are thus precipitated by weak traditional regimes; Eastern
revolutions by narrow modernizing ones."[19]

Moore, by contrast, sees revolution as a matter of making or
failing to make a decisive break with the past. He sees, depending on the occurrence of revolution and its type, four possible

outcomes: successful "bourgeois revolutions," such as those in England and France, producing capitalism and democratic government; failed bourgeois revolutions, such as those in Japan and Germany, producing capitalism but not democracy; successful proletarian and peasant revolutions, such as those in Russia and China, producing communism and dictatorship; and the lack of any revolution at all, such as in India, producing no modernization of either the democratic, fascist, or communist form.[20]

Huntington's and Moore's theories are both very powerful. They are obviously germane, for example, to an analysis of the causes of the Iranian revolution of 1978–79 (Huntington), and to an analysis of the failure of high levels of economic development to be accompanied by democracy in countries such as Korea (Moore). However, by factoring out the element of process, they appear, like all structural theories, dogmatic and lacking in nuance. Huntington, since he ignores the *contingencies* that arise in rapidly changing societies, glosses over the chances for reform that exist in them prior to a revolution. Albert Hirschman's comments are relevant here: "There are many . . . less rigid situations in which change by methods short of revolution is or has become possible, but where, because of the force of habit or some similar cultural lag, change is still visualized primarily as something that requires a revolution. . . . It requires at least as much imagination and sophistication to perceive that two groups whose interests were universally assumed to be wholly divergent actually have some important interests in common as to notice an opposition of interests between groups that were hitherto thought to be, and thought of themselves as, partners travelling along the same road toward common objectives."[21] Since Huntington's theory does not take these considerations fully into account, he has trouble conceptualizing modernizing regimes that do not elicit broad-based revolts against themselves (e.g., Japan, Israel, Singapore, Korea, and Taiwan during much of the postwar period).

Moore's indifference to process leads to different kinds of

rigidities. In his theory the onus for the dictatorships that resulted in Russia and China after their revolutions is placed squarely on the proletarians and the peasants of these countries, as if they could not possibly have conceived of better governments than the ones they got. But there is little reason to suppose that the Russian and Chinese people have less political imagination than the English or the French. Michael Walzer's process-oriented theory, for example, avoids such an assumption. He relates revolutionary outcomes to the conflict of interests that develops during and immediately following a revolutionary struggle between revolutionary vanguards and revolutionary classes, and his two different outcomes follow naturally: "First, the vanguard wins and holds power, making its dictatorship permanent, dominating and controlling weak social classes. It attempts for awhile to act out its radical ideology but undergoes a gradual routinization. Leaving aside the precise history and character of the routinization, it is fair to say that this was the foreseeable outcome of the Bolshevik revolution. The dictatorial rule of the vanguard was determined by the radical inability of any social class to sustain a Thermidorean politics. Thermidor, then, represents the second possibility: the revolutionary class resists and replaces the vanguard and slowly, through the routines of its everyday life, creates a new society in its own image. It reabsorbs the vanguard intellectuals into the social roles occupied by their parents, that is, into professional and official roles without any special political significance."[22] This, it seems to me, is a more historically valid way to portray abstractly the varying outcomes of the "classic" revolutions. Nonetheless, it is only in the broad structural perspective that questions of the enduring historical impact of revolutions, such as those discussed by Moore, get raised at all.

Conjunction theories, which attempt to combine actor-oriented and structural theories, make up the mainstream of research on revolutions. They commonly place revolutionary movements within the more inclusive context of social movements, seeing revolutionary movements as a subclass of the latter that arise in response to formidable countermovements to social change. The conjunction theorist seeks to understand the origins of social movements, their ideological content, their structural aspects, and their sources of recruitment and commitment; and he analyzes the factors that cause such movements to achieve social change through reform, to attempt social change through revolution, to be routinized at a lesser level of change, or to be defeated. Since conjunction theories are concerned with how particular leaders and followers come together to constitute movements, and with what happens to such movements, they also emphasize the "careers," "life cycles," or "stages" of revolutionary movements. Thus for Neil Smelser the examination of "value-oriented" social movements involves six stages: one must study the structural conditions leading to the movements, their psychological impact, the generation of ideologies and belief systems, mobilization and group formation, processes of conflict and control, and outcomes.[23]

Writing in the *International Encyclopedia of the Social Sciences*, Joseph R. Gusfield defines social movements as "socially shared demands for change in some aspect of the social order. . . . A social movement . . . is not the unnoticed accretion of many unrecognized changes. Rather, it has the character of an explicit and conscious indictment of [the] whole or part of the social order, together with a conscious demand for change. It also has an ideological component—that is, a set of ideas which specify discontents, prescribe solutions, and justify change."[24] Whether or not social movements strive to gain political power, *all* have political implications. However, *revolutionary* social movements are those that locate their major grievances in a constituted political order or see the seizure and exclusive exercise of political power as necessary for the achievement of their aims.

Movements that consciously seek a radically different social order became possible, as Rudolf Heberle observes, "only when the social order is seen not as a divine creation but as a work of man, subject to man's will. . . . This is why such movements have occurred in the West only since the eighteenth century."[25] Before the Enlightenment, radical attempts at social change took the form of millenarian religious or quasi-religious movements.

Such movements still occur today in countries where the transition to modern society has only begun or where its achievement is contested and still in doubt (e.g., in Iran during the late 1970's).[26]

Although some social movements may draw on nonrational motivations and attract maladjusted people, their ultimate causes lie in the tensions created by a changing social order—what we have described as a dissynchronized social system. Aberrant people exist in unchanging societies, but either control their personal tensions in some private way or are isolated as criminals or lunatics. A study of the *causes* of social movements must therefore look first at how a system's dissynchronization has rendered long-standing social relationships among particular groups of people no longer appropriate. If the system is not dissynchronized, then the violence that occurs in it is not evidence of an incipient social movement, regardless of what its perpetrators or suppressors may call it. Structural variables thus contribute to conjunction theories by revealing the degree and nature of the incongruence between the values of a social system and its division of labor. A good example of just such an analysis is Robert Dahl's dissection of the basic value conflicts— those concerning racial discrimination and the distribution of resources—in American society.[27] Needless to say, the discovery of the bases of change is not the same thing as predicting the occurrence of a revolution.

Actor-oriented variables are introduced into conjunction theories to explain why activists (or vanguards) and followers are drawn to a particular social movement. They are used to analyze the degree to which interpersonal relationships built up through participation have replaced or reinforced ideological commitments, and to reveal the personalities and capabilities of a movement's leaders and ideologues. (As we have seen, "The founders, the leaders, and the framers of the belief system in class movements are often alienated members of another class."[28]) Actor-oriented variables are also used to identify the personalities and capabilities of the members of a society who have been mobilized to resist a movement.[29]

Structural variables reenter the analysis when it comes to assessing the likelihood of a movement's becoming revolutionary. A useful concept here is Smelser's "structural conduciveness," the degree to which dissent in a given society is condoned or prohibited.[30] Does a society have the structural capability to transform a potentially revolutionary movement into a nonviolent protest movement? Can disputes about norms be restricted to questions about their *propriety* (whether they are good, fair, or reasonable, and how they might be changed to make them more so), or is it likely to escalate to the level of their *validity* (whether the rules that govern their enactment and make them binding on all members of society remain in force)?[31] Arguments over the validity of the normative order are characteristic of revolutionary situations.

Various types of political arrangements may affect a society's structural conduciveness. If a society has a sufficient number of intermediary associations that can absorb, pacify, and routinize protests, the probability of revolutionary violence is low. Because peasant societies have many traditional and voluntary intermediary associations, peasant revolutions are likely to occur only when some sudden, overwhelming shock to the system (such as the Japanese invasion of China in 1937) obliterates these social networks. Democratic political philosophy allows for a similar array of intermediary associations in modernized societies. A social and political structure conducive to reform is thus the most formidable barrier to revolution. "I do not assert," wrote Tocqueville, "that men living in democratic communities are naturally stationary; I think, on the contrary, that a perpetual stir prevails in the bosom of those societies, and that rest is unknown there. . . . They are forever varying, altering, and restoring secondary matters; but they carefully abstain from touching what is fundamental. They love change, but they dread revolutions."[32]

Political structures that allow people to vent their frustrations and organize protests seek to keep disputes about norms at the level of propriety. They also try to tolerate small groups that cannot be satisfied with anything less than a challenge to the

validity of norms but whose adherents are so few that they
constitute only minor police problems. Toleration provides time
for such groups slowly to "routinize" their activities and to dis-
solve their ideologies through association—for sects to become
churches and social movements to become interest groups—
while the system as a whole seeks the kernel of truth, if any, in
their protests. By contrast, political structures that overcentra-
lize power and isolate people are conducive to social movements
that must, for structural reasons, challenge the very validity of
the normative order. It has long been observed that when authoritarian regimes begin to relax their controls over society,
they paradoxically invite revolutions. This occurs not because
people are necessarily opposed to a moderation of controls but
because, given the opportunity for the first time to voice some of
their grievances, they "go too far." They have no other tradition
of protest, no target other than the entire system. This phenomenon has occurred often in the Soviet Union's Eastern European
satellites since the death of Stalin (Hungary in 1956, Czechoslovakia in 1968, and Poland in 1981).

Alienation, recruitment, ideological conversion, protest, and
structural conduciveness—these are some of the main elements
of conjunction theory. Conjunction theorists also try to establish
modal patterns or paths that some important revolutions have
followed and to generalize on this basis. They know that these
models are abstractions, that not all revolutions will go through
the same stages (compare, for example, the American and Mexi-
can revolutions), and that what happens at one stage will affect
whether the next stage will occur at all. Nonetheless, such life-
cycle or stage-by-stage descriptions provide very useful interpretations of a few revolutions. Their main strength *and* weakness come from the small number of cases they compare and
from their refusal or inability to account for examples that do not
fit their patterns.

The most famous and still the most powerful stage or life-
cycle theory is Crane Brinton's. He divides the process of revolution into five great stages: (1) the "prodromal" symptoms of

revolution in the old regimes; (2) the actual "fever"; (3) the accession of the extremists and the "delirium"; (4) the reaction to the resultant Terror and the onset of Thermidor; and (5) the restoration of equilibrium.[33] There is room to argue over Brinton's descriptions of particular stages and over whether these actually occurred in all four of the revolutions he compares (the English, American, French, and Russian). As we have already noted, Walzer questions whether Thermidor ever came to the Russian Revolution; he sees its outcome as a permanent institutionalization of the Terror. Nonetheless, Brinton's remains our richest and most elegantly written elaboration of stage theory.

Perhaps Brinton's most original insight, and the one with the longest philosophical pedigree, deals with the occurrence of dissension within the ruling class. Brinton is unique among modern theorists of revolution in actually studying ruling classes and their attributes, even though every writer from Trotsky to Skocpol mentions divisions in the ruling class as the key to the success of a revolution and usually even to its occurrence. Brinton writes: "A mixture of the military virtues, of respect for established ways of thinking and behaving, and of willingness to compromise, and if necessary, to innovate, is probably an adequate rough approximation of the qualities of a successful ruling class. . . . When numerous and influential members of such a class begin to believe that they hold power unjustly, or that all men are brothers, equal in the eyes of eternal justice, or that the beliefs they were brought up on are silly, or that 'after us the deluge,' they are not likely to resist successfully any serious attacks on their social, economic, and political positions. . . . Successful ruling classes have not infrequently been quite addicted to cruel sports, drinking, gambling, adultery, and other similar pursuits which we should no doubt all agree to condemn. It is a reasonable assertion that the virtuous Lafayette was a much clearer sign of the unfitness of the French aristocracy to rule than were Pompadour or even Du Barry."[34]

Dissension within the elite is only one of the symptoms of impending revolution that Brinton derived from his four cases.

Another is his famous "desertion of the intellectuals," which he called "the most reliable of symptoms," though he acknowledged that without a "syndrome" of other symptoms this symptom is meaningless, since intellectuals by definition have weak class loyalties and make Cassandra-like pronouncements about social problems.[35] Other of Brinton's symptoms are a narrowing of class distances, and rapid social and economic development that make political arrangements obsolete (the same thing as Huntington's major structural variable). But Brinton does not try to be exhaustive about these symptoms, and he is indifferent to the absence or weak occurrence of some of them among his four cases (the American Revolution displays the least "fit"). Moreover, he has no explanation for the movement from one phase of revolution to another. We must ask of Brinton's stage theory the same thing we asked of Skocpol's structural theory: What would happen to the model if different cases were used as the main source of data? What is the importance of defeat in a foreign war, urban rioting, racial and ethnic conflict, and the employment of terrorist tactics, all of which occurred in America during the late 1960's and early 1970's? Why do some social systems with all these symptoms of dissynchronization still manage to avoid revolution, whereas others succumb?

Such problems are inherent in conjunction theory. Conjunction theory identifies many common features of revolutionary movements and situations, and explains them in terms of the conjunction of a wide range of actor and structural variables; but the range is seldom wide enough. The theory is analogous to a simple chemical reaction: pour some revolutionaries into a system laboring under structural distortion and it will explode into revolution. Incidentally, something like this did happen during the First World War when Germany secretly transported exiled Bolshevik leaders back into Russia. What is needed, however, is a theory of chain reaction, one that can account for all the major contingencies that arise *during* an actual revolutionary situation: the nature of the resistance, foreign aid or intervention, changes in the character of the initial adherents, variations in strategy and tactics, and so forth. Conjunction theories stop short of trying to account for these contingencies theoretically and in a manner useful for cross-cultural comparison.

Process theories seek to overcome the limitations of conjunction theories by emphasizing the notion of contingency. This notion reflects the fact that changes beget changes—that after the leaders of a social movement make their first moves, their succeeding moves and those of their opponents can no longer be understood in terms of the state of affairs that existed at the outset. New information and situations develop continuously, and an outcome can never be predicted simply on the basis of an explanation of a movement's origins. As Cohen puts it, "Pathways are not predictable from initial states or initial acts alone; prediction is contingent on the state of affairs following each move. . . . For example, while one is deliberating about breaking into a car, his buddy may get cold feet and 'chicken out,' or a policeman may just happen to turn the corner. There are now new problems and possibilities to conjure with. Certain moves are now foreclosed and others, scarcely anticipated at the outset, are now inviting or may even seem inescapable."[36]

There is of course nothing unusual about seeing social action as a contingent process. This conception comes closest to the full complexity of the real world and is the one normally adopted by the narrative historian. Many revolutionaries, particularly successful ones, also adopt process theory, at least while they are still making a revolution; afterward they may concoct a more rigid theory that explains why their success was "inevitable." Lenin, for example, demanded that his revolutionary organization have the "ability to adapt itself immediately to the most diverse and rapidly changing conditions of struggle, an ability to renounce an open fight against overwhelming and concentrated forces, and yet capable of taking advantage of the awkwardness and immobility of the enemy and attack at a time and place where he least expects attack."[37] At a more abstract level, Mao Tse-tung's flexible concept of primary and secondary "social contradictions" enabled his party to avoid dogmatic definitions and to shift its emphasis from one discontent to another as these changed in salience for the Chinese people. Among other things, this meant that he was able to take advantage of the rapid political mobilization of the North China peasantry in the wake of the Japanese invasion of 1937.[38]

Contingency theory is useful for explaining not only the changing strategic vision of the parties to a conflict, but also the unintended consequences of direct action, what Toch calls momentum: "Once collective action has been initiated, it acquires a momentum of its own; even if people did not suffer from grievances, riots would attract and recruit participants. They would do so because they appeal to boredom, anger, frustration, desire for adventure; because they provide a ready-made opportunity to discharge feelings; because they furnish festive activity with the sanction of peers and under the aegis of principle."[39] Momentum often thus has the effect of broadening the composition of a social movement to include a far larger and more heterogeneous group of people.

A contingent process can always be displayed and studied historically, given the availability of information. But can it be portrayed analytically, in a way that fully takes account of contingency without becoming trapped by specific details? It can, but the result is inevitably highly abstract, usually mathematical, and often tends toward the purely formal, leading to serious problems of definition when the theory is applied to actual cases. This is the world of cybernetics, game theory, and Markov processes.*

---

* "In a Markov process the probability of any recent event is dependent on the probability of the event that has preceded it. In other words, given that event A has occurred, what is the probability that the next event will be B? Each link in the chain of events derives directly and wholly from its predecessor without regard to the earlier states which are part of its history. Once the probabilities associated with the passing from one state of the system into another are known, that is, once the transition probabilities are known, the probability associated with the whole sequence of states can be determined." E. Feit, "Insurgency in Organizations: A Theoretical Analysis," *General Systems*, 14 (1969), 162. See also Anatol Rapoport, *Prisoner's Dilemma: A Study in Conflict and Cooperation* (Ann Arbor, Mich., 1965).

Since contingencies in the real world are limitless, what the empirical researcher needs is not a mathematical model displaying all possible probability coefficients, but a model of the revolutionary process that encompasses all the aspects of revolution, incorporates both actor-oriented and structural variables, and is sensitive to the contingencies that may arise when all the different variables are combined. This is the kind of model I have tried to present in this book. My intention has been to indicate the diverse types of data required for analyzing a revolution and to suggest how such data should be combined. I have not offered a process theory of any given revolution, but a guide to the creation of such a theory—in short, a model. As Feit comments about models in general, "A model is an abstraction. Although it is a translation of real variables into model variables, from which model solutions are generated, these solutions cannot be applied to the real world without another translation."[40]

I have tried to portray the process of revolution at three levels, each level involving variables that may move a potentially revolutionary situation toward violence or away from violence. It is the interaction of these variables at each level and among the three levels that produces variation among revolutionary situations and that determines their outcomes. The three levels are (1) the level of structural distortion; (2) the level of conscious political choice; and (3) the level of strategies and tactics.

Conditions at the level of structural distortion determine whether people are receptive to proposals for changing their normative order. We have described this level in terms of the degree of synchronization between the values of a collectivity of people and the ensemble of roles they require in order to adapt to their political and economic environment. Dissynchronized conditions generate demands for change; that is, they generate social movements.

It should go without saying that such terms as social system, equilibrium, and homeostasis are not meant to be envalued; they do not suggest a preference for any one state of the system over another. As concepts, they have a long pedigree in social

research. Crane Brinton implicitly adopts the concept of homeostasis in his recognition of a social *vis medicatrix naturae* (i.e., the
social body's capacity for self-healing); and he states, although
he does not adopt it, that the "conceptual scheme of the social
equilibrium is probably in the long run the most useful for the
sociologist of revolution." His idea of equilibrium is similar to
the one presented here, although it is couched in different
terms: "Obviously any human society can be but in imperfect
equilibrium, a condition in which the varying and conflicting
desires and habits of individuals and groups of individuals are
in complex mutual adjustment, an adjustment so complex that
no mathematical treatment of it seems possible at present. As
new desires arise, or as old desires grow stronger in various
groups, or as environmental conditions change, and as institutions fail to change, a relative disequilibrium may arise, and
what we call a revolution break out."[41]

The view presented in this book also benefits from Pitirim
Sorokin's concept of culture and of cultural sectors (i.e., the
view that when the various elements of a culture are sufficiently
integrated they supply people with a coherent set of "fundamental premises" about the nature of reality and morality). As
Sorokin says, "The coordination or integration [of cultural sec-
tors] is not perfect, first because each compartment has a certain
'margin of autonomy,' so that some achieve a certain stage or
move out of it before others do; and second because there are
other, albeit secondary, factors that do not operate equally on all
compartments."[42] For such a system to be in equilibrium obviously does not imply the elimination of all violence, protest,
crime, conflict, or deviancy. However, it does imply that such
behavior is not disorienting to people: they know what they
think about such events, what the events signify, and what to
do about them; and they have a culturally specific understanding of the human imperfections that cause them.

The researcher must analyze social conditions at this level in
order to determine whether the "political" violence occurring in
a social system has revolutionary potential, regardless of what

either its perpetrators or suppressors call it. If the system is in homeostatic equilibrium, the violence is a sign of crime, deviancy, permissiveness, inattention, misunderstanding, faulty socialization, or some other nonpolitical source of violent behavior (the ostensibly "political" terrorism of the Symbionese Liberation Army now appears to have been of this variety). If the system is disequilibrated, the violence may signify the existence of a social movement, one that may attract both genuine status protesters and people who are projecting their private tensions onto public objects. To alleviate the conditions causing this kind of violence requires political action. Often, of course, ruling elites misdiagnose an instance of violence and help to dissynchronize an otherwise equilibrated system or turn a social movement into a revolutionary movement.

The second level, that of conscious political choice, determines the *kind* of social change that will result from disequilibrated social conditions: either processual change, revolutionary change, systemic decay, or disintegration of the system. Some of the main contingencies at this level are the structural conduciveness of the system to disputes over the propriety or validity of norms, the unity of the ruling class and its external and internal allies, the qualities of the ruling class (including its willingness to co-opt status protesters into its ranks), and the discipline and reliability of the system's armed forces. Analysis at this level concerns the justice of a social movement's cause and the effectiveness (seeming or real) of the various political policies adopted to overcome the discontent feeding the movement. Ideas of social justice will figure prominently in the ideological disputation that takes place at this level. As Gusfield observes, "The concept of a 'social movement' is . . . suggestive of people who, on the one hand, are in process of rejecting existing social values and arrangements, while, on the other, they are both striving to make converts to their way of seeing things and dealing with the resistance that their activities inevitably call forth. But while the movement is often carried by associations, it is not wholly an associational phenomenon. It is in the *system*

of generalized beliefs, and in partisan commitment to such beliefs, that we find the characterizing features of a social movement."[43]

There is nothing deterministic about the choices made at this
second level. Even in highly dissynchronized situations a government may so thoroughly overreact as to make either processual change or revolution virtually impossible (e.g., the government of South Africa, which is not subject to idealistic appeals,
cannot be infiltrated, and is realistically prepared to fight a revolution). Under these circumstances the result is likely to be social
stagnation, decay, disintegration, or foreign conquest, but not
revolution. Conversely, governmental underreaction in the face
of widespread misery is itself not necessarily conducive to revolution. As Brinton observes, French and Russian history—and
we could certainly add Chinese history—are filled with famines,
plagues, and bad harvests, many of which led to sporadic rioting; but in each society, this rioting led only once to revolution.[44]
The political choices that turn a situation of social change into
one of revolutionary change are *mistakes* in the application and
interpretation of a people's conception of justice. It is up to
the researcher to discover what a people thinks is just—not to
posit it.

Accelerators, or precipitating events, inaugurate revolutionary violence. These are the most contingent events of all, but
they are not difficult to recognize or conceptualize. As Overholt
puts it: "A precipitant provokes a decision by a group to pursue
actively and explicitly the destruction of the government. . . .
The decision process need not be formal. In [some] crowds, only
the attitudes of the single leader count; revolutionary violence
will begin if he demands it. In a Leninist Party the decision may
be made by a small Politburo, based on clearly defined expectations—for instance, of economic crisis. In a democratic group,
the majority view becomes the decision. When two angry mobs
face each other, a single rock thrown by any man may initiate
revolutionary violence. In any concrete case we can identify the
groups which have the ability and desire to initiate a revolution,

and in principle we can discover the attitudes of the members and the process by which those attitudes are aggregated into a decision. Sometimes such knowledge may even make possible avoidance of precipitants until a crisis is past—as when political leaders strive to avoid creating martyrs."[45]

The outbreak of revolutionary violence brings into urgent focus our third level of variables, the level of strategies and tactics. Even governments bent on social reform and sensitive to the meaning of justice in a particular situation may still have to contend with revolutionary violence. Such violence may, in fact, improve the government's chances of bringing about its reforms. Once the revolutionaries have resorted to violence, they have lost their initial flexibility to operate at various levels and have made their threat recognizable to all. The government may now begin to bring its own forces of violence and propaganda to bear against them. Needless to repeat, if the resort to revolutionary violence is accompanied by dissension within the standing army or by the creation of new revolutionary armies, the conflict will take the form of a civil war.

One important contingency at this third level is the appropriateness (i.e., the justice) of the forms and targets of revolutionary and counterrevolutionary violence. The resort to terrorism by either side is often self-defeating. Equally important, however, when the opponents of a revolution find their home territory and population largely immune from attack (e.g., France in Algeria, the United States in Vietnam, or the Soviet Union in Afghanistan), the revolutionary side may try to exploit its clear military disadvantage by appealing to public opinion within the immune country. This tactic only works when there is a sentiment in favor of underdogs in the immune country, the revolutionaries can gain access to it (e.g., through terrorism, the media, the United Nations), and the sentiment makes some difference at the level of policy."[46]

All the military variables, including the balance of forces and their leadership, come into play in a violent revolutionary struggle. Even in an equilibrated system with an enlightened government, the "revolutionaries" may still win their war (military coups d'état do this all the time). In such a case, the so-called revolution was not a revolution at all, but a source of change (usurpation of power, subversion, foreign conquest) impinging on an equilibrated system—though the change may well lead to true dissynchronization and revolution. Conversely, it is equally possible that the counterrevolutionaries may win their war, even in a totally disequilibrated system, with the result that the revolutionary situation becomes chronic and the "social system" is replaced by a form of concentration camp (e.g., Czechoslovakia after 1968, Tibet during the 1960's, and Eritrea under Ethiopian domination). The variables at this third level thus have as great an influence on the other levels as the first two levels have in determining the occurrence and outcome of revolutionary conflicts themselves.

The three levels discussed here are analytically separable congeries of variables, not stages of a process. Since a revolutionary process by definition takes place over time, one of these levels may be more salient than another at a particular moment, but none of them ever loses its contingent influence completely until the process as a whole comes to an end. Even quite late in the game new contingencies affecting the synchronization of the system may transform or make obsolete policies and ideologies being contested at the time (for example, the outbreak of a foreign war or the occurrence of a domestic technological innovation of great significance, such as the harnessing of atomic energy). Similarly, elites may consciously upstage and trivialize problems caused by a system's dissynchronization through policies of distraction (e.g., the precipitation of a foreign crisis).

The model presented in this book does not stipulate the direction of influence among the three levels; it provides the tools to discover the direction. Some critics of this approach have labeled it tautological, arguing that influences at one level can be determined only by an outcome at another level (e.g., whereas dissynchronization is said to be prerequisite to revolution, the only way to know that a system is dissynchronized is because a revolution has broken out). But the difference between the level of structural distortion and the level of political choice is not tautological. (No one has ever doubted that the level of strategies and tactics is separable.) The first two levels are different analytically, empirically, and operationally. Long-term systematic interactions among people joined in a collectivity, and conscious alterations in systematic behavior, are easily observed as separate phenomena. It is also possible to devise ways of measuring dissynchronization for a given social system that are independent of events at the second level; indeed, the entire field of social and economic indicators is devoted to doing precisely that.[47] The refusal to differentiate the first two levels analytically also ignores the important cases in which genuine dissynchronization has been overcome by policies of reform (e.g., the United States during the late 1960's and early 1970's).

The question of tautology does, however, serve to remind us of several dangers in the study of revolutions. One is the not uncommon fallacy in social research of defining a problem in terms of itself, which is not so much a matter of tautology as of simple semantic confusion—for example, saying that "fatigue" is caused by "exhaustion."[48] Something like this can be found in the staff report submitted to the U.S. National Commission on the Causes and Prevention of Violence in 1969, which comes close to concluding that violence in America during the 1960's was caused by a "history of violence" in America.[49] Since there was no way to change the past, this conclusion had obvious policy implications.

Another danger is premature quantitative measurement of revolutionary conditions, before their various contingencies have been studied and understood. Simpleminded schemes for the construction of "indexes of revolution" or, even worse, transcultural quantitative comparisons of revolutions have been responsible for deep confusion in the field. Premature quantification has even misled those coping with actual revolutionary struggles (for example, the hamlet evaluation surveys and the "body counts" of the Vietnam War, which consistently showed South Vietnam to be winning).

This book suggests a method for analyzing and understanding the complex phenomenon of revolution, and it tries to bring the four main ways social scientists have looked at revolution (through actor-oriented, structural, conjunction, and process theories) into congruence with each other. It is also designed to give its readers the wherewithal to determine whether any so-called revolution is in fact a revolution. In short, it is intended as a modest aid to thinking about real-world politics. If it does this, it will have served its purpose.

Notes

Notes

Chapter 1. Revolution: The Implications of a Political Concept

1. Arthur Bauer, *Essai sur les Révolutions* (Paris, 1908), Bibliothèque Sociologique Internationale, 36: 11.

2. Hannah Arendt, *On Revolution* (New York, 1963), p. 9.

3. Arthur Hatto, "'Revolution': An Enquiry into the Usefulness of an Historical Term," *Mind*, 58, no. 232 (October 1949), 495–517.

4. Aristotle, *Politics*, Benjamin Jowett, trans.; reprinted in William Ebenstein, *Great Political Thinkers* (New York, 1951), p. 106.

5. Gaetano Salvemini quoted by Kenneth E. Bock, "Evolution and Historical Process," *American Anthropologist*, 54 (1952), 494.

6. Crane Brinton, *The Anatomy of Revolution* (Englewood Cliffs, N.J., 1938).

7. Harry Eckstein, ed., *Internal War: Problems and Approaches* (New York, 1964), p. 23. For surveys of analytical approaches to the study of revolution, see Lawrence Stone, "Theories of Revolution," *World Politics*, 18, no. 2 (January 1966), 159–76; Perez Zagorin, "Theories of Revolution in Contemporary Historiography," *Political Science Quarterly*, 88, no. 1 (March 1973), 23–52; and Jack A. Goldstone, "Theories of Revolution: The Third Generation," *World Politics*, 32, no. 3 (April 1980), 425–53.

8. Alfred H. Stanton and Stewart E. Percy, eds., *Personality and Political Crisis* (Glencoe, Ill., 1951), p. 10. Another objection to comparative analyses of revolutions in the absence of a thorough conceptualization of revolution is that "In human affairs a causal generalization derived entirely from a set of analogous events is undependable, for the simple reason that human beings sometimes profit from experience." Louis Gottschalk, "Causes of Revolution," *American Journal of Sociology*, 50, no. 1 (July 1944), 3.

9. Max Weber, *The Theory of Social and Economic Organization*, A. M. Henderson and Talcott Parsons, trans. (New York, 1964 ed.), p. 88.

10. Thomas Hobbes, *Leviathan*, Part I, Chapter 13.

11. Norton Long, "The Political Act as an Act of Will," *American Journal of Sociology*, 69, no. 1 (July 1963), 1.

12. For example, Stanislaw Andrzejewski, *Military Organization and Society* (London, 1954), p. 22.

13. Lewis Coser, *The Functions of Social Conflict* (Glencoe, Ill., 1956), p. 21.

14. Talcott Parsons and Edward A. Shils, *Toward a General Theory of Action: Theoretical Foundations for the Social Sciences* (New York, 1962 ed.), p. 231. Emphasis in the original.

15. Reinhard Bendix, *Nation-Building and Citizenship* (New York, 1964), p. 45.

16. Ortega y Gasset, *The Revolt of the Masses* (New York, 1932), p. 82. See also Charner Perry, "Violence—Visible and Invisible," *Ethics*, 81, no. 1 (October 1970), 1–21.

17. Eckstein, *Internal War*, p. 13.

18. Arendt, *On Revolution*, p. 2.

19. See Max Gluckman, *Order and Rebellion in Tribal Africa* (New York, 1963).

Chapter 2. The Social System: Coercion and Values

1. Dorothy Emmet, *Function, Purpose, and Powers* (London, 1958), p. 23.

2. *Ibid.*, p. 16.

3. Thomas Hobbes, *Leviathan*, Part I, Chapter 13.

4. Ralf Dahrendorf, *Class and Class Conflict in Industrial Society* (Stanford, Calif., 1959), p. 64.

5. Max Weber, *From Max Weber: Essays in Sociology*, H. H. Gerth and C. Wright Mills, trans. (New York, 1958), p. 78. Emphasis in the original.

6. Dahrendorf, *Class and Class Conflict*, pp. 21, 30–31, 137.

7. *Ibid.*, p. 165.

8. Translated and quoted by Dahrendorf, *ibid.*, p. 14.

9. Talcott Parsons, "Some Reflections on the Place of Force in Social Process," in Harry Eckstein, ed., *Internal War: Problems and Approaches* (New York, 1964), p. 34.

10. Talcott Parsons, *The Social System* (New York, 1964 ed.), p. 42.

11. Thomas Kuhn, *The Structure of Scientific Revolutions* (Chicago, 1962), p. x.

12. Talcott Parsons, "Authority, Legitimation, and Political Action," in C. J. Friedrich, ed., *Authority* (Cambridge, Mass., 1958), p. 199.

13. Philip E. Jacob, "The Influence of Values in Political Integration," in P. E. Jacob et al., eds., *The Integration of Political Communities* (Philadelphia, 1964 ed.), p. 220.

14. D. F. Aberle, A. K. Cohen, A. K. Davis, M. J. Levy, and F. X. Sutton, "The Functional Prerequisites of a Society," *Ethics*, 60, no. 2 (January 1950), 100–111.

15. Anthony F. C. Wallace, *Culture and Personality* (New York, 1961 ed.), pp. 26–27.

16. *Ibid.*, p. 40.

17. *Ibid.*, p. 41.

18. See James C. Davies, *Human Nature in Politics* (New York, 1963), p. 9. For an extended discussion of needs and a different conception of them, see H. G. Barnett, *Innovation: The Basis of Cultural Change* (New York, 1953 ed.), Part 2, pp. 97–180.

19. Thomas Carlyle, *On Heroes and Hero-Worship* (New York, Dolphin paperbound ed., n.d.), pp. 13–14. Compare K. E. Boulding, "The Place of the Image in the Dynamics of Society," in G. K. Zollschan and W. Hirsch, eds., *Explorations in Social Change* (Boston, 1964), pp. 5–16, particularly pp. 10–13. See also Michael Walzer, "On the Role of Symbolism in Political Thought," *Political Science Quarterly*, 82, no. 2 (June 1967), 191–204.

20. On the question of whether these inescapable discriminations are, indeed, inescapable, see Kingsley Davis and Wilbert E. Moore, "Some Principles of Stratification," *American Sociological Review*, 10 (April 1945), 242–49; Melvin Tumin, "Some Principles of Stratification: A Critical Analysis," *American Sociological Review*, 18 (August 1953), 387–97 (with replies by Davis and Moore); and Dennis H. Wrong, "The Functional Theory of Stratification: Some Neglected Considerations," *American Sociological Review*, 24 (December 1959), 772–82. Cf. Anthony Giddens, *The Class Structure of the Advanced Societies* (New York, 1975).

21. Max Weber, *The Theory of Social and Economic Organization*, A. M. Henderson and Talcott Parsons, trans. (New York, 1964 ed.), p. 152.

22. Dahrendorf, *Class and Class Conflict*, p. 166.

23. Parsons, "Some Reflections on the Place of Force in Social Process," p. 42.

24. *Ibid.*, p. 45.

25. *Ibid.*, p. 46.

26. *Ibid.*, p. 47.

27. *Ibid.*, pp. 34–39.

28. Hannah Arendt, *On Revolution* (New York, 1963), p. 153.

29. *Ibid.*, p. 112.

30. See Parsons, *The Social System*, pp. 252, 267 et seq.

31. Quoted by George Woodcock, *Anarchism* (Cleveland, 1962), p. 276.

32. Cf. Norton Long, "The Political Act as an Act of Will," *American Journal of Sociology*, 69 (July 1963), 1–2.

33. See James Joll, *The Anarchists* (London, 1964), p. 55.

34. Quoted by Joll, *ibid.*, pp. 75–76.

35. Dahrendorf, *Class and Class Conflict*, p. 135.

36. See Vilhelm Aubert, "Competition and Dissensus: Two Types of Conflict and of Conflict Resolution," *Journal of Conflict Resolution*, 7, no. 1 (1963), 26–42.

37. For a survey of the diverse ways in which relations of conflict can be "managed," see Dennis C. Pirages, "Political Stability and Conflict Management," in Ted R. Gurr, ed., *Handbook of Political Conflict* (New York, 1980), pp. 425–60.

38. Dahrendorf, *Class and Class Conflict*, p. 178.

39. David Lockwood, "Some Remarks on 'The Social System,'" *British Journal of Sociology*, 7, no. 2 (June 1956), 140. Also see Lockwood, "Social Integration and System Integration," in Zollschan and Hirsch, *Explorations in Social Change*, pp. 244–57.

Chapter 3. The Social System: Structure and Function

1. See Alvin W. Gouldner, "Reciprocity and Autonomy in Functional Theory," in Llewellyn Gross, ed., *Symposium on Sociological Theory* (New York, 1959), p. 242.

2. D. F. Aberle et al., "The Functional Prerequisites of a Society," *Ethics*, 60 (January 1950), 101.

3. Alfred H. Stanton and Stewart E. Percy, eds., *Personality and Political Crisis* (Glencoe, Ill., 1951), p. 81.

4. For a discussion of variations in role performances of Supreme Court justices, see, for example, Anthony Lewis, *Gideon's Trumpet* (New York, 1964).

5. Wilbert E. Moore, *Social Change* (Englewood Cliffs, N.J., 1963), p. 13.

6. Aberle, "Functional Prerequisites," p. 105.

7. Dorothy Emmet, *Function, Purpose, and Powers* (London, 1958), p. 26. For a particularly lucid exposition of role theory, see Ralf Dahrendorf, "Homo Sociologicus," in his *Essays in the Theory of Society* (Stanford, Calif., 1968), pp. 19–87.

8. Ralf Dahrendorf, *Class and Class Conflict in Industrial Society* (Stanford, Calif., 1959), p. 120.

9. Emmet, *Function, Purpose, and Powers*, p. 113.

10. *Ibid.*, p. 57. See also Charles Taylor, *The Explanation of Behaviour* (London, 1964).

11. Emmet, *Function, Purpose, and Powers*, pp. 84, 96.

12. For warnings concerning the dangers of "normative functionalism," see Lewis Coser, "Social Conflict and the Theory of Social Change," *British Journal of Sociology*, 8 (September 1957), 206–7, n. 22; and David Lockwood, in G. K. Zollschan and W. Hirsch, eds., *Explorations in Social Change* (Boston, 1964), p. 245.

13. Talcott Parsons, *Essays in Sociological Theory: Pure and Applied* (Glencoe, Ill., 1949), p. 21. Quoted by Gouldner, "Functional Theory," p. 243.

14. Gouldner, "Functional Theory," p. 241.

15. Aberle, "Functional Prerequisites." The Aberle prerequisites have been rephrased as positive actions rather than left as conditions.

16. For a summary and application of the Parsonian "functional imperatives," see Karl Deutsch, "Integration and the Social System: Implications of Functional Analysis," in P. E. Jacob et al., eds., *The Integration of Political Communities* (Philadelphia, 1964 ed.), pp. 179–208.

17. Carl Hempel, in L. Gross, *Symposium on Sociological Theory*, p. 294.

18. Emmet, *Function, Purpose, and Powers*, p. 74.

19. *Ibid.*, p. 62.

20. Anthony F. C. Wallace, "Revitalization Movements," *American Anthropologist*, 58 (April 1956), 265.

21. Dahrendorf, *Class and Class Conflict*, p. 225.

22. *Ibid.*, p. 121.

Chapter 4. The Disequilibrated Social System

1. Eric Hoffer, *The Ordeal of Change* (New York, 1964 ed.), pp. 4–5.

2. T. H. Wintringham, *Mutiny* (London, 1936), p. 10.

3. Louis Gottschalk, "Causes of Revolution," *American Journal of Sociology*, 50, no. 1 (July 1944), 5.

4. Anthony F. C. Wallace, *Culture and Personality* (New York, 1961 ed.), p. 144.

5. Alexis de Tocqueville, *The Old Régime and the French Revolution*, Stuart Gilbert, trans. (New York, 1955 ed.), p. 176.

6. James C. Davies, "Toward a Theory of Revolution," *American Sociological Review*, 27, no. 1 (February 1962), 6, 8; and *Human Nature in Politics* (New York, 1963), p. 350.

7. Alfred Meusel, "Revolution and Counter-Revolution," *Encyclopedia of the Social Sciences*, 13 (1934), 367.

8. H. G. Barnett, *Innovation: The Basis of Cultural Change* (New York, 1953 ed.), p. 80.

9. Wilbert E. Moore, *Social Change* (Englewood Cliffs, N.J., 1963), p. 18.

10. Quoted by Arthur Bauer, *Essai sur les Révolutions* (Paris, 1908), Bibliothèque Sociologique Internationale, 36: 41.

11. Everett Hagen, *On the Theory of Social Change* (Homewood, Ill., 1962), p. 6.

12. See Wallace, *Culture and Personality*, p. 125; and Everett M. Rogers, *Diffusion of Innovations* (New York, 1962).

13. Barnett, *Innovation*, p. 181 et seq.

14. *Ibid.*, p. 56.

15. See George M. Foster, *Traditional Cultures: And the Impact of Technological Change* (New York, 1962), pp. 112–15; and Everett C. Hughes, "Social Change and Status Protest: An Essay on the Marginal Man," *Phylon*, 10 (First quarter, 1949), 58–65.

16. On modernizing oligarchs, see Edward Shils, *Political Development in the New States* (The Hague, 1962), p. 67 et seq.

17. For a case study of a high-status innovator, see L. Pospisil, "Social Change and Primitive Law: Consequences of a Papuan Legal Case," *American Anthropologist*, 60 (1958), 832–37; and E. R. Leach, "Social Change and Primitive Law [Rejoinder]," *American Anthropologist*, 61 (1959), 1096–97.

18. Karl Deutsch, "Social Mobilization and Political Development," *American Political Science Review*, 55, no. 3 (September 1961), 493–514.

19. Hoffer, *Ordeal*, pp. 120–21.

20. Basic bibliography is included in A. James Gregor, "Black Nationalism: A Preliminary Analysis of Negro Radicalism," *Science and Society*, 27, no. 4 (Fall 1963), 415–32. See also *Report of the National Advisory Commission on Civil Disorders* (New York, 1968 ed.); and Edward C. Banfield, *The Unheavenly City* (Boston, 1970).

21. George S. Pettee, *The Process of Revolution* (New York, 1938), p. 66.

22. Anthony F. C. Wallace, "Revitalization Movements," *American Anthropologist*, 58 (April 1956), 266.

23. Wallace, *Culture and Personality*, p. 20.

24. Emile Durkheim, *The Rules of Sociological Method* (Glencoe, Ill., 1938), pp. lvi–lvii, n. 7.

25. Talcott Parsons, "Personality and Social Structure," in Alfred H. Stanton and Stewart E. Percy, eds., *Personality and Political Crisis* (Glencoe, Ill., 1951), p. 74. Emphasis added.

26. Donald R. Cressey, "The Respectable Criminal," *Trans-Action*, March–April 1965, pp. 12–15.

27. Parsons, "Personality and Social Structure," pp. 72–74.

28. Herbert Phillips, "Personality and Social Structure in a Siamese Community," *Human Organization*, 22, no. 2 (1963), 105.

29. See, for example, Eric Hoffer, *The True Believer* (New York, 1951).

30. Harold D. Lasswell, *Psychopathology and Politics* (New York, 1960 ed.), pp. 180–81. For other examples of psychological reductionism, see Chalmers Johnson, "Pregnant with 'Meaning!': Mao and the Revolutionary Ascetic," *Journal of Interdisciplinary History*, 7, no. 3 (Winter 1977), 499–508.

31. P. M. Yap, "The Mental Illness of Hung Hsiu-ch'üan, Leader of the Taiping Rebellion," *Far Eastern Quarterly*, 13, no. 3 (May 1954), 287–304.

32. Wallace, *Culture and Personality*, p. 152.

33. A. Inkeles and D. J. Levinson, "National Character: The Study of Modal Personality and Sociocultural Systems," in Gardner Lindzey, ed., *Handbook of Social Psychology* (Reading, Mass., 1954), p. 982.

34. Lewis Coser, *The Functions of Social Conflict* (New York, 1964 ed.), p. 78.

35. Talcott Parsons, *The Social System* (New York, 1964 ed.), p. 521.

36. Kurt Riezler, "On the Psychology of the Modern Revolution," *Social Research*, 10, no. 3 (September 1943), 320–26.

37. Erik Erikson, *Young Man Luther* (New York, 1962 ed.), p. 22.

38. Talcott Parsons, "Some Reflections on the Place of Force in Social Process," in Harry Eckstein, ed., *Internal War: Problems and Approaches* (New York, 1964), p. 66.

39. Clifford Geertz, "Ideology as a Cultural System," in David E. Apter, ed., *Ideology and Discontent* (New York, 1964), p. 64.

40. Wallace, *Culture and Personality*, p. 148.

41. See James J. Maguire, *The Philosophy of Modern Revolution* (Washington, D.C., 1943), 76–77; and Chalmers Johnson, *Revolution and the Social System* (Stanford, Calif., 1964), 35–39.

42. Parsons, *The Social System*, p. 530.

43. An excellent case study of the transformation of Bolshevik revolutionary ideology into the value structure of the Soviet Union is Raymond A. Bauer, *The New Man in Soviet Psychology* (Cambridge, Mass., 1959).

44. Alexis de Tocqueville, *The Old Régime and the French Revolution*, Stuart Gilbert, trans. (New York, 1955 ed.), p. 13.

45. Thomas Carlyle, *On Heroes and Hero-Worship* (New York, Dolphin paperbound ed., n.d.), pp. 121–22.

Chapter 5. Revolution

1. Karl Popper, *The Poverty of Historicism* (New York, 1964 ed.), p. 66.

2. Dorothy Emmet, *Function, Purpose, and Powers* (London, 1958), pp. 105–6.

3. Niccolò Machiavelli, *The Prince and The Discourses* (New York, 1940 ed.), p. 81.

4. Lucian Pye, "Roots of Insurgency," in Harry Eckstein, ed., *Internal War: Problems and Approaches* (New York, 1964), pp. 159–60.

5. Lewis Namier, *1848: The Revolution of the Intellectuals* (New York, 1964 ed.), p. 3.

6. *Ibid.*, p. 26.

7. George S. Pettee, *The Process of Revolution* (New York, 1938), p. 91.

8. See the *New York Times*, May 7, 8, 1965.

9. Pettee, *Process of Revolution*, p. 11.

10. Stanislaw Andrzejewski, *Military Organization and Society* (London, 1954), pp. 158, 127.

11. Alexis de Tocqueville, *The Old Régime and the French Revolution*, Stuart Gilbert, trans. (New York, 1955 ed.), p. 20.

12. Louis Gottschalk, "Causes of Revolution," *American Journal of Sociology*, 50, no. 1 (July 1944), 8.

13. Peter Amann, "Revolution: A Redefinition," *Political Science Quarterly*, 77, no. 1 (March 1962), 39.

14. Pettee, *Process of Revolution*, p. 100.

15. Katharine C. Chorley, *Armies and the Art of Revolution* (London, 1943), pp. 11, 16.

16. Cecil Woodham-Smith, *The Reason Why* (New York, 1953), p. 26.

17. Chorley, *Armies*, p. 87.

18. United Nations, XI General Assembly, *Report of the Special Committee on the Problem of Hungary* (A/3592, 1957), pp. 24–25, s. v. pars. 159, 166.

19. F. M. Cornford, trans., *The Republic of Plato* (New York, 1945), p. 268.

20. International Institute for Strategic Studies, *Strategic Survey 1978* (London, 1979), p. 53.

21. Chorley, *Armies*, p. 108.

22. For the relationship between war and revolution in China and Yugoslavia, see Chalmers Johnson, *Peasant Nationalism and Communist Power* (Stanford, Calif., 1962).

23. Chorley, *Armies*, p. 76.

24. Anthony F. C. Wallace, *Culture and Personality* (New York, 1961 ed.), pp. 143–44.

25. Anthony F. C. Wallace, "Revitalization Movements," *American Anthropologist*, 58 (April 1956), 264.

26. Wallace, *Culture and Personality*, p. 144. Italics added.

27. *Ibid.*, 147.

28. *Ibid.*

29. *Ibid.*

30. *Ibid.*, p. 148.

31. *Ibid.*, p. 149.

32. *Ibid.*, p. 151.

33. Hannah Arendt, *On Revolution* (New York, 1963), p. 235.

34. Wallace, *Culture and Personality*, pp. 160–61.

35. Thomas Kuhn, *The Structure of Scientific Revolutions* (Chicago, 1962), pp. 65, 77, 144.

36. Wallace, *Culture and Personality*, p. 161.

37. John Locke, *Two Treatises of Government*, Thomas I. Cook, ed. (New York, 1947), p. 233.

38. *Ibid.*, p. 207.

39. *Ibid.*, p. 238.

40. *Ibid.*, p. 235.

41. *Ibid.*, p. 225.

42. *Ibid.*, p. 236.

43. *Ibid.*, p. 244.

44. *Ibid.*, pp. 233–34.

45. Arendt, *On Revolution*, p. 18.

46. *Ibid.*, p. 158.

47. *Ibid.*, p. 28.

48. *Ibid.*, p. 121.

49. *Ibid.*

50. *Ibid.*, p. 221.

Chapter 6. Varieties of Revolution

1. Hannah Arendt, *On Revolution* (New York, 1963), p. 33.

2. E. J. Hobsbawm, *The Age of Revolution, 1789–1848* (Cleveland, 1962), p. 160.

3. George Woodcock, *Anarchism* (Cleveland, 1962), p. 469.

4. The present use of the terms "government," "regime," and "community" follows that of David Easton, "Political Anthropology," in B. J. Siegel, ed., *Biennial Review of Anthropology 1959* (Stanford, Calif., 1959), pp. 228–29.

5. James Rosenau, ed., *International Aspects of Civil Strife* (Princeton, N.J., 1964), pp. 63–64.

6. Anthony F. C. Wallace, "Revitalization Movements," *American Anthropologist*, 58 (April 1956), 275.

7. *Ibid.*, p. 276.

8. An example of research that roots revolution in the context of the disequilibrated system is Charles Tilly, *The Vendée: A Sociological Analysis of the Counterrevolution of 1793* (Cambridge, Mass., 1964).

9. Talcott Parsons and Edward A. Shils, eds., *Toward a General Theory of Action: Theoretical Foundations for the Social Sciences* (New York, 1962 ed.), p. 76.

10. For a study of interdependence and equilibrium as variables that differentiate types of social systems, see Alvin W. Gouldner, "Reciprocity and Autonomy in Functional Theory," in Llewellyn Gross, ed., *Symposium on Sociological Theory* (New York, 1959), pp. 241–70. On the highly controversial subject of the determinants of rebellion or revolution in peasant societies, see Karl D. Jackson, *Traditional Authority, Islam, and Rebellion* (Berkeley, Calif., 1980); John W. Lewis, ed., *Peasant Rebellion and Communist Revolution in Asia* (Stanford, Calif., 1974); Samuel Popkin, *The Rational Peasant* (Berkeley, Calif., 1979); and James C. Scott, *The Moral Economy of the Peasant* (New Haven, Conn., 1976).

11. Cf. Tilly, *The Vendée*, p. 16.

12. *Ibid.*, p. 17.

13. Arnold Feldman, "Violence and Volatility: The Likelihood of Revolution," in Harry Eckstein, ed., *Internal War: Problems and Approaches* (New York, 1964), pp. 120–21. See also Alexander Yanov, *The Origins of Autocracy* (Berkeley, Calif., 1981), pp. 27–70.

Chapter 7. Strategies of Revolution

1. Thomas Schelling, *The Strategy of Conflict* (New York, 1963 ed.), p. 3. Italics in original.

2. *Ibid.*, p. 90.

3. Andrew C. Janos, *The Seizure of Power: A Study of Force and Popular Consent* (Princeton, N.J., 1964), pp. 36–39.

4. See Chalmers Johnson, *Revolution and the Social System* (Stanford, Calif., 1964), pp. 49–57. For a complete discussion of Leninist tactics of infiltration, see Philip Selznick, *The Organizational Weapon* (Glencoe, Ill., 1960). Tactical details are discussed by Edward Luttwak, *Coup d'Etat: A Practical Handbook* (New York, 1969).

5. Franz Borkenau, *World Communism* (Ann Arbor, Mich., 1962 ed.), p. 191.

6. V. I. Lenin, *'Left-Wing' Communism, An Infantile Disorder* (Moscow, n.d.), p. 85. Italics added.

7. In Gunther Nollau, *International Communism and World Revolution: History and Methods* (New York, 1961), p. 341.

8. Leon Trotsky, *The Russian Revolution*, abridged ed. (New York, 1959), p. 318.

9. For more detailed studies of guerrilla warfare, see Douglas S. Blaufarb, *The Counterinsurgency Era* (New York, 1977); Chalmers Johnson, "The Third Generation of Guerrilla Warfare," *Asian Survey*, 8, no. 6 (June 1968), 435–47; Chalmers Johnson, *Autopsy on People's War* (Berkeley, Calif., 1973); and Sam C. Sarkesian, ed., *Revolutionary Guerrilla Warfare* (Chicago, 1975).

10. *Mao Tse-tung hsüan-chi* [Selected Works of Mao Tse-tung] (Peking, 1964), I, 107.

11. Peter Paret, "The French Army and *La Guerre Révolutionnaire*," *Journal of the Royal United Service Institution*, 104, no. 613 (February 1959), 59.

12. *Mao Tse-tung on Guerrilla Warfare*, S. Griffith, trans. (New York, 1961), p. 44.

13. *Peking Review*, no. 15 (April 9, 1965), p. 12.

14. *Mao Tse-tung hsüan-chi*, I, 219.

Chapter 8. Terrorism

1. Jordan J. Paust, "A Survey of Possible Legal Responses to International Terrorism: Prevention, Punishment, and Cooperative Action," *Georgia Journal of International and Comparative Law*, 5 (1975), 434–35 (emphasis added).

2. Raymond Aron, *Peace and War* (Garden City, N.Y., 1966), p. 170.

3. Augustus R. Norton and Martin H. Greenberg, *International Terrorism: An Annotated Bibliography and Research Guide* (Boulder, Colo., 1980), p. 2.

4. Brian Jenkins, "International Terrorism: A Balance Sheet," *Survival*, 17, no. 4 (July–August 1975), 158.

5. Melvin J. Lasky, "Ulrike Meinhof and the Baader-Meinhof Gang," *Encounter*, June 1975, p. 17.

6. Eugene V. Walter, "Violence and the Process of Terror," in Joan V. Bondurant, ed., *Conflict: Violence and Nonviolence* (Chicago, 1971), p. 105. On attempts to impose order without law from below, see H. Jon Rosenbaum and Peter C. Sederberg, eds., *Vigilante Politics* (Philadelphia, 1976).

7. On the types of terrorism, see National Advisory Committee on Criminal Justice Standards and Goals, *Report of the Task Force on Disorders and Terrorism* (Washington, D.C., 1976), pp. 3–6.

8. On reigns of terror in general, see Walter, "Violence and the Process of Terror." On the Stalinist case, see Alexander Dallin and George Breslauer, *Political Terror in Communist Systems* (Stanford, Calif., 1970). For an important study that relates the reigns of terror of Hitler and Stalin to their personalities, see Robert C. Tucker, "The Dictator and Totalitarianism," in Fred I. Greenstein and Michael Lerner, eds., *A Source Book for the Study of Personality and Politics* (Chicago, 1971), pp. 456–76.

9. On collaboration between the Red Brigades and professional criminals, see Claire Sterling, "Italian Terrorists: Life and Death in a Violent Generation," *Encounter*, July 1981, 18–31. On Okamoto, see Yoshihiro Kuriyama, "Terrorism at Tel Aviv International Airport and a 'New Left' Group in Japan," *Asian Survey*, 13, no. 3 (March 1973), 336–46; and Patricia G. Steinhoff, "Portrait of a Terrorist: An Interview with Kozo Okamoto," *Asian Survey*, 16, no. 9 (September 1976), 830–45.

10. Herman Blei, "Terrorism, Domestic and International: The West German Experience," in National Advisory Committee, *Disorders and Terrorism*, p. 500.

11. H. Edward Price, Jr., "The Strategy and Tactics of Revolutionary Terrorism," *Comparative Studies in Society and History*, 19, no. 1 (January 1977), p. 53.

12. Quoted in Robert Moss, *Urban Guerrillas: The New Face of Political Violence* (London, 1972), p. 13.

13. National Advisory Committee, *Disorders and Terrorism*, p. 420.

14. Alistair Horne, *A Savage War of Peace: Algeria 1954–1962* (Harmondsworth, England, 1979), pp. 122–23.

15. Lasky, "Ulrike Meinhof and the Baader-Meinhof Gang," p. 15.

16. Desmond Smith, "The Hearst Story: Kidnapping the News," *National Observer*, April 6, 1974.

17. On the concept of revolutionary paradigm, see Chalmers Johnson, *Autopsy on People's War* (Berkeley, Calif., 1973), pp. 109–14.

18. For figures on the frequency of various forms of revolutionary violence, see Edward Luttwak, *Coup d'Etat: A Practical Handbook* (New York, 1969), pp. 208–9. The bibliography on military coups is extensive, but excellent analytical introductions are Edward Feit, *The Armed Bureaucrats* (Boston, 1973); S. E. Finer, *The Man on Horseback* (New York, 1962); and Morris Janowitz, *The Military in the Political Development of New Nations* (Chicago, 1964).

19. National Advisory Committee, *Disorders and Terrorism*, p. 7.

20. U.S. Central Intelligence Agency, *International and Transnational Terrorism: Diagnosis and Prognosis* (Report PR 76 10030, April 1976), p. 10. One of the most reliable statistical series, because it has been com-

piled longer and because the instances are unambiguous, is that for aerial hijackings. This series also shows a significant rise in such incidents starting in 1968. See U.S. 93d Congress, 2d Session, House of Representatives, Committee on Internal Security, *Terrorism* (Washington, D.C., 1974), pp. 97, 165–67. Claire Sterling also emphasizes 1968 as the year when the terrorist offensive began. See her *The Terror Network* (New York, 1981), p. 5.

21. For an important firsthand account of the Latin American kidnappings, see Sir Geoffrey Jackson, *Surviving the Long Night* (New York, 1974). Jackson was the British Ambassador to Uruguay when, in 1971, he was kidnapped by the Tupamaros.

22. Central Intelligence Agency, *International and Transnational Terrorism*, p. 10; *U.S. News and World Report* (on the CIA compilations for 1979 and 1980), June 16, 1980, p. 40, and May 4, 1981, p. 28; and Chalmers Johnson, "Perspectives on Terrorism," in Walter Laqueur, ed., *The Terrorism Reader* (New York, 1978), pp. 269–70.

23. National Advisory Committee, *Disorders and Terrorism*, pp. 170–73, 376–78 (including bibliography on the new field of "design for security").

24. R. W. Mengel, "Terrorism and New Technologies of Destruction: An Overview of the Potential Risk," in National Advisory Committee, *Disorders and Terrorism*, pp. 443–73; and David M. Rosenbaum, "Nuclear Terror," *International Security*, 1, no. 3 (Winter 1977), 140–61.

25. "The Terrorists: Thriving Black Market Puts Military Weapons into Amateurs' Hands," *Wall Street Journal*, January 11, 1977.

26. Central Intelligence Agency, *International and Transnational Terrorism*, p. 19.

27. See Sterling, *The Terror Network*; and Herbert Romerstein, *Soviet Support for International Terrorism* (Washington, D.C., 1981). Romerstein is a staff member of the Permanent Select Committee on Intelligence of the U.S. House of Representatives.

28. Jenkins, "International Terrorism," p. 164.

29. Sterling, "Italian Terrorists," p. 31.

30. James Q. Wilson, "Thinking About Terrorism," *Commentary*, July 1981, p. 38.

31. Central Intelligence Agency, *International and Transnational Terrorism*, p. 22.

Chapter 9. Theories of Revolution

1. Harry Eckstein, "Theoretical Approaches to Explaining Collective Political Violence," in Ted R. Gurr, ed., *Handbook of Political Conflict*

(New York, 1980), p. 135; U.S. 90th Congress, 2d Session, Senate, Committee on Foreign Relations, *The Nature of Revolution* (Washington, D.C., 1968); Robert A. Dahl, *After the Revolution?* (New Haven, Conn., 1970), p. 3; Stanislav Andreski, *Prospects of a Revolution in the U.S.A.* (New York, 1974); Hannah Arendt, "Civil Disobedience," *New Yorker*, September 12, 1970.

2. Eckstein, "Theoretical Approaches," p. 138.

3. *Ibid.*, p. 161; Albert K. Cohen, *Deviance and Control* (Englewood Cliffs, N.J., 1966), p. 59.

4. This categorization is adapted from a standard taxonomy of psychological theories. See Cohen, *Deviance and Control*, pp. 41–47.

5. See, among other works, M. Rejai (with Kay Phillips), *Leaders of Revolution* (Beverly Hills, Calif., 1979), pp. 26–27; D. V. Segre and J. H. Adler, "The Ecology of Terrorism," *Survival*, 15, no. 4 (July–August 1973), 180; and Harold D. Lasswell, *Psychopathology and Politics* (New York, 1960 ed.), pp. 262–64.

6. See J. Bowyer Bell, "Trends on Terror: The Analysis of Political Violence," *World Politics*, 29, no. 3 (April 1977), 476–88; and Augustus R. Norton and Martin H. Greenberg, *International Terrorism: An Annotated Bibliography and Research Guide* (Boulder, Colo., 1980).

7. Michael Walzer, "A Theory of Revolution," *Marxist Perspectives*, 2, no. 1 (Spring 1979), 31.

8. For further details, see Herman Blei, "Terrorism, Domestic and International: The West German Experience," in National Advisory Committee on Criminal Justice Standards and Goals, *Report of the Task Force on Disorders and Terrorism* (Washington, D.C., 1976), pp. 497–99; and Jillian Becker, *Hitler's Children* (London, 1978).

9. Cohen, *Deviance and Control*, p. 70.

10. Ted R. Gurr, *Why Men Rebel* (Princeton, N.J., 1970). For further bibliography, see Gurr, *Handbook*, pp. 518–19.

11. Edward N. Muller, "The Psychology of Political Protest and Violence," in Gurr, *Handbook*, p. 72.

12. *Ibid.*, pp. 96–97. For another critical attempt to apply various theories, including Gurr's, to concrete cases, see Waltraud Q. Morales, *Social Revolution: Theory and Historical Application* (Denver, Colo., 1973).

13. Theda Skocpol, *States and Social Revolutions* (Cambridge, England, 1979), p. 291.

14. *Ibid.*, pp. 19, 23.

15. *Ibid.*, pp. 112–13.

16. *Ibid.*, pp. 161–62. Compare Ellul's definition: "Revolution is finally the crisis of the development of the state." Jacques Ellul, *Autopsy of Revolution* (New York, 1971), pp. 160, 162–63.

17. The classic study of the vanguard victory in Soviet communism is

Milovan Djilas, *The New Class: An Analysis of the Communist System* (New York, 1957).

18. Samuel P. Huntington, *Political Order in Changing Societies* (New Haven, Conn., 1968), p. 265.

19. *Ibid.*, p. 273.

20. Barrington Moore, Jr., *Social Origins of Dictatorship and Democracy* (Boston, 1966), pp. 314, 413–14.

21. Albert O. Hirschman, *Journeys Toward Progress* (New York, 1963), pp. 256, 270.

22. Walzer, "A Theory of Revolution," p. 43. See also Richard Lowenthal, "The 'Missing Revolution' of Our Times: Reflections on New Post-Marxist Fundamentals of Social Change," *Encounter*, February–March 1981, pp. 10–18.

23. Neil J. Smelser, *Theory of Collective Behavior* (London, 1962), Chap. 10, "The Value-Oriented Movement," particularly pp. 316–17.

24. Joseph R. Gusfield, "The Study of Social Movements," in David L. Sills, ed., *International Encyclopedia of the Social Sciences* (New York, 1968), 14: 445.

25. Rudolf Heberle, "Types and Functions of Social Movements," in Sills, *International Encyclopedia*, 14: 440.

26. On millenarian movements, see Kenelm Burridge, *New Heaven, New Earth: A Study of Millenarian Activities* (New York, 1969).

27. Dahl, *After the Revolution?*, pp. 112–15.

28. Heberle, "Types and Functions of Social Movements," p. 443.

29. On actor-oriented variables, see Hans Toch, *Violent Men: An Inquiry into the Psychology of Violence* (Chicago, 1969).

30. Smelser, *Theory of Collective Behavior*, p. 15.

31. Cohen, *Deviance and Control*, p. 17.

32. Alexis de Tocqueville, *Democracy in America*, Richard D. Heffner, ed. (New York, 1956), p. 267.

33. Crane Brinton, *The Anatomy of Revolution* (New York, 1957 ed.), pp. 17–18.

34. *Ibid.*, pp. 53–54.

35. *Ibid.*, pp. 69, 265.

36. Cohen, *Deviance and Control*, pp. 44–45.

37. V. I. Lenin, *What Is To Be Done?* (New York, 1929 ed.), p. 162.

38. Chalmers Johnson, "Chinese Communist Leadership and Mass Response," in Ping-ti Ho and Tang Tsou, eds., *China in Crisis* (Chicago, 1968), 1: 409.

39. Toch, *Violent Men*, p. 211.

40. E. Feit, "Insurgency in Organizations: A Theoretical Analysis," *General Systems*, 14 (1969), 157.

41. Brinton, *Anatomy*, pp. 16–17.

42. Pitirim Sorokin, *Social and Cultural Dynamics* (New York, 1937), quoted in Cohen, *Deviance and Control*, p. 33.

43. Gusfield, "The Study of Social Movements," p. 446. Italics in original.

44. Brinton, *Anatomy*, p. 33.

45. William H. Overholt, "An Organizational Conflict Theory of Revolution," *American Behavioral Scientist*, 20, no. 4 (March–April 1977), 511.

46. Chalmers Johnson, *Autopsy on People's War* (Berkeley, Calif., 1973); Andrew Mack, "Why Big Nations Lose Small Wars: The Politics of Asymmetric Conflict," *World Politics*, 27, no. 2 (January 1975), 175–200.

47. See, among other works, Louis I. Dublin, *Suicide: A Sociological and Statistical Study* (New York, 1963); Val R. Lorwin and Jacob M. Price, *The Dimensions of the Past: Materials, Problems, and Opportunities for Quantitative Work in History* (New Haven, Conn., 1972); and Eugene J. Webb, Donald T. Campbell, Richard D. Schwartz, and Lee Sechrest, *Unobtrusive Measures: Nonreactive Research in the Social Sciences* (Chicago, 1966).

48. Cohen, *Deviance and Control*, p. 61.

49. Hugh D. Graham and Ted R. Gurr, eds., *Violence in America: Historical and Comparative Perspectives* (New York, 1969).

Index

QM LIBRARY
(MILE END)

WITHDRAWN
FROM STOCK
QMUL LIBRARY

Printed in the United States
15704LVS00001B/451-453

HM 281 JOH

QM Library

23 1331304 7

Revolutionary Change

WITHDRAWN
FROM STOCK
QMUL LIBRARY

Woe to him that claims obedience when it is not due;
Woe to him that refuses it when it is.

THOMAS CARLYLE

The nature of things does not madden us: only
ill will does.

JEAN JACQUES ROUSSEAU

WITHDRAWN
FROM STOCK
QMUL LIBRARY